Communications in Computer and Information Science 1530

More information about this series at https://link.springer.com/bookseries/7899

Luis A. Leiva · Cédric Pruski · Réka Markovich ·
Amro Najjar · Christoph Schommer (Eds.)

Artificial Intelligence and Machine Learning

33rd Benelux Conference
on Artificial Intelligence, BNAIC/Benelearn 2021
Esch-sur-Alzette, Luxembourg, November 10–12, 2021
Revised Selected Papers

 Springer

Editors
Luis A. Leiva (ID)
University of Luxembourg
Esch-sur-Alzette, Luxembourg

Cédric Pruski (ID)
Luxembourg Institute of Science
and Technology
Esch-sur-Alzette, Luxembourg

Réka Markovich (ID)
University of Luxembourg
Esch-sur-Alzette, Luxembourg

Amro Najjar (ID)
University of Luxembourg
Esch-sur-Alzette, Luxembourg

Christoph Schommer (ID)
University of Luxembourg
Esch-sur-Alzette, Luxembourg

ISSN 1865-0929   ISSN 1865-0937 (electronic)
Communications in Computer and Information Science
ISBN 978-3-030-93841-3   ISBN 978-3-030-93842-0 (eBook)
https://doi.org/10.1007/978-3-030-93842-0

This Springer imprint is published by the registered company Springer Nature Switzerland AG
The registered company address is: Gewerbestrasse 11, 6330 Cham, Switzerland

Preface

Welcome to the proceedings of BNAIC/Benelearn 2021, the 33rd edition of the annual Benelux Conference on Artificial Intelligence and the 30th edition of the annual Belgian-Dutch Conference on Machine Learning.

In 2021, this joint conference was organized by the University of Luxembourg, under the auspices of the Faculty of Science, Technology, and Medicine (FSTM) and the Interdisciplinary Lab for Intelligent and Adaptive Systems (ILIAS), and the IT for Innovative Services (ITIS) research department from the Luxembourg Institute of Science and Technology (LIST).

Held yearly, the objective of BNAIC/Benelearn is to promote and disseminate recent research developments in Artificial Intelligence in the Benelux. In 2021 we returned to in-person attendance, under CovidCheck regulations, as a three-day event: the conference taking place from Wednesday, November 10 to Friday, November 12, 2021.

BNAIC/Benelearn 2021 included invited keynote speakers, research presentations, posters, and demonstrations. The conference provided ample opportunity for interaction between academia and industry. This year, the chosen motto of the conference was "AI in ACTION", to reflect the aforementioned synergies between academia and industry.

For the scientific part, we welcomed four types of contributions, namely, a) regular papers, b) encore abstracts of work already published in 2021, c) posters, and demonstrations, and d) thesis abstracts. We received 105 submissions overall, out of which 46 were regular papers. Of these, 14 were selected for inclusion in this volume of the Springer CCIS series after a second round of reviewing by members of the Program Committee, representing a 30% acceptance rate. All regular papers, posters, and demonstrations received three expert single-blind reviews on average, whereas thesis and encore abstracts were reviewed by at least one Program Committee member.

All scientific contributions were presented as 20-minute talks, for which the conference program comprised four parallel tracks. In addition to these scientific presentations, we had keynote presentations by Fosca Giannotti (ISTI-CNR Pisa, Italy), Katie Atkinson (University of Liverpool, UK), Carles Sierra (IIIA of CSIC, Spain), Manuela Naveau (Kunstuniversität Linz, Austria), Julie Bernauer (NVIDIA Corporation, USA), and Iris von der Tuin (Utrecht University). We also held a special FACt (FACulty focusing on the FACts of AI) session with presentations by Benoit Macq (Polytechnic School of UCLouvain, Belgium), Gilles Louppe (University of Liège, Belgium), and Christoph Schommer (University of Luxembourg, Luxembourg).

To conclude, we want to express our gratitude to everyone who made this conference possible. Without their efforts, this conference could not have taken place. In addition to all invited speakers mentioned above, many thanks go to our sponsors: Luxembourg's National Research Fund (FNR), the Dutch Foundation for Neural Networks (SNN), the Foundation for Knowledge-Based Systems (SKBS), and the Benelux Association for AI (BNVKI). We also thank all the organizing and Program Committee members for their hard work to guarantee the high quality of this conference, both before and during the conference. We sincerely appreciate all the student volunteers, administrative and secretarial assistants, and, of course, all the academic as well as business sponsors. Finally, we also thank all the authors who made important contributions to the conference.

November 2021

Luis A. Leiva
Cédric Pruski
Réka Markovich
Amro Najjar
Christoph Schommer

Organization

General Chairs

Thibaud Latour   University of Luxembourg, Luxembourg
Leon van der Torre   University of Luxembourg, Luxembourg

Program Committee Chairs

Luis A. Leiva   University of Luxembourg, Luxembourg
Reka Markovich   University of Luxembourg, Luxembourg
Amro Najjar   University of Luxembourg, Luxembourg
Cédric Pruski   Luxembourg Institute of Science and Technology, Luxembourg
Christoph Schommer   University of Luxembourg, Luxembourg

Additional Conference Chairs

Vladimir Despotovic   University of Luxembourg, Luxembourg
Sviatlana Höhn   University of Luxembourg, Luxembourg
Nina Hosseini-Kivanani   University of Luxembourg, Luxembourg

Program Committee

Mitra Baratchi   Leiden University, The Netherlands
Floris Bex   Utrecht University, The Netherlands
Hendrik Blockeel   KU Leuven, Belgium
Bart Bogaerts   Vrije Universiteit Brussel, Belgium
Chiara Boldrini   CNR, Italy
Tibor Bosse   Radboud Universiteit, The Netherlands
Bert Bredeweg   University of Amsterdam, The Netherlands
Lu Cao   Leiden University, The Netherlands
Tom Claassen   Radboud Universiteit, The Netherlands
Walter Daelemans   University of Antwerp, Belgium
Mehdi Dastani   Utrecht University, The Netherlands
Mateusz Dubiel   University of Luxembourg, Luxembourg
Sebastijan Dumancic   TU Delft, The Netherlands
Ad Feelders   Utrecht University, The Netherlands
Miguel A. Ferrer   ULPGC, Spain
Emma Frid   IRCAM, France
Nicolas Gillis   Université de Mons, Belgium

Tom Heskes	Radboud Universiteit, The Netherlands
Arjen Hommersom	Open University of the Netherlands, The Netherlands
Mark Hoogendoorn	Vrije Universiteit Amsterdam
Michel Klein	Vrije Universiteit Amsterdam, The Netherlands
Jana Koehler	DFKI, Germany
Walter Kosters	Leiden University, The Netherlands
Johan Kwisthout	Radboud Universiteit, The Netherlands
John A. Lee	UCLouvain, Belgium
Jan Lemeire	Vrije Universiteit Brussel, Belgium
Tom Lenaerts	Vrije Universiteit Brussel, Belgium
Jefrey Lijffijt	Ghent University, Belgium
Gilles Louppe	University of Liège, Belgium
Peter Lucas	Leiden University, The Netherlands
Sven Mayer	LMU Munich, Germany
Wannes Meert	KU Leuven, Belgium
Vlado Menkovski	Eindhoven University of Technology, The Netherlands
John-Jules Meyer	Utrecht University, The Netherlands
Aske Plaat	Leiden University, The Netherlands
Henry Prakken	Utrecht University, The Netherlands
Verónica Romero	Universitat de València, Spain
Yvan Saeys	Ghent University, Belgium
Fatiha Saïs	LRI, Université Paris Sud, France
Stephan Sigg	Aalto University, Finland
Marija Slavkovik	University of Bergen, Norway
Jonas Soenen	KU Leuven, Belgium
Gerasimos Spanakis	Maastricht University, The Netherlands
Jennifer Spenader	University of Groningen, The Netherlands
Yolanda Spinola	University of Seville, Spain
Siham Tabik	University of Granada, Spain
Dirk Thierens	Utrecht University, The Netherlands
V. Javier Traver	Universitat Jaume I, Spain
Frans Oliehoek	TU Delft, The Netherlands
Egon L. van den Broek	Utrecht University, The Netherlands
Tim van Erven	University of Amsterdam, The Netherlands
Peter van der Putten	Leiden University, The Netherlands
Frank van Harmelen	Vrije Universiteit Amsterdam, The Netherlands
Nanne van Noord	University of Amsterdam, The Netherlands
Marieke van Vugt	University of Groningen, The Netherlands
Menno van Zaanen	North-West University, South Africa
Remco Veltkamp	Utrecht University, The Netherlands
Joost Vennekens	KU Leuven, Belgium
Arnoud Visser	Universiteit van Amsterdam, The Netherlands
Hui Wang	Leiden University, The Netherlands
Jef Wijsen	University of Mons, Belgium
Mark H. M. Winands	Maastricht University, The Netherlands
Yingqian Zhang	Eindhoven University of Technology, The Netherlands

Contents

Understanding Language

Reinforcing Decisions

Annotating Data

Active Learning for Reducing Labeling Effort in Text Classification Tasks

Pieter Floris Jacobs[1]([⊠])(iD), Gideon Maillette de Buy Wenniger[1,2]([⊠])(iD),
Marco Wiering[1]([⊠])(iD), and Lambert Schomaker[1]([⊠])(iD)

[1] University of Groningen, Groningen, The Netherlands
p.f.jacobs@student.rug.nl, {m.a.wiering,l.r.b.schomaker}@rug.nl
[2] Open University of the Netherlands, Heerlen, The Netherlands
gideon.maillettedebuywenniger@ou.nl

Abstract. Labeling data can be an expensive task as it is usually performed manually by domain experts. This is cumbersome for deep learning, as it is dependent on large labeled datasets. Active learning (AL) is a paradigm that aims to reduce labeling effort by only using the data which the used model deems most informative. Little research has been done on AL in a text classification setting and next to none has involved the more recent, state-of-the-art Natural Language Processing (NLP) models. Here, we present an empirical study that compares different uncertainty-based algorithms with BERT$_{base}$ as the used classifier. We evaluate the algorithms on two NLP classification datasets: Stanford Sentiment Treebank and KvK-Frontpages. Additionally, we explore heuristics that aim to solve presupposed problems of uncertainty-based AL; namely, that it is unscalable and that it is prone to selecting outliers. Furthermore, we explore the influence of the query-pool size on the performance of AL. Whereas it was found that the proposed heuristics for AL did not improve performance of AL; our results show that using uncertainty-based AL with BERT$_{base}$ outperforms random sampling of data. This difference in performance can decrease as the query-pool size gets larger.

Keywords: Active Learning · Text classification · Deep Learning · BERT

1 Introduction

Deep Learning (DL) is a field in machine learning in which neural networks with a large number of layers are made to perform complicated human tasks. These networks have to be trained on a large amount of data to be able to learn the underlying distribution of the task they are trying to model. In supervised learning, this data is required to be labeled with the desired output. This allows the network to learn to map the input to the desired output. This study will focus on an instance of supervised learning, called text classification. Data labeling is usually done manually and can grow to be an expensive and time-consuming

© Springer Nature Switzerland AG 2022
L. A. Leiva et al. (Eds.): BNAIC/Benelearn 2021, CCIS 1530, pp. 3–29, 2022.
https://doi.org/10.1007/978-3-030-93842-0_1

task for larger datasets, like those used in DL. This begs the question of whether there is no way to reduce the labeling effort while preserving good performance on the chosen task. Similarly to lossy compression [1], we want to retain a good approximation of the original dataset while at the same time reducing its size as much as possible. More specifically: given a training set, how can we optimally choose a limited number of examples based on the amount of relevant information they contain for the target task?

Conceptually, answering this question requires quantifying the amount of information contained in each data point. This finds its roots, like lossy compression, in information theory [31]. A model trained on limited data has an entropy associated with its target variable predictions. Our goal is to greedily select the data for labeling, while reducing entropy as much as possible, similar to how it is done in research on decision trees [13]. In essence, we aim to incrementally, optimally select a subset of data points; such that the distribution encoded by the learned model maximizes the information gain or equivalently minimizes the Kullback-Leibler divergence [21] with respect to the unknown distribution of the full labeled data. However, there are two problems. First, the labels of the data are not known until labeling, and additional held-out labeled data to aid the selection is typically not available either. This contrasts with the easier case of summarizing a known dataset by a subset of data, in which the Kullback-Leibler divergence of a selected subset with the full set can be measured and minimized. Second, because the parameters of a neural network change during training, predictions and certainty of new data points also change. Because of these two problems, examples can only be greedily selected based on their expected utility for improving the current, incrementally improved model. As the actual labels for examples are lacking before their selection, their real utility cannot be known during selection. Therefore, only proxies for this utility such as model uncertainty can be used, as discussed next.

A machine-learning technique called Active Learning (AL) [30] can be used to combat these problems. In AL, a human labeler is queried for data points that the network finds most informative given its current parameter configuration. The human labeler assigns labels to these queried data points and then the network is retrained on them. This process is repeated until the model shows robust performance, which indicates that the data that was labeled is a sufficient approximation of the complete dataset. There are multiple types of informativeness by which to determine what data to query the oracle for. For instance calculating what results in the largest model change [3] or through treating the model as a multi-arm bandit [2]. However, the existing literature predominantly utilizes different measures of model uncertainty [5,7–9,37], which is also done in this research. Bayesian probability theory provides us with the necessary mathematical tools to reason about uncertainty, but for DL has its complications. The reason is that (typical) neural networks, as used for classification and regression, are discriminative models. These produce a single output, a so called point estimate. Even in the case of softmax outputs this is not a true probability density function [7,8]. Another view on this is that modern neural networks often lack adequate *confidence calibration*, meaning they fail at predicting probability estimates representative of the true correctness likelihood [14].

This poses a problem to Bayesian probability theory as it prevents us from being able to perform Bayesian inference. With Bayesian inference we can determine the probability of a certain output y* given a certain input point x*:

$$p(y*|x*, X, Y) = \int p(y*|x*, \omega)p(\omega, X, Y)d\omega \tag{1}$$

Unfortunately, for the discriminative neural network models there is no probability distribution: the output is always the same for a given input. What is more, even if we suppose the network was generative (Eq. 1), the integral is not analytically solvable due to the fact that we need to integrate over all possible parameter settings ω. However, it can be approximated. Existing literature has explored different methods of achieving this, with Monte Carlo Dropout (MCDO) being the most popular one [5,8,38]. In MCDO, the network applies dropout [34] to make the network generative. Multiple stochastic forward passes are performed to produce multiple outputs for the same input. The outputs can then be used to summarize the uncertainty of the model in a variety of ways.

This research uses the MCDO approximation to compare different uncertainty-related AL query methods for text classification, noting there is still little literature on the usability of AL for modern NLP models. We strive to answer the following research question:

Research Question. *How can uncertainty-based Active Learning be used to reduce labeling effort for text classification tasks?*

Where previous literature focused on comparing AL strategies on small datasets and on the test accuracy of the final classifier, this paper will try and explore the usability of AL on a real-world setting, in which factors like the effect of transfer learning and considerations such as scalability have to be taken into account. The goal is to reach a performance similar to the state-of-the-art text-classification models that use a large randomly sampled set of labeled examples as training set. This should show whether AL can be applied to reduce labeling effort.

2   Related Work

Active Learning Applied to Deep Learning for Image Classification
Multiple methods of incorporating AL into Deep Neural Networks (DNNs) have been proposed in the past. Most of these focus on image classification tasks.

Houlsby et al. [16] proposed an information theoretic approach to AL: Bayesian Active Learning by Disagreement (BALD). In hopes of achieving state-of-the-art performance and making minimal approximations for achieving tractability, they used a Gaussian process classifier and compared the performance of BALD to nine other AL algorithms. Their findings included that BALD, which we use in this study, makes the smallest number of approximations across all tested algorithms.

Gal et al. [9] used a Bayesian convolutional network together with MCD to be able to approximate Bayesian inference and thereby proposed an AL framework that makes working with high dimensional data possible. They compared results of a variety of uncertainty-based query functions (including BALD and variation ratio) to random sampling and found that their approach to scaling AL to be able to use high dimensional data was a significant improvement to previous research, with variation ratio achieving the best results.

Drost [5] provided a more extensive discussion of the different ways of incorporating uncertainty into DNNs. He tried to learn which way of computing the uncertainty for DNNs worked best. Using a convolutional neural network, he compared the use of dropout, batch normalization, using an Ensemble of NNs and a novel method named Error Output for approximating Bayesian inference. His main conclusion was that using dropout, batch normalization and ensembles were all useful ways of lowering uncertainty in model predictions. He found that the Ensemble method provided the best uncertainty estimation and accuracy but that it was very slow to train and required a large amount of memory. He concluded MCDO, which is what we use in this study, to be a promising strategy of uncertainty estimation, albeit that one has to take into account slow inference times.

Gikunda and Jouandeau [10] explored an approach for preventing the selection of outlier examples. They combined the uncertainty measure with a correlation measure, measuring the correlation of each unlabeled example with all other unlabeled examples. A higher correlation indicated that an example was less likely to be an outlier. Their method is similar to using a local KNN-based example density as discussed in [41], which is one of the methods we used in this work. The main difference with the KNN-density approach is that their correlation-based density does not consider local neighborhoods in the density estimation. As uncertainty measure they used so-called sampling margin, which is based on the difference in probability between the most likely and second most likely class according to softmax outputs. This is somewhat similar to variation ratio, but does not use stochastic forward passes. It uses plain softmax outputs instead, making it quite distinct from the dropout-sampling based approach we adopt in this work.

Active Learning Applied to Deep Learning for Text Classification

A survey of deep learning work on using AL for text classification is given in [29]. They present a taxonomy of different query functions, including those focused on prediction and model uncertainty that we use. They also discuss the incorporation of word embeddings into DNN-based AL, which is something that we attempt in this study.

BERT is used in combination with AL in [6]. They presented a large-scale empirical study on AL techniques for BERT-based classification, covering a diverse set of AL strategies and datasets; focusing on binary text classification with small annotation budgets. They concluded that AL can be used to boost BERT performance.

Active Learning for Regression
Whereas our work is on classification, dropout-based AL can be adapted for regression as well, and this was done by [38]. They used the set of T sample predictions from the forward passes to compute sample standard deviation for the T predictions, using this as a measure of uncertainty. Evaluation was done on standard open multivariate datasets of the UCI Machine Learning repository.

Confidence Calibration
Dropout sampling as used in this work aims to solve the problem that softmax outputs are not reliable representations of the true class probabilities. This problem is known as *confidence calibration*, and dropout sampling is not the only solution to it.

Guo et al. [14] evaluated the performance of various post-processing techniques that took the neural network outputs and transformed them into values closer to representative probabilities. They found that in particular a simplified form of *Platt Scaling*, known as *temperature scaling*, was effective in calibrating predictions on many datasets. This method conceptually puts a logistic regression model with just one learnable 'temperature' parameter behind the softmax outputs, and is trained by optimizing negative log likelihood (NLL) loss over the validation set. It thus learns to spread out or peak the probabilities further in a way that helps to decrease NLL loss, thereby as a side-effect increasing calibration. Recently, using a new procedure inspired by Platt Scaling, Kuleshov et al. [20] generalized an effective approach for confidence calibration to be usable for regression problems as well.

Discriminative Active Learning and Cartography Active Learning
Gissin and Shalev-Shwartz [11] proposed an AL method, called Discriminative Active Learning (DAL). Their method uses a separate binary classifier trained to distinguish examples from the labeled and unlabeled set. Using this classifier, the acquisition function is then set to prefer examples predicted to belong to the unlabeled set, with the aim of greedily making the labeled set more similar to the unlabeled one. The classifier uses as input the representation learned by the model, but not the labels. Their approach was evaluated on image classification tasks. While it was competitive when using large batch sizes and labeling budgets, it fell behind uncertainty-based methods in other settings.

Zhang and Plank [40] proposed a new AL method called Cartography Active Learning (CAL), which takes inspiration from work on *Data Maps* [35] as well as DAL [11]. Like DAL, they used a separate binary classifier as the basis for their acquisition function. Different from DAL however, they used the available labels when determining example informativeness. Their method uses the information about the model performance on the currently labeled dataset to predict the informativeness of currently unlabeled examples. They trained a classifier that predicts whether training examples have been correctly classified across training epochs, for a fraction of times above a chosen threshold. The used acquisition function favors unlabeled examples closest to the decision boundary of this classifier, as these *ambiguous* yet not overly easy or hard examples were hypothesized to be the most beneficial for training the model.

The method was evaluated on text classification tasks. Significant improvements over state-of-the-art AL methods, as well as analysis based on confidence, variability and correctness statistics [35] provide evidence for the effectiveness of the method. The model used for evaluating the method utilizes averaged word embeddings as inputs to a Multi-layer Perceptron; as opposed to more context-aware sentence encodings such as those provided by BERT.

3   Methods

This section will go on to describe the general AL loop, the model architecture, the used query functions, the implemented heuristics, and finally the experimental setup.

3.1   Active Learning

An implementation of the general AL loop/round is shown in Appendix A.2 (Algorithm 1). It consists of four steps:

1. **Train:** The model is reset to its initial parameters. After this, the model is trained on the labeled dataset $\mathcal{L}$. The model is reset before training because otherwise the model would overfit on data from previous rounds [17].
2. **Query:** A predefined query function is used to determine what data is to be labeled in this AL round. As discussed, this can be done in various ways, but the guiding principle is that the data that the model finds most useful for the chosen task gets queried.
3. **Annotate:** The queried data is parsed to a human expert, often referred to as the oracle. The oracle then labels the queried examples.
4. **Append:** The newly-labeled examples are transferred from the unlabeled dataset $\mathcal{U}$ to $\mathcal{L}$. The model is now ready to be retrained to recompute the informativeness of the examples in $\mathcal{U}$ now that the underlying distribution of $\mathcal{L}$ has been altered.

Please note that the datasets used for the experiments (Sect. 3.5) were fully labeled and the annotation step thus got skipped in this research. $\mathcal{U}$ existed out of labeled data that was only trained on from the moment it got queried. This was done to speed up the process and to enable scalable and replicable experiments with varying experimental setups.

3.2   Model Architecture

BERT. The model used to classify the texts was $BERT_{base}$ [4], a state-of-the-art language model which is a variant of the Transformer model [39]. Specifically, we used the uncased version of $BERT_{base}$, as the information of capitalization and accent markers was judged to be not helpful for the used tasks and datasets. Due to computational constraints, only the first sentence of the used texts was put into the tokenizer and the maximal length to which the tokenizer either padded or cut down this sentence was set to 50. To better deal with unknown words and shorter text, we used the option of the $BERT_{base}$ tokenizer to make use of special tokens for sentence separation, padding, masking and to generalize unknown vocabulary. Finally, a softmax layer was added to the end of $BERT_{base}$, which is essential as the implemented query functions (Sect. 3.3) compute uncertainty based on sampled output probability distributions.

Monte Carlo Dropout. Monte Carlo dropout (MCDO) is, as discussed in Sect. 1, a technique that enables reasoning about uncertainty with neural networks. Dropout [34] essentially 'turns off' neurons during the forward pass with a predefined probability. Dropout is normally used during training to prevent overfitting and create a more generalized model. In MCDO though, it is used to approximate Bayesian inference [8] through creating T predictions for all data points, using T slightly different models induced by different dropout samples. The result of these so-called stochastic forward passes (SFP's) can then be used by the query function to compute the uncertainty, as will be explained in Sect. 3.3. The way MCDO is incorporated in the AL loop is shown in green in the Appendix (Algorithm 2). $BERT_{base}$ has two different types of dropout layers: hidden dropout and attention dropout. Both were turned on when performing a stochastic forward pass. Note that there are other ways of approximating Bayesian inference with neural networks. Frequently used ones are:

- Having an ensemble of neural networks vote on the label [19].
- Monte Carlo Batch Normalization (MCBN) [37].

MCDO was chosen over the ensemble method due to it being easier to implement and quicker to train. MCBN was not chosen as it has been shown to be more inconsistent than MCDO [5].

Sentence-BERT. Textual data offers the advantage of having access to the use of pre-trained word embeddings. These are learned representations of words into a vector space in which semantically similar words are close together. Textual embeddings can be computed in a variety of ways. BERT specific ones include averaging the pooled BERT embeddings and looking at the BERT CLS token output. Other more general ways are averaging over Glove word embeddings [26] and averaging embeddings created by a Word2Vec model [23]. We have opted to make use of Sentence-BERT [27], a Siamese BERT architecture trained to produce embeddings that can be adequately compared using cosine-similarity. For our purposes this provides better performance than the other embedding computations. Sentence-BERT was used separately from the previously discussed $BERT_{base}$ model, and was used only for assigning embeddings to each sentence in the dataset that were used by the heuristics described in Sect. 3.4.

3.3   Query Functions

The query functions determine data selection choices of the model in the AL loop. This paper will focus on functions that reason about uncertainty, obtained from approximated Bayesian distributions [8]. For every data point, the distribution is derived from T stochastic forward passes and resulting T (in our case) softmax probability distributions. The following subsections will go on to discuss the implemented query functions. One is encouraged to look at [7] for an extensive discussion that highlights the difference between these functions.

Variation Ratio. The variation ratio is a measure of dispersion around the class that the model predicts most often (the mode). The intuition here is that the model is uncertain about a data point when it has predicted the mode class a relatively small number of times. This indicates that it has predicted other classes a relatively large number of times. Equation 2 shows how the variation ratio is computed, where f_x denotes the mode count and T the number of stochastic forward passes.

$$v[x] = 1 - \frac{f_x}{T} \tag{2}$$

The function attains its maximum value when the model predicts all classes an equal amount of times and its minimum value when the model only predicts one class across all stochastic forward passes. Variation ratio only captures the uncertainty contained in the predictions, not the model, as it only takes into account the spread around the most predicted class. It is thus a form of predictive uncertainty.

Predictive Entropy. Entropy $H(x)$ in the context of information theory is defined as:

$$H(x) = -\sum_{i=1}^{n} p(x_i) \log_2 p(x_i) \tag{3}$$

This formula expresses the entropy in bits per symbol to be communicated, in which $p(x_i)$ gives the probability of the i-th possible value for the symbol. Entropy is used to quantify the information of data. In our case we want to know the chance of the model classifying a data point as a certain class given the input and model parameters ($p(y = c|\mathbf{x}, \boldsymbol{\omega})$). We can compute this chance by averaging over the softmax probability distributions across the T stochastic forward passes. This adjusted version of entropy is denoted in Eq. 4, where $\hat{\omega}_t$ denotes the stochastic forward pass t, and c the number associated to the class-label.

$$H[y|\mathbf{x}, \mathcal{D}_{train}] = -\sum_c \left(\frac{1}{T} \sum_t p(y = c|\mathbf{x}, \hat{\omega}_t) \right) \\ \log \left(\frac{1}{T} \sum_t p(y = c|\mathbf{x}, \hat{\omega}_t) \right) \tag{4}$$

To exemplify: in binary classification, the predictive entropy is highest when the model its softmax classifications consist of T times $[0.5, 0.5]$. In that case, expected surprise when we would come to know the real class-label is at its highest. The uncertainty is computed by averaging over all predictions and thus falls under predictive uncertainty.

Bayesian Active Learning by Disagreement. Predictive entropy (Sect. 3.3) is used to quantify the information in one variable. Mutual information or joint entropy is very similar but is used to calculate the amount of information one variable conveys about another. In our case, we'll be looking at what the average model prediction will convey about the model posterior, given the training data. This is a form of conditional mutual information, the condition or the third variable being the training data $\mathcal{D}_{train}$. Houlsby et al. [16] used this form of mutual information in an AL setting and dubbed it Bayesian active learning by disagreement (BALD).

$$
\begin{aligned}
I[y, \omega | \mathbf{x}, \mathcal{D}_{train}] = - \sum_c & \left(\frac{1}{T} \sum_t p(y = c | \mathbf{x}, \hat{\omega}_t) \right) \\
& \log \left(\frac{1}{T} \sum_t p(y = c | \mathbf{x}, \hat{\omega}_t) \right) \\
& - \frac{1}{T} \sum_{c,t} p(y = c | \mathbf{x}, \hat{\omega}_t) \\
& \log p(y = c | \mathbf{x}, \hat{\omega}_t)
\end{aligned}
\tag{5}
$$

The difference between Eqs. 5 and 4 is that the conditional entropy is subtracted from the predictive entropy. The conditional entropy is the probability of the full output being generated from the training data and the input. This is the reason we do not average the predictions for every single class. We first sum over all classes, so that we do not average over the model parameters for every single class and thus take into account the fact that we are looking at the chance of the complete probability distribution being generated.

BALD is maximized when the T predictions are strongly disagreeing about what label to assign to the example. So in the binary case, it would be highest when the predictions would alter between $[1, 0]$ and $[0, 1]$ as these two predictions are each others complete opposite. Unlike the variation ratio and predictive entropy, BALD is a form of model uncertainty. When the softmax outputs would be equal to T times $[0.5, 0.5]$, the minimal BALD value would be returned as the predictions are the same and the model is thus very confident about its prediction.

3.4   Heuristics

Redundancy Elimination. In AL, a larger query-pool size (from now on referred to as q) results in the model being retrained less and the uncertainties of examples being re-evaluated less frequently. Consequently, the model gets to make less informed decisions as it uses less up-to-date uncertainty estimates. Larger q could therefore theoretically cause the model to collect many similar examples for specific example types with high model uncertainty in an AL round. Say for instance we were dealing with texts about different movie genres. Suppose the data contained a lot of texts about the exact same movie. When the model would be uncertain about this type of text, a large q would result in a large amount of these texts getting queried. This could be wasteful, as querying this type of text a small amount of times would likely result in the model no longer being uncertain about that type of text. Note however, that low model uncertainty by itself is no guarantee for robustly making accurate predictions for a type of examples. Yet provided such robust performance is achieved, additional examples of the same type would be a waste.

The above could form a problem as although a smaller q should theoretically provide us with better results, it also requires more frequent uncertainties re-computation. Every computation of the uncertainties requires T stochastic forward passes on the unlabeled dataset $\mathcal{U}$. This entails that, next to the computation, the time required to label a dataset would increase as well, which is not in line with our goal. In hopes of improving performance with larger q, we propose two heuristics:

1. Redundancy Elimination by Training (RET)
2. Redundancy Elimination by Cosine Similarity (RECS).

For both of these heuristics, a new pool, which we will refer to as the redundancy-pool $\mathcal{RP}$, is introduced. The query-pool $\mathcal{QP}$ will be a subset of $\mathcal{RP}$ of which we will try to select the most dissimilar examples.

RET tries to eliminate redundant data out of $\mathcal{RP}$ by using it as a pool to retrain on. The data point with the highest uncertainty is trained on for one epoch and then the uncertainties of the examples in $\mathcal{RP}$ are recomputed. This process gets repeated until $\mathcal{QP}$ is of the desired size. Note that although this strategy seems similar to having a q of one, it is less computationally expensive as only the uncertainties for the examples in $\mathcal{RP}$ have to be recomputed (which also shrinks after each repetition). Algorithm 3 of Appendix A.2 shows how RET is integrated in the AL loop.

The main purpose of RET is to enable the use of larger q. However, one needs to be mindful of the fact that when q is increased, $\mathcal{RP}$ is to be increased in size well. This being due to the fact that smaller differences between the sizes of $\mathcal{RP}$ and $\mathcal{QP}$ result in less influence of the heuristic. In the RET algorithm, forward passes over $\mathcal{RP}$ contribute to the total amount of forward passes. Furthermore, this contribution increases linearly with the redundancy-pool size ($|\mathcal{RP}|$) and in practice coupled query-pool size q. Using $|\mathcal{RP}| = 1.5 \times q$, this contribution starts to dominate the total amount of forward passes (approximately) once $q > \sqrt{|\text{data}|}$. This is explained in more detail in Appendix A.1. This limits its use for decreasing computation by increasing q. Because of this, RECS is aimed at being computationally cheaper.

Instead of retraining the model and constantly taking into account recomputed uncertainties, RECS makes use of the sentence embeddings created by Sentence-BERT (Sect. 3.2). The assumption made is that semantically similar data conveys the same type of information to the model. The examples are selected based on their cosine similarity to other examples. $\mathcal{RP}$ is looped through and examples are only added to $\mathcal{QP}$ if their cosine similarity to all other points that are already in $\mathcal{QP}$ is lower than the chosen threshold l. If not enough examples are selected to get the desired q, the threshold gets decreased by 0.01. Algorithm 4 of Appendix A.2 shows how this heuristic is added to the AL loop.

Sampling by Uncertainty and Density (SUD). Schomaker and Oosten [25] showed that the distinction between separability and prototypicality is important to account for. In their use case of the SVM, data points that had a high margin to the decision boundary were not always representative of the class prototype. Uncertainty sampling also tries to sample examples close to the decision boundary, but has been shown to often select outliers [28,36]. Outliers contain a lot of information that the model has not encountered yet, but this information is not necessarily useful. As with the previously described RECS heuristic, we hypothesize that semantically similar sentences provide the same type of information. In that situation, outliers are very far from other examples in embedding space.

Zhu et al. [41] proposed a K-Nearest-Neighbor-based density approach called Sampling by Uncertainty and Density (SUD) to avoid outliers based on their distance in embedding space. In this approach, the mean cosine similarity between every data point and its K most similar neighbors is computed. A low value indicates that a data point is not very similar to others. This value is then multiplied with the uncertainty and the dataset is sorted based on this Uncertainty-Density measure. They showed that this measure improved performance of the maximum entropy model classifier. We will explore whether this approach also works for BERT combined with the embeddings computed by Sentence-BERT. The adjusted pseudocode is shown in Appendix A.2 (Algorithm 5).

3.5   Experimental Setup

Data. (The code used for the experiments can be found at https://github.com/Pieter-Jacobs/bachelor-thesis.) Two datasets were used to validate and compare the performance of the different AL implementations. Table 1 shows an overview of the amount of examples and classes of each dataset. The first of the used datasets was the Stanford Sentiment Treebank [33] (SST). SST exists out of 215,154 phrases from movies with fine-grained sentiment labels in the range of 0 to 1. These phrases are contained in the parse trees of 11,855 sentences. Only these full sentences were used in the experiments, and the sentiment labels were mapped to five categories in the following way:

Table 1. An overview of the two datasets used in the experiments

Dataset	Examples	Number of classes
SST	11,850	5
KvK	2212	15

- $0 \leq$ label < 0.2: very negative
- $0.2 \leq$ label < 0.4: negative
- $0.4 \leq$ label ≤ 0.6: neutral
- $0.6 <$ label ≤ 0.8: positive
- $0.8 <$ label ≤ 1: very positive

Use of the SST dataset was motivated by its size as well as by it being a benchmark for language models. It allowed for the evaluation of AL for a larger dataset and for comparison with results found in related work such as [24]. This helped to check whether BERT$_{base}$ was achieving desirable performance.

The second dataset that was used consists of the descriptions of companies located in Utrecht. The companies are all registered at the Dutch Chamber of Commerce, or Kamer van Koophandel (KvK) and were mapped to their corresponding SBI-code. The SBI code denotes the sector a company operates in, as defined by the KvK. The HTML of the companies websites was scraped and the meta content that was tagged as the description was extracted. In nearly all cases, this contained a short description about what the company was involved in. Note that only English descriptions were used. The KvK dataset provided us with the opportunity to evaluate AL for a classification problem with a large amount of classes as well as the ability to compare results between a dataset with a limited number of examples and one with a relatively large amount of examples (SST). Testing AL on a dataset with a limited number of examples was deemed necessary due to the fact that most of the positive results found in related work were achieved by making use of very small datasets. The dataset will not be shared and is not available online due to the fact that it was constructed as part of an internship at Dialogic.

Evaluation Metrics. To evaluate and compare the performance of the different AL strategies, two evaluation metrics were reported: the accuracy and an altered version of the deficiency metric proposed in [41].

The variant of deficiency that was used is shown in Eq. 6, in which n denotes the amount of accuracy scores, $acc(R)$ denotes the accuracy of the reference strategy and $acc(C)$ the accuracy of the strategy to be compared to this reference strategy. In our case, n is equal to $\frac{|\mathcal{U}|}{q} + 1$ (+1 comes from the accuracy achieved after training on the seed), as we computed the test accuracy after every AL round.[1] Furthermore, instead of using the accuracy that was achieved in the final AL round for $acc(C)$ and $acc(R)$ like [41], we use the overall maximum accuracy. This accounts for the fact that the last achieved accuracy in a

---

[1] For our experiments, this resulted in our n ranging from 20 to 191 for the SST dataset and from 17 to 152 for the KvK dataset (the used q can be found in Sect. 3.5).

classification task is not necessarily the best value, while still returning a metric which provides a summary of the entire learning curve. This in turn means that a decrease/increase in its value is analogical to a decrease/increase in overall performance of the comparison strategy. However, the deficiency does not convey whether there were points at which the accuracy of a strategy was higher than usual and would serve as a good point to cut-down the dataset to reduce labeling effort. A deficiency of <1 indicates a better performance than the reference strategy whereas a value of >1 indicates a worse performance.

$$DEF(AL, R) = \frac{\sum_{t=1}^{n}(max(acc(R)) - acc_t(C))}{\sum_{t=1}^{n}(max(acc(R)) - acc_t(R))} \tag{6}$$

Experiments. The goal of the experiments was to answer the question of whether overall labeling effort could be reduced through making use of AL. We split this into the following three sub-questions:

1. Does AL achieve better performance with less data when compared to plain random sampling?
2. What is the relation between query-pool size q and the achieved performance?
3. Do the proposed heuristics (SUD, RET, RECS) improve the performance of AL?

The statistical setup used for the experiments can be found in Table 2. The setup for SST was based on the proposed setup in [33]. To reiterate, the following AL strategies were implemented:

1. Variation Ratio (Sect. 3.3)
2. Predictive Entropy (Sect. 3.3)
3. BALD (Sect. 3.3)

4. RET (Sect. 3.4)
5. RECS (Sect. 3.4)
6. SUD (Sect. 3.4)

Table 2. The statistical setup used for both datasets. The percentages used are relative to the full dataset size.

Dataset	Seed	$\mathcal{U}$	Dev	Test
SST	594 (5%)	7951 (67%)	1101 (9%)	2210 (19%)
KvK	111 (5%)	1659 (75%)	221 (10%)	221 (10%)

To answer subquestion 1, these strategies were compared to the performance of random sampling using a q of 1% of the dataset size. For subquestion 2, the three query functions were be compared across three q: 0.5%, 1% and 5% of the dataset size. Finally, to be able to answer subquestion 3, RET, RECT and SUD were compared with a q of 1%. As RET, RECS and SUD were meant as additions to general problems of uncertainty-based AL, they were only tested for the variation ratio query function. This function was chosen, because it was reported in [7] to give the best result. To make the results more generalizable, all the experiments mentioned above were run three times.

Moreover, to test the assumption of the RECT strategy, we measured whether there was a relation between how the model softmax predictions changed towards the one-hot vector of the actual label and the cosine similarity to the data point that was trained on. The relationship was quantified by means of Kendall's τ between the ranking of the examples based on which one had the largest change in KL divergence after training on the top example and the ranking of the examples based on cosine similarity to the example being trained on.

Hyperparameters. Table 4 gives an overview of used hyperparameters. Model weights were randomly initialized using the various PyTorch initialization defaults for the respective model components. In addition to the randomness of weight initialization, randomness determines dropout choices during training. These two forms of randomness influence model performance. For each system/setting, we averaged results over three repeated runs which were identical except for these random elements. This helps to prevent false conclusions due to performance differences caused by effects of these elements.

Both dropout rate and l (the cosine-similarity threshold used in RECS) were chosen based on a grid search across both datasets. The amount of stochastic forward passes T was based on [6] and was set to 10 across all experiments.[2] Early stopping was applied on each training phase of the AL loop, Table 3 shows the amount of epochs used for each dataset. The model yielding the lowest validation loss across all epochs was used for evaluation and uncertainties computation. Note that in a normal AL setting, validation sets are usually not available due to the labelling effort required and this strategy would be less feasible.

The Adam algorithm [18] was used for optimization and its learning rate was tuned based on the CLR method [32]. The best performing computationally feasible batch size (128), out of the tried batch sizes (32, 64, 128, 256), was used in all experiments. The betas and ϵ were set to their default values. The size of $\mathcal{RP}$ was chosen arbitrarily, determining its optimal choice is left future research.

Finally, dimensionality reduction using PCA was tried to determine whether this would result in better class-separability. For every data point in the full dataset, the classes of the group of ten most similar data points (based on cosine similarity) were determined. By maximizing the average of the number of within-group same-class data points, the used dimensionality was determined.

---

[2] Larger values up to 100 were tested, but induced much larger training times without noteworthy performance gains.

Table 3. The amount of epochs used for early stopping for the different datasets.

Dataset	# Epochs
SST	15
KvK	25

Table 4. Hyperparameters values

Parameter	Value
Dropout rate	0.2
T	10
l	0
β_1, β_2	0.9, 0.999
ϵ	$1 * 10^{-8}$
Learning rate	$2 * 10^{-5}$
Batch size	128
$\mathcal{RP}$ size	$1.5*q$
Embedding dim.	768

4   Results

This section will go onto visualize and describe the achieved results for all three experiments described in Sect. 3.5. Note that for all figures, the results were averaged over three runs with the error bars showing one standard deviation. Furthermore, all deficiencies were rounded to two decimal places. For deficiency values <1 (improvements over the reference strategy), we show the smallest value in the comparison in bold. For the sake of readability and to keep graph points aligned, in the graphs for query-pool sizes of 0.5% and 1% the points shown are respectively those at every 10th and 5th and interval.

4.1   Active Learning

Figure 1a shows how the query functions performed on the KvK dataset. All query functions outperform random sampling when the labeled dataset is less than 200 examples large. After this, in particular BALD and variation ratio continue to mostly outperform random sampling until near the maximum labeled data size. Notably, many of the performance differences are larger than one standard deviation.

Figure 1b shows how random sampling and the implemented query functions performed on the SST dataset. On this dataset the results for the random sampling baseline and the other systems is much smaller, and there does not seem to be a clear winner.

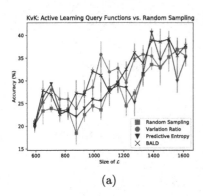 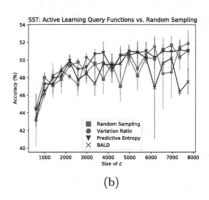

(a)   (b)

Fig. 1. The achieved test accuracy on the KvK dataset (a) and on the SST dataset (b) by random sampling and the uncertainty-based query functions.

Finally, the deficiencies shown in Table 5 show a positive result (<1) for all query functions except for predictive entropy for the SST dataset. Matching the graphs, the performance gains as measured by the deficiency scores are overall more substantial on the KvK dataset. BALD has the lowest deficiency for both datasets.

Table 5. The deficiencies (Eq. 6) of the uncertainty-based query functions. Random sampling was the reference strategy.

Dataset	VR	PE	BALD
SST	0.95	1.01	**0.89**
KvK	0.67	0.9	**0.64**

4.2   Query-Pool Size

Figure 2a shows the performance of variation ratio across different q when used on the KvK dataset. In the middle range of the graph, variation ratio with a q of 5% has a worse performance than the other q. The q of 0.5% and 1% achieve similar performance with the accuracy scores always staying within one standard deviation of each other.

Figure 2b shows the performance of the different q on the SST dataset. The performance of variation ratio with a q of 0.5% fluctuates more when compared to the other q. Moreover, it results in an overall worse performance when compared to the other sizes. The q of 5% shows to have the best and most consistent performance over the whole learning curve in terms accuracy. However, the q of 0.5% manages to outperform the other q at about 5000 labeled examples.

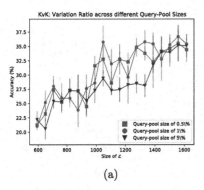
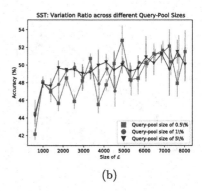

(a)   (b)

Fig. 2. The achieved test accuracy on the KvK dataset (a) and the SST dataset (b) by using the variation ratio query function with different q.

The deficiencies for the different q across both datasets are shown in Table 6. For the SST dataset, the q of 5% had a lower deficiency across the learning curve whereas the q of 0.5% shows a relatively high deficiency. For the KvK dataset however, we see that the q of 5% has a relatively high deficiency when compared to the similarly performing q of 0.5% and 1%.

Table 6. The achieved deficiencies (Eq. 6) by the different q for the different datasets. A q of 1% was the reference strategy.

Dataset	0.5%	5%
SST	1.65	**0.62**
KvK	**0.91**	1.33

4.3 Heuristics

Figure 3a shows the performance of using variation ratio with heuristics together with the performance of solely using variation ratio on the KvK dataset (also shown in Fig. 1b). Both RET and RECT show no clear improvement over solely using variation ratio. The same can be gathered from the results of the SST dataset shown in Fig. 3b as their accuracy scores stay within one standard deviation for the entire learning curve. Moreover, Table 7 shows that the average Kendall's τ is around 0 with a relatively large standard deviation; indicating that there is no relationship between the compared rankings.

Lastly, SUD shows an overall worse performance for both the SST and KvK datasets. The deficiencies shown in Table 8 also show high values for SUD across both datasets.

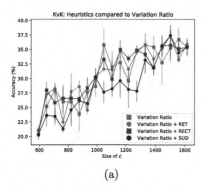 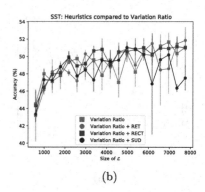

(a)   (b)

Fig. 3. The achieved test accuracy on the KvK dataset (a) and on the SST dataset (b) by the different heuristics.

Table 7. The mean and the 1 SD range of Kendall's τ from the described ranking experiment across the two datasets (rounded to two decimal places).

Dataset	Mean	σ
SST	0.14	0.33
KvK	0.02	0.47

Table 8. The achieved deficiencies by the different heuristics. Variation ratio was the reference strategy.

Dataset	RET	RECT	SUD
SST	1.02	1.05	1.23
KvK	0.98	**0.96**	1.33

5   Discussion

This research investigated whether AL could be used to reduce labeling effort while at the same time maintaining similar performance to a model trained on a full dataset. To achieve this, the performance and scalability of different AL query-strategies was tested for the state-of-the-art NLP model: BERT.

Conclusions. The results showed that uncertainty-based AL can provide improved performance over random sampling for cut-down datasets. This difference was not consistent throughout the whole training curve: at specific points AL outperformed random sampling and at others at it achieved similar performance. BALD was the query function with the overall best performance. This could be the case due to the fact that it is the only query function used which measures model uncertainty. The found results differs from what was found in [7,9], where variation ratio achieved the best overall performance.

Unfortunately, the results found for the KvK dataset show that the found improvement can diminish as query-pool sizes get larger, which corresponds to what was theorized hypothesized in Sect. 3.4.

Moreover, the two proposed heuristics aimed at improving scalability did not help in improving performance for either dataset and the heuristic aimed at avoiding outliers even resulted in worse performance. This was surprising due to the favorable results found in [41], albeit that they only tested it for training sets of up to 150 examples.

An unexpected result was found in that the assumption that semantically similar data conveyed the same type of information did not hold according to the conducted ranking experiment. A possible explanation for this could be that the texts were not mapped to embeddings in a way in which semantically similar data was close enough to each other. Another curious finding was that for the SST dataset, the smallest q resulted in the worse performance, especially at the beginning of the learning curve. This is counter-intuitive due to the fact that performance seems to suffer from more frequent uncertainty estimates. A potential justification for this could be that updating too frequently at the beginning of the learning curve results in the model not being able to train enough on high frequency classes. This could result in the model focusing too much on the long tail of the class distribution due to the fact that it is more uncertain about texts with low frequency classes at the start of the learning curve. Further research is needed to build a better understanding of this. Conversely, given that AL was shown to have little influence on the achieved accuracy and that most of the differences between the different q are within one standard deviation, one could argue that that the size of q did have an influence on the results whatsoever and that we thus cannot conclude anything from the found results.

From the above, we conclude that uncertainty-based AL with $BERT_{base}$ can be used to decrease labeling effort. This supports what was concluded by [12].

When looking at the bigger picture, we showed that AL can still provide an improvement in performance over random sampling for large datasets. The improvement of performance of AL with BERT is however limited when compared to what it achieved for older NLP models [28,36,41] and even more so when compared to image classifiers [5,9,16]. Performance did show to increase more when used on the KvK dataset. A possible explanation for this is its smaller size. BERT is pretrained on a large amount of data and only needs fine-tuning for achieving good performance on a specific task. Transfer learning models [15] like BERT have the ability to perform well on new tasks with just a limited amount of data. The power of this few-shot learning also became apparent on a dataset which we decided not to use. Here, BERT was able to get a low validation error on the seed alone, while at the same time having a training accuracy of 100%.

An additional explanation can be found in the nature of the two tasks and their examples. The SST dataset belongs to a sentiment analysis task, with sentiment scores in the range 0–1. These were binned into spans of 0.2 to get a five-class classification task. Furthermore, bag-of-words (BOW) models such as Naive Bayes were shown to perform relatively really well on this task, because specific individual words provide substantial information about the class. As a consequence, each example is actually *compound*: it indirectly provides information about not just that example but about the sentiment contributions of all the words in that example as well. In contrast, the KvK dataset provides is a real classification task as opposed to a regression task converted to classification task, with 15 distinct classes. A subset of words in each example can be expected to be informative for the class label, as opposed to words giving nearly independent contributions as is the case in sentiment analysis.

A limitation of the research was that, due to computational constraints, only the first sentence of texts was used. There were data points where the first sentence did not contain any clear indication of its label. Take for example the following description from the KvK dataset:

> *"**Hi, I'm Barbara Goudsmit.** Welcome to my woven world! I am a passionate hand weaver from the Netherlands who loves creating patterns and bringing them to live on my 8-shaft loom."*

This type of data could have resulted in the network learning suboptimal mappings, which could in turn have had an influence on the performance of AL.

Future Research. This work focused on classification tasks. A future direction could be to investigate the influence of AL on BERT's performance in the context of regression tasks and also to examine how the proposed heuristics perform there. Moreover, more recent BERT variants, like for instance RoBERTa [22], could be tested to see whether AL still outperforms the random sampling benchmark. Furthermore, the used query functions were mostly developed for and used in computer vision. Query functions aimed at text classification or at the fact that BERT is a pretrained model could be further investigated. Lastly, an important direction for future work remains making AL more scalable by finding ways to preserve performance with larger query-pool sizes.

Acknowledgments. We would like to express our thanks and gratitude to the people at Dialogic (Utrecht) of which Nick Jelicic in particular, for the useful advice on the writing style of the paper and the suggested improvements for the source code.

Appendix

A.1   RET Algorithm Computational Cost Analysis

The number of forward passes required by the RET algorithm depends on two factors:

1. *Basic passes*: The forward passes required by the "normal" computation of uncertainty at the beginning of the computation for every query-pool.
2. *RP passes*: The forward passed required for intermediate updates, using the redundancy pool RP.

In this analysis we will assume that the size of the redundancy pool $|\mathcal{RP}|$ is chosen as a factor $f > 1$ of the size of the query-pool q. A reasonable assumption, considering that making $|\mathcal{RP}|$ larger than needed incurs unnecessary computational cost, whereas a too small value is expected to diminish the effect of the RET algorithm. We furthermore notice that given this assumption, and assuming a fixed total number of examples to label, there are two factors influencing the required amount of *RP passes*:

- Linearly increasing the query-pool size and coupled redundancy pool size causes a quadratic increase in the number of required forward passes per query pool round.
- At the same time, a linearly increased query-pool size also induces a corresponding linear decrease in the number of required query-pool rounds.

We will see that these two factors will cause a net linear contribution to the number of *RP passes* starts causing a net increase of total passes once the query-size comes above a certain value. Looking at (1) more precisely, the amount of passes over $\mathcal{RP}$ that needs to be performed per query-pool round can be computed as an *arithmetic progression*:

$$|\mathcal{RP}| + (|\mathcal{RP}| - 1) + (|\mathcal{RP}| - 2) + \ldots + (|\mathcal{RP} - q) \tag{7}$$

$$= \frac{1}{2} \times (q + 1) \times (|\mathcal{RP}| + |\mathcal{RP}| - q) \tag{8}$$

$$= \frac{1}{2} \times (q + 1) \times ((2f - 1) \times q) \tag{9}$$

$$= \frac{1}{2} \times (q + 1) \times f' \times q \tag{10}$$

$$= \frac{1}{2} \times f' \times (q^2 + q)) \tag{11}$$

Let's assume we use $f = 1.5$ (as also used in our experiments), and consequently, $f' = 2f - 1 = 2$. The number of forward passes over $\mathcal{RP}$ then becomes exactly $q^2 + q$.

The complexity can then be expressed by the following formula:

$$T \times \lceil \frac{\#\text{Samples}}{q} \rceil \times (|\text{data}| + q^2 + q) \tag{12}$$

This can be approximately rewritten as:

$$T \times \#\text{Samples} \times (\frac{|\text{data}|}{q} + \frac{q^2 + q}{\text{query-pool}}) \tag{13}$$

$$= T \times \#\text{Samples} \times (\frac{|\text{data}|}{q} + q + 1) \tag{14}$$

Note that the second term query-pool-size + 1 only starts dominating the number of forward passes in this formula as soon as:

$$q + 1 \approx q > \frac{|\text{data}|}{q}$$

This is the case when

$$q > \sqrt{(|\text{data}|)}$$

Until then, the computational gains of less *basic passes* outweighs the cost of more *RP passes*. In practice though, this may happen fairly quickly. For example, assuming we have a data size of 10000 examples, and we use as mentioned $q = 1.5| \times \mathcal{RP}|$, then as soon as $q \geq 100$ the increased computation of the *RP passes* starts dominating the gains made by less *basic passes* when further increasing the query-pool size, and the net effect is that the total amount of computation increases.

In summary, for the RET algorithm, *RP passes* contribute to the total amount of forward passes. Furthermore, this contribution increases linearly with redundancy-pool size and coupled query-pool size, and starts to dominate the total amount of forward passes once redundancy-pool-size $> \sqrt{\text{data-size}}$. This limits its use for decreasing computation by increasing the query-pool size.

A.2   Algorithms

Algorithm 1. The general AL loop.

Input Labeled dataset $\mathcal{L} = \{(x_i, y_i)\}_i^n$, the unlabeled data $\mathcal{U} = \{(x_i, \emptyset)\}_i^n$ and the untrained classifier $f(x; \theta)$.
Output Fully labeled dataset $\mathcal{L} = \{(x_i, y_i)\}_i^n$ and trained classifier $f(x; \theta)$

  1: $n \leftarrow$ Desired length of $\mathcal{L}$
  2: $q \leftarrow$ Query-pool size
  3: $Q(x) \leftarrow$ Query Function
  4: **while** $\mathcal{L}$ length $< n$ **do**
  5:     Retrain $f(x; \theta)$ on $\mathcal{L}$
  6:     Sort $\mathcal{U}$ based on $Q(\mathcal{U})$
  7:     Let Oracle assign labels to $\mathcal{U}_0^q$
  8:     Insert $\mathcal{U}_0^q$ into $\mathcal{L}$
  9:     Remove $\mathcal{U}_0^q$ from $\mathcal{U}$
 10: **end while**

Algorithm 2. The AL loop with MCD.

Input Labeled dataset $\mathcal{L} = \{(x_i, y_i)\}_i^n$, the unlabeled data $\mathcal{U} = \{(x_i, \emptyset)\}_i^n$ and the untrained classifier $f(x; \theta)$.
Output Fully labeled dataset $\mathcal{L} = \{(x_i, y_i)\}_i^n$ and trained classifier $f(x; \theta)$

1: $n \leftarrow$ Desired dataset length
2: $q \leftarrow$ Query-pool size
3: $Q(x) \leftarrow$ Query Function
4: $T \leftarrow$ Number of SFP's
5: **while** $\mathcal{L}$ length $< n$ **do**
6:     Retrain $f(x; \theta)$ on $\mathcal{L}$
7:     $P \leftarrow \emptyset$
8:     **for** $t = 0, ..., T$ **do**
9:         insert $f(\mathcal{U}; \theta_t)$ into P
10:     **end for**
11:     Sort $\mathcal{U}$ based on $Q(P)$
12:     Let Oracle assign labels to $\mathcal{U}_0^q$
13:     Insert $\mathcal{U}_0^q$ into $\mathcal{L}$
14:     Remove $\mathcal{U}_0^q$ from $\mathcal{U}$
15: **end while**

Algorithm 3. The AL loop with Redundancy Elimination by Training (RET).

Input Labeled dataset $\mathcal{L} = \{(x_i, y_i)\}_i^n$, the unlabeled data $\mathcal{U} = \{(x_i, \emptyset)\}_i^n$ and the untrained classifier $f(x; \theta)$.
Output Fully labeled dataset $\mathcal{L} = \{(x_i, y_i)\}_i^n$ and trained classifier $f(x; \theta)$

1: $n \leftarrow$ Desired dataset length
2: $r \leftarrow$ Redundancy-pool size
3: $q \leftarrow$ Query-pool size
4: $T \leftarrow$ Number of SFP's
5: $Q(x) \leftarrow$ Query Function
6: **while** $\mathcal{L}$ length $< n$ **do**
7:     Retrain $f(x; \theta)$ on $\mathcal{L}$
8:     $P \leftarrow \emptyset$
9:     **for** $t = 0, ..., T$ **do**
10:         insert $f(\mathcal{U}; \theta_t)$ into P
11:     **end for**
12:     Sort $\mathcal{U}$ based on $Q(P)$
13:     $U \leftarrow \emptyset$
14:     $queried \leftarrow 0$
15:     **while** $queried < q$ **do**
16:         **for** $t = 0, ..., T$ **do**
17:             insert $f(\mathcal{RP}; \theta_t)$ into U
18:         **end for**
19:         $i \leftarrow argmin(U)$
20:         Let Oracle assign label to $\mathcal{U}_i$
21:         Train $f(x; \theta)$ on $\mathcal{U}_i$
22:         Insert $\mathcal{U}_i$ into $\mathcal{L}$
23:         Remove $\mathcal{U}_i$ from $\mathcal{U}$
24:         $queried \leftarrow queried + 1$
25:     **end while**
26: **end while**

Algorithm 4. The AL loop with Redundancy Elimination by Cosine Similarity (RECS).

Input Labeled dataset $\mathcal{L} = \{(x_i, y_i)\}_i^n$, the unlabeled data $\mathcal{U} = \{(x_i, \emptyset)\}_i^n$ and the untrained classifier $f(x; \theta)$.
Output Fully labeled dataset $\mathcal{L} = \{(x_i, y_i)\}_i^n$ and trained classifier $f(x; \theta)$

1: $n \leftarrow$ Desired dataset length
2: $u \leftarrow$ Redundancy-pool size
3: $q \leftarrow$ Query-pool size
4: $l \leftarrow$ Cosine similarity threshold
5: $T \leftarrow$ Number of SFP's
6: $Q(x) \leftarrow$ Query Function
7: $Cos(x, y) \leftarrow$ Cosine similarity between x and y
8: **while** $\mathcal{L}$ length $< n$ **do**
9:     Retrain $f(x; \theta)$ on $\mathcal{L}$
10:     $P \leftarrow \emptyset$
11:     **for** $t = 0, ..., T$ **do**
12:         insert $f(\mathcal{U}; \theta_t)$ into P
13:     **end for**
14:     Sort $\mathcal{U}$ based on $Q(P)$
15:     $U \leftarrow \emptyset$
16:     **while** $Ulength < q$ **do**
17:         **for** $i = 0, ..., u$ **do**
18:             **if** $Cos(\mathcal{U}_i, U_0^{Ulength}) < l$ **then**
19:                 insert $\mathcal{U}_i$ into U
20:             **end if**
21:         **end for**
22:         $l \leftarrow l - 0.01$
23:     **end while**
24:     Reset l to initial value
25:     Let Oracle assign labels to U
26:     Insert U into $\mathcal{L}$
27:     Remove U from $\mathcal{U}$
28: **end while**

Algorithm 5. The AL loop with SUD.

Input Labeled dataset $\mathcal{L} = \{(x_i, y_i)\}_i^n$, the unlabeled data $\mathcal{U} = \{(x_i, \emptyset)\}_i^n$ and the untrained classifier $f(x; \theta)$.

Output Fully labeled dataset $\mathcal{L} = \{(x_i, y_i)\}_i^n$ and trained classifier $f(x; \theta)$

1: $n \leftarrow$ Desired dataset length
2: $q \leftarrow$ Query-pool size
3: $k \leftarrow$ Amount of similar examples to compute density with
4: $T \leftarrow$ Number of SFP's
5: $Q(x) \leftarrow$ Query Function
6: $Cos(x, y) \leftarrow$ Cosine similarity between x and y
7: **while** $\mathcal{L}$ length $< n$ **do**
8:      Retrain $f(x; \theta)$ on $\mathcal{L}$
9:      $P \leftarrow \emptyset$
10:     $E \leftarrow \emptyset$
11:     **for** $t = 0, ..., T$ **do**
12:         Insert $f(\mathcal{U}; \theta_t)$ into P
13:     **end for**
14:     **for** $example$ in $\mathcal{U}$ **do**
15:         $similar \leftarrow Sort(Cos(example, U))$
16:         Insert $\frac{sum(similar_0^k))}{k}$ into E
17:     **end for**
18:     Sort $\mathcal{U}$ based on $Q(P * E)$
19:     Let Oracle assign labels to $\mathcal{U}_0^q$
20:     Insert $\mathcal{U}_0^q$ into $\mathcal{L}$
21:     Remove $\mathcal{U}_0^q$ from $\mathcal{U}$
22: **end while**

References

1. Ahmed, W., Natarajan, T., Rao, K.R.: Discrete cosine transform. IEEE Trans. Comput. **23**(1), 90–93 (1974)
2. Bouneffouf, D., Laroche, R., Urvoy, T., Feraud, R., Allesiardo, R.: Contextual bandit for active learning: active Thompson sampling. In: Loo, C.K., Yap, K.S., Wong, K.W., Teoh, A., Huang, K. (eds.) ICONIP 2014. LNCS, vol. 8834, pp. 405–412. Springer, Cham (2014). https://doi.org/10.1007/978-3-319-12637-1_51
3. Cai, W., Zhang, Y., Zhou, J.: Maximizing expected model change for active learning in regression. In: Proceedings - IEEE International Conference on Data Mining, ICDM, pp. 51–60 (2013)
4. Devlin, J., Chang, M.W., Lee, K., Toutanova, K.: BERT: pre-training of deep bidirectional transformers for language understanding. In: North American Association for Computational Linguistics (NAACL), pp. 4171–4186 (2019)
5. Drost, F.: Uncertainty estimation in deep neural networks for image classification. Master's thesis, University of Groningen (2020)
6. Ein-Dor, L., et al.: Active learning for BERT: an empirical study. In: Proceedings of the 2020 Conference on Empirical Methods in Natural Language Processing (EMNLP), pp. 7949–7962 (2020)

7. Gal, Y.: Uncertainty in deep learning. Master's thesis, University of Cambridge (2016)
8. Gal, Y., Ghahramani, Z.: Dropout as a Bayesian approximation: representing model uncertainty in deep learning. In: Proceedings of The 33rd International Conference on Machine Learning, vol. 48, pp. 1050–1059. PMLR (2016)
9. Gal, Y., Islam, R., Ghahramani, Z.: Deep Bayesian active learning with image data. In: Proceedings of the 34th International Conference on Machine Learning, vol. 70, pp. 1183–1192. PMLR (2017)
10. Gikunda, P.K., Jouandeau, N.: Budget active learning for deep networks. In: Intelligent Systems and Applications, pp. 488–504 (2021)
11. Gissin, D., Shalev-Shwartz, S.: Discriminative active learning. CoRR abs/1907.06347 (2019)
12. Grießhaber, D., Maucher, J., Vu, N.T.: Fine-tuning BERT for low-resource natural language understanding via active learning. CoRR abs/2012.02462 (2020)
13. Gulati, P., Sharma, A., Gupta, M.: Theoretical study of decision tree algorithms to identify pivotal factors for performance improvement: a review. Int. J. Comput. Appl. **141**(14), 19–25 (2016)
14. Guo, C., Pleiss, G., Sun, Y., Weinberger, K.Q.: On calibration of modern neural networks. In: International Conference on Machine Learning, pp. 1321–1330 (2017)
15. Gupta, A., Thadani, K., O'Hare, N.: Effective few-shot classification with transfer learning. In: Proceedings of the 28th International Conference on Computational Linguistics, pp. 1061–1066 (2020)
16. Houlsby, N., Huszár, F., Ghahramani, Z., Lengyel, M.: Bayesian active learning for classification and preference learning (2011)
17. Hu, P., Lipton, Z.C., Anandkumar, A., Ramanan, D.: Active learning with partial feedback. CoRR abs/1802.07427 (2018)
18. Kingma, D., Ba, J.: Adam: a method for stochastic optimization. CoRR abs/1412.6980 (2015)
19. Krogh, A., Vedelsby, J.: Neural network ensembles, cross validation and active learning. In: Proceedings of the 7th International Conference on Neural Information Processing Systems, pp. 231–238. MIT Press (1994)
20. Kuleshov, V., Fenner, N., Ermon, S.: Accurate uncertainties for deep learning using calibrated regression. In: Proceedings of the 35th International Conference on Machine Learning. Proceedings of Machine Learning Research, vol. 80, pp. 2796–2804 (2018)
21. Kullback, S., Leibler, R.A.: On information and sufficiency. Ann. Math. Stat. **22**(1), 79–86 (1951)
22. Liu, Y., et al.: RoBERTa: a robustly optimized BERT pretraining approach. CoRR abs/1907.11692 (2019)
23. Mikolov, T., Chen, K., Corrado, G., Dean, J.: Efficient estimation of word representations in vector space. In: Proceedings of Workshop at ICLR, pp. 1–12 (2013)
24. Munikar, M., Shakya, S., Shrestha, A.: Fine-grained sentiment classification using BERT (2019)
25. Oosten, J.P., Schomaker, L.: Separability versus prototypicality in handwritten word-image retrieval. Pattern Recogn. **47**(3), 1031–1038 (2014)
26. Pennington, J., Socher, R., Manning, C.: GloVe: global vectors for word representation. In: Proceedings of the 2014 Conference on Empirical Methods in Natural Language Processing (EMNLP), pp. 1532–1543 (2014)
27. Reimers, N., Gurevych, I.: Sentence-BERT: sentence embeddings using Siamese BERT-networks. CoRR abs/1908.10084 (2019)

28. Roy, N., McCallum, A.: Toward optimal active learning through sampling estimation of error reduction. In: Proceedings of the Eighteenth International Conference on Machine Learning, pp. 441–448 (2001)
29. Schröder, C., Niekler, A.: A survey of active learning for text classification using deep neural networks. CoRR abs/2008.07267 (2020)
30. Settles, B.: Active learning literature survey. Synth. Lect. Artif. Intell. Mach. Learn. **6**(1), 1–114 (2012)
31. Shannon, C.E.: A mathematical theory of communication. Bell Syst. Tech. J. **27**(3), 379–423 (1948)
32. Smith, L.N.: No more pesky learning rate guessing games. CoRR abs/1506.01186 (2015)
33. Socher, R., et al.: Recursive deep models for semantic compositionality over a sentiment treebank. In: Proceedings of the 2013 Conference on Empirical Methods in Natural Language Processing, pp. 1631–1642 (2013)
34. Srivastava, N., Hinton, G., Krizhevsky, A., Sutskever, I., Salakhutdinov, R.: Dropout: a simple way to prevent neural networks from overfitting. J. Mach. Learn. Res. **15**(56), 1929–1958 (2014)
35. Swayamdipta, S., et al.: Dataset cartography: mapping and diagnosing datasets with training dynamics. In: Proceedings of the 2020 Conference on Empirical Methods in Natural Language Processing (EMNLP), pp. 9275–9293. Online (2020)
36. Tang, M., Luo, X., Roukos, S.: Active learning for statistical natural language parsing. In: Proceedings of ACL 2002, pp. 120–127 (2002)
37. Teye, M., Azizpour, H., Smith, K.: Bayesian uncertainty estimation for batch normalized deep networks. In: Proceedings of the 35th International Conference on Machine Learning, vol. 80, pp. 4907–4916. PMLR (2018)
38. Tsymbalov, E., Panov, M., Shapeev, A.: Dropout-based active learning for regression. In: van der Aalst, W.M.P., et al. (eds.) AIST 2018. LNCS, vol. 11179, pp. 247–258. Springer, Cham (2018). https://doi.org/10.1007/978-3-030-11027-7_24
39. Vaswani, A., et al.: Attention is all you need. In: Proceedings of the 31st International Conference on Neural Information Processing Systems, pp. 6000–6010 (2017)
40. Zhang, M., Plank, B.: Cartography active learning. CoRR abs/2109.04282 (2021)
41. Zhu, J., Wang, H., Yao, T., Tsou, B.K.: Active learning with sampling by uncertainty and density for word sense disambiguation and text classification. In: Proceedings of the 22nd International Conference on Computational Linguistics (Coling 2008), pp. 1137–1144 (2008)

Refining Weakly-Supervised Free Space Estimation Through Data Augmentation and Recursive Training

François Robinet$^{(\boxtimes)}$ (iD) and Raphaël Frank (iD)

Interdisciplinary Centre for Security, Reliability and Trust (SnT),
University of Luxembourg, Esch-sur-Alzette, Luxembourg
{francois.robinet,raphael.frank}@uni.lu

Abstract. Free space estimation is an important problem for autonomous robot navigation. Traditional camera-based approaches rely on pixel-wise ground truth annotations to train a segmentation model. To cover the wide variety of environments and lighting conditions encountered on roads, training supervised models requires large datasets. This makes the annotation cost prohibitively high. In this work, we propose a novel approach for obtaining free space estimates from images taken with a single road-facing camera. We rely on a technique that generates weak free space labels without any supervision, which are then used as ground truth to train a segmentation model for free space estimation. We study the impact of different data augmentation techniques on the performances of free space predictions, and propose to use a recursive training strategy. Our results are benchmarked using the Cityscapes dataset and improve over comparable published work across all evaluation metrics. Our best model reaches 83.64% IoU (+2.3%), 91.75% Precision (+2.4%) and 91.29% Recall (+0.4%). These results correspond to 88.8% of the IoU, 94.3% of the Precision and 93.1% of the Recall obtained by an equivalent fully-supervised baseline, while using no ground truth annotation. Our code and models are freely available online.

Keywords: Weak supervision · Free space estimation · Data augmentation · Recursive training

1 Introduction

Perception is the first step towards autonomous robot navigation. To be able to safely act in the world, a robot needs to perceive its environment and identify traversable free space. In the context of autonomous driving, free space is usually defined as road areas that are not occupied by either static objects such as traffic signs and road dividers, or by dynamic entities such pedestrians and cars [18].

This work is supported by the Fonds National de la Recherche, Luxembourg (MASSIVE Project). The authors also thank Foyer Assurances Luxembourg for their support.

© Springer Nature Switzerland AG 2022
L. A. Leiva et al. (Eds.): BNAIC/Benelearn 2021, CCIS 1530, pp. 30–45, 2022.
https://doi.org/10.1007/978-3-030-93842-0_2

Since collision-free planning requires a fine-grained understanding of the environment around the vehicle, we attempt to label each pixel of a front-facing camera as traversable or not.

This work focuses on systems that use a single road-facing camera. Monocular free space segmentation has traditionally been approached using supervised segmentation techniques. Although effective, these techniques require vast amounts of pixel-wise annotated frames. Studies have shown that such pixel-level ground truth is significantly more expensive to craft than image-level labels or bounding boxes [27]. In addition to the large labor costs entailed by labeling each frame [7], such approaches are held back by the wide variety of environments and lighting conditions that are present at runtime and need to be captured in training data. This need for ever larger annotated datasets makes supervised learning unsuitable for solving this problem. Instead, we tackle it in a different way: relying on a method that generates weak, noisy, free space annotations without any supervision [42], we train a neural network to generalize past the label noise using data augmentation and recursive training.

Our contributions can be summarized as follows: (1) we study the impact of data augmentation on weakly-supervised free space segmentation, (2) we propose a recursive training scheme that uses a progressively refined ground truth, (3) we establish a new state-of-the-art for weakly supervised free space estimation on the Cityscapes dataset, improving over previous efforts by +2.3% in IoU, +2.4% in Precision, and 0.4% in Recall, (4) we discuss the limitations of our simple recursive training approach, and (5) we release our code and models for reproduction and further work.

The remainder of this paper is organized as follows: In Sect. 2, we review the recent literature for free space estimation, data augmentation in the context of semantic segmentation, and recursive training. In Sect. 3, we introduce our data augmentation and recursive training schemes. In Sect. 4, we describe our use of the Cityscapes dataset [7] and detail the experimental setup of this study. In Sect. 5, we carry out experiments and present the qualitative and quantitative results achieved. Finally, we summarize our contributions and share further research directions.

2   Related Work

Over the last decades, free space estimation has been approached with methods that leverage a wide variety of sensors, *e.g.* GNSS [24], LiDAR [45] or cameras [35]. In this work, we place a particular focus on recent camera-based learning methods that use Convolutional Neural Networks (CNNs). Our work builds on recent advances in network architectures for segmentation and on unsupervised methods specific to free space estimation. We present this background material in the following sections.

2.1   Supervised Learning for Segmentation

As a segmentation task, supervised free space estimation has directly benefited from progress in semantic segmentation. Pixel-level prediction carries a crucial challenge for network design: an optimal prediction can only be achieved by combining fine-grained local information with global contextual cues. Fully Convolutional Networks (FCNs) rely on skip connections to carry these cues in their encoder-decoder architecture [28], while SegNets ease the upsampling task by reusing encoder max-pooling indices in the decoder [3]. Building on similar ideas, U-Nets combine entire encoder feature maps with decoder features at each step of the expansion path of the network [40]. U-Nets have attracted a lot of attention in recent years, and researchers have proposed refinements such as the use of dense connections [19] and dilated convolutions [51], the integration of attention mechanisms [34], or extensions to volumetric images [32]. In this work, we will rely on a simple U-Net architecture. Our choice is motivated by a recent finding that many recent architecture improvements are outperformed by a well-tuned vanilla U-Net [17].

2.2   Weakly-Supervised Semantic Segmentation

The major drawback of supervised techniques is their reliance on extensive human-annotated datasets. The cost of labeling is particularly important in segmentation tasks, where the total time required to annotate every pixel in a single frame can reach 1.5 h in some cases [7]. The reuse of models pre-trained on very large datasets such as ImageNet [11] partially alleviates this problem, but several thousands of training images are still routinely needed to reach adequate performance. In recent years, researchers have devised strategies to reduce or eliminate the need for human annotations during training.

In cases where fine-grained annotations are available for at least a subset of the data, semi-supervised approaches such as Co-Training can be applied [37]. In the complete absence of pixel-wise ground truth labels, researchers have proposed to use domain adaptation from synthetic datasets [16], or to rely on weaker ground truth. Existing techniques rely on coarser labels, such as bounding boxes [9,20,21,46], image-level labels [12,38,43], class activation maps [5], single points [4], or scribbles [26].

2.3   Unsupervised and Weakly-Supervised Monocular Free Space Segmentation

Monocular free space estimation has been approached in many different ways that differ in the representation they use. Stixel-like approaches represent obstacles as vertical sticks [2,8] or horizontal curves [48], but ignore free space lying behind obstacles. Monocular SLAM relies on video sequences to obtain point-clouds which do not explicitly represent free space [10,13,33]. Using temporal sequences and structure-from-motion to jointly learn an explicit representation of free space and obstacle footprints has also been recently proposed [44]. Our work uses a different strategy: we learn dense free space estimates from single frames using approximate masks that are obtained without human-supervision. Such *weak labels* have historically been generated using depth information from stereo pairs before localizing the ground plane, for example using the v-Disparity algorithm [14,23,31]. Other attempts exploit strong road texture and location priors, by dividing the input into superpixels and clustering them based on saliency maps [43] or semantic features [35]. We stress that using weak labels departs from previously mentioned approaches that leverage coarse ground truth, since weak labels contain false positives and negatives.

2.4   Training Strategies for Weakly-Supervised Segmentation

Recent research shows that it is possible to train over-parametrized models to generalize past some of the label noise using Stochastic Gradient Descent (SGD) schemes combined with early stopping [25]. Dealing with label noise at training time has become an important research area over the past few years. Solutions to this problem include label cleaning [6], noise-aware network architectures [41], or noise reduction through robust loss functions [29,30,39].

Besides work on training algorithms themselves, researchers have also largely explored regularization through data augmentation in unsupervised settings. Traditional augmentation strategies (scaling, color jittering, flipping, cropping, *etc.*) change pixel values in a single input image without altering its semantic content. More recently, researchers have proposed augmentations that combine several images and their labels. Two notable examples are MixUp [50] and Cut-Mix [49]. MixUp is a method that augments the training set using convex combinations of image pairs and labels, while CutMix overlays random crops of other samples on top of original frames.

3   Methodology

In this work, we train U-Net models to predict dense free space from RGB images by learning on approximate labels that can be generated without any supervision. Since our focus is on improving training aspects rather than on improving weak labels generation, we will reuse the weak labels from [42]. We look at improving training across two dimensions: data augmentation and recursive training.

3.1   Data Augmentation

We study the impact of data augmentation on weakly-supervised free space estimation. We cover both traditional augmentation techniques that operate on single images, as well as MixUp and CutMix, which are more recent and combine multiple samples.

Color-Flip-Crop. To represent traditional augmentation techniques, we use a combination of color jittering, horizontal flips and random cropping, which we will refer to as *Color-Flip-Crop* or *CFC* in the remainder of the text. Each augmentation is independently applied with a 50% probability. The color jittering randomly affects brightness, contrast, saturation, and hue using the bounds defined in the Torchvision implementation [1]. In order to preserve most of the original image, cropping is performed with a randomly chosen rectangle that occupies between 25% and 50% of the image area. The aspect ratio is also randomly chosen, with the constraint that the height is at least 10% of the height of the original image. Figure 1 shows some examples of the effect of CFC on a single randomly chosen training image.

Fig. 1. Seven possible Color-Flip-Crop augmentations on a random training sample. The original sample is on the top-left. We show ground truth mask for illustration purposes, they are not used during training.

MixUp. Rather than augmenting isolated images, Mixup trains models on convex combinations of samples [50]. By training on synthesized samples that lie between the original training samples, MixUp encourages the network to exhibit a linear behavior between samples and helps preventing memorization. During training, each sample (x_1, y_1) is combined with another random sample (x_2, y_2) from the batch using Eqs. 1 and 2, where we sample λ uniformly in $[0, 1]$. The effect of combining input samples is illustrated on Fig. 2.

$$x_{mixup} = \lambda x_1 + (1 - \lambda)x_2 \tag{1}$$
$$y_{mixup} = \lambda y_1 + (1 - \lambda)y_2 \tag{2}$$

(a)   (b)   (c)

Fig. 2. MixUp augmentation combining two random samples (a) and (b) from the training set. The convex combination using $\lambda = 0.5$ is shown as (c). We show ground truth mask for illustration purposes, they are not used during training.

CutMix. Similar to Mixup in spirit, CutMix also combines two random input samples (x_1, y_1) and (x_2, y_2) from the same batch [49]. Rather than combining them over the entire image, CutMix overlays a crop of x_2 over x_1, and the same crop of y_2 over y_1. Equations 3 and 4 formalize this process using a random binary mask $M \in \{0,1\}^{H \times W}$ to denote the cropped area ($\circ$ denotes the element-wise product). Like for the CFC augmentation, the cropping mask M occupies between 25% and 50% of the image area with a random aspect ratio. Figure 3 illustrates four different instances of CutMix augmentation on a chosen training sample. CutMix generates more natural images than MixUp and allows the network to learn more localizable features since the transformation is only applied to a fraction of the input image.

$$x_{cutmix} = (1 - M) \circ x_1 + M \circ x_2 \qquad (3)$$
$$y_{cutmix} = (1 - M) \circ y_1 + M \circ y_2 \qquad (4)$$

3.2   Recursive Training

We are training neural networks to estimate free space by learning on approximate labels y_{weak}. Since neural networks trained with SGD variants are partially robust to noise in their training targets [25], the outputs y will tend to approximate the unknown ground truth y^* better than y_{weak}. Assuming the outputs y are better estimates of free space than y_{weak}, it is natural to treat them as cleaner targets for a second round of training. This process can in principle be iterated to obtain progressively cleaner outputs y_2, y_3, *etc.*. This approach was already attempted in the context weakly-supervision free space segmentation [43], but

Fig. 3. Four instances of the CutMix augmentation on a random training sample. We show ground truth mask for illustration purposes, they are not used during training.

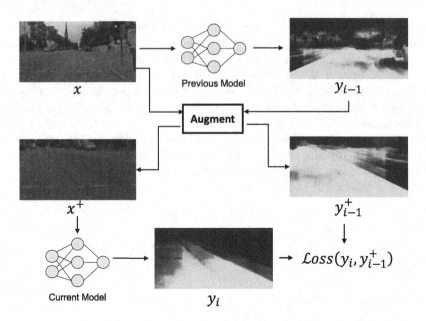

Fig. 4. Recursive training procedure. The current model is trained on augmented outputs from the model obtained at the previous training round. In this example, CFC is used for augmentation. The process is similar for other augmentation strategies.

we revisit its impact in the presence of data augmentation and with different weak labels. Figure 4 illustrates the process for a given training round.

4   Experimental Setup

4.1   Dataset

Our experiments leverage the Cityscapes dataset, which provides pixel-wise ground truth labels for 30 visual classes in 5000 frames [7]. The official test set has no public annotation, and we therefore treat the 500 frames of its validation set as our test set and randomly split the Cityscapes training set into 2380 training and 595 validation frames. Since we are interested in estimating drivable free space in the context of autonomous vehicle navigation, we consider free space equivalent to the *road* class. Cityscapes also contains 1.6% of frames with no *road* pixel. For these frames, visual inspection confirmed that free space correspond to the *ground* class, and that label was used for free space instead of *road*. Finally, the semantic labels include 6 *void* classes such as *unlabeled, out of the region of interest* or *ego-vehicle*. Following official Cityscapes segmentation benchmarks, we ignore pixels corresponding to such classes at evaluation time using a binary evaluation mask. We note that this evaluation mask is never used during training or validation, only to evaluate models on the test set.

4.2   Evaluation Metrics

We use three evaluation metrics: the Intersection-over-Union (IoU), Precision and Recall. IoU is a standard metric in segmentation tasks to reflect the overall quality of the predictions. However, IoU does not immediately capture *false free space positives*. These pixels that are labeled as part of the road but are actually occupied are extremely harmful in robotic path-planning scenarios. For this reason, we also monitor the Precision of the free space class, *i.e.* the fraction of our free space prediction that is indeed free space. To obtain a complete picture of prediction quality, we also monitor Recall. We however note that missing free space in predictions has less impact than false free space positives in robot navigation contexts. Given a single free space prediction $\hat{y}$, ground truth y, and evaluation mask m, the metrics for a single frame of shape $H \times W$ are computed with Eqs. 5, 6 and 7, where $\hat{y}$, y, $m \in \{0,1\}^{H \times W}$.

$$IoU = \frac{\sum_i \hat{y}_i y_i m_i}{\sum_i (\hat{y}_i + y_i - \hat{y}_i y_i) m_i} \tag{5}$$

$$Precision = \frac{\sum_i \hat{y}_i y_i m_i}{\sum_i \hat{y}_i m_i} \tag{6}$$

$$Recall = \frac{\sum_i \hat{y}_i y_i m_i}{\sum_i y_i m_i} \tag{7}$$

4.3   Network Architectures

Following recent research that shows that a well-tuned vanilla U-Net can outperform many refined variants on most segmentation tasks [17], we opt for a U-Net structure based on a ResNet18 residual network backbone [15,40,47]. To allow for comparison with prior art, we also implement and train the SegNet model described in [42]. For computational reasons, we use a 512×1024 input resolution in all experiments. Outputs are however re-scaled using nearest neighbor interpolation in order to compute IoU and Precision in the original 1024×2048 resolution.

4.4   Training Procedure

We use the PyTorch framework [36] and train randomly initialized models to minimize a binary cross-entropy loss using the Adam optimizer [22], a batch size of 8 and an initial learning rate of 0.001. We train our models on single NVIDIA V100 for up to 200 epochs, with an early stopping strategy that halts training when the validation loss has not improved by at least 10^{-4} for 50 consecutive epochs. For each experiment, we select the model that minimizes the validation loss.

4.5   Use of Ground Truth Data

The Cityscapes dataset provides ground truth annotations for all training and validation frames used in this study. We stress that these annotations are only used to train the fully-supervised baseline for comparison with our weakly-supervised approach. Outside of the fully-supervised experiment, ground truth labels are never used for training, hyperparameter tuning, or to perform early stopping. Ground truth IoU, Precision and Recall are computed only once on the test set, after all these steps have been performed.

5   Results

This section describes the experiments carried out to benchmark our proposed method, using Precision, IoU and Recall. We present results for three main categories of models: 1) a fully-supervised upper-bound, 2) unsupervised and weakly-supervised baselines, and 3) U-Nets trained on the weak labels using recursive training and different augmentation strategies. The quantitative results for each category are summarized in Table 1. In this section, we analyze the results of each category, discuss the limitations of recursive training, and present qualitative results.

5.1   Fully-Supervised Results

Since Cityscapes provides pixel-wise ground truth annotations for our training and validation data, we use it to train a fully-supervised U-Net for comparison with its unsupervised counterpart. When trained on ground-truth labels, our U-Net model reaches high IoU (94.12%), Precision (97.26%) and Recall (97.27%). Since this fully-supervised model is the only one that uses ground truth labels at any point during training and validation, it is expected to produce an upper-bound for our unsupervised experiments.

5.2   Unsupervised and Weakly-Supervised Baselines

Competing unsupervised approaches are often focused on generic semantic segmentation rather than free space estimation, and use other datasets than Cityscapes as benchmarks [5,9,12,38,46]. Among weakly-supervised approaches that tackle free space estimation [14,16,43,48], only two publish results for Cityscapes. *Distant Supervision* [43] and *Unsupervised Domain Adaptation* [16] respectively obtain an IoU of 80% and 70.4%, but do not report Precision or Recall values.

We generate approximate labels without supervision using the technique described in [42]. Evaluating these raw weak labels, we obtain an IoU of 79%, a Precision of 87.78% and a Recall of 89.24%. These results can be further improved by training a neural network to generalize beyond the noise in these labels. This was already attempted using the SegNet architecture in [42], which we also implement and train for comparison. SegNet is able to improve results over raw weak labels in IoU (+2.3%), Precision (+1.58%) and Recall (+0.91%).

5.3   Data Augmentation and Recursive Training

We train the same U-Net model using different data augmentation strategies. Since the outputs of our different augmented U-Nets are better than the initial weak labels, we use them as target for a second round of training. We iterate this recursive training process four times for each of the data augmentation strategies under study. We limit training to four rounds for computational reasons and because it is enough for IoU values to reach their peak.

No Augmentation. We start by training a U-Net with the weak labels as targets and without any data augmentation. We observe that it compares favorably with the results from SegNet, reaching an IoU of 81.85%, a Precision of 90.65%, and a Recall of 89.76%. Without resorting to data augmentation, recursive training over several rounds is unable to meaningfully improve IoU, and slightly decreases Precision in favor of Recall.

MixUp. Applying MixUp allows to improve Precision compared to not using data augmentation by 0.5% in the first training round. IoU is maintained, but Recall decreases by 0.45%. Iterative training is however not effective when combined with MixUp, since we observe a drop in Precision after each round. As discussed in Sect. 4.2, free space IoU and Precision are more important than Recall in an autonomous navigation scenario. In this case, increases in Recall are not enough to compensate this effect, and we observe a steady decrease in IoU.

Color-Flip-Crop. Traditional data augmentation consisting of color jittering, horizontal flips and random cropping is able to improve IoU over not using augmentation and over using MixUp. After a single training round, CFC allows to reach an IoU of 81.99% through increasing Recall by 1.47% compared to the first round without augmentation. Subsequent training rounds are able to improve both Precision and IoU. After 3 iterations, the model reaches an IoU of 82.34% and a Precision of 90.75%.

CutMix. The CutMix augmentation can be seen as providing the advantages of cropping and MixUp. Like MixUp, it synthesizes new input samples by combining pairs of existing ones. However, CutMix produces more natural images and its effect is localized since it only affects the area of a random crop. The locality of CutMix has been shown to allow models to learn more localizable features in classification scenarios [49], and it is not surprising that such features are helpful in this segmentation context. Indeed, models trained with CutMix augmentation outperform all other models by a wide margin. After a single training round, CutMix improves over not using augmentations in IoU (+1.2%), Precision (+0.5%), and Recall (+0.26%).

Since our application scenario favors Precision over Recall, our best overall model is obtained after the fourth training round, reaching an IoU of 83.64% and a Precision of 91.75%. Compared to the prior state-of-the-art results from SegNet [42], it improves IoU by 2.3%, Precision by 2.4% and Recall by 0.4%. Although our model does not rely on any human-annotated ground truth, its relative performance compared to the fully-supervised variant is impressive: we reach 88.8% of its IoU, 94.3% of its Precision, and 93.1% of its Recall.

5.4   Limits of Recursive Training

While CutMix results are impressive, we note that the success of recursive training is limited. When not applying data augmentation or when using MixUp, recursive training does not improve on IoU or Precision. In the case of CFC and CutMix augmentations, results are more encouraging, but the improvements are limited to three rounds of training. Starting with the fourth round of training, IoU results start to degrade, sometimes getting worse than those obtained after a single round of training. Explaining this effect is not straightforward: given that target labels on round 4 are superior to those used on round 3 in both IoU and Precision, we would expect to either observe improved or plateauing results. Such recursive training strategy has been successfully used in foreground class segmentation contexts with results improving over more than 10 rounds [21]. As opposed to our completely unsupervised approach, the authors of [21] could exploit coarser ground truth in the form of bounding boxes in order to refine predictions after each round. We postulate that the absence of such refinement step in our approach is the reason

Table 1. Results on the Cityscapes validation set, which we treat as our test set. The best results for a given data augmentation strategy are underlined, and the best overall results are reported in bold.

	Training/Validation Labels	Test IoU	Test precision	Test recall
Fully-supervised U-Net	Ground truth	94.12%	97.26%	97.27%
Unsup. domain adaptation [16]	Synthetic data	70.40%	Not reported	Not reported
Distant supervision [43]	Image labels	80.00%	Not reported	Not reported
Weak labels [42]	No training	79.00%	87.78%	89.24%
SegNet (repr. from [42])	Weak labels	81.30%	89.36%	90.15%
U-Net (no augmentation)				
Round 1	Weak labels	81.85%	90.65%	89.76%
Round 2	Output of round 1	81.79%	89.53%	90.80%
Round 3	Output of round 2	81.86%	90.15%	90.27%
Round 4	output of round 3	81.82%	90.11%	90.25%
U-Net + MixUp				
Round 1	Weak labels	81.89%	91.14%	89.31%
Round 2	Output of round 1	81.97%	90.89%	89.60%
Round 3	Output of round 2	81.62%	90.13%	89.97%
Round 4	Output of round 3	81.45%	89.91%	90.02%
U-Net + Color-Flip-Crop				
Round 1	Weak labels	81.99%	88.80%	91.23%
Round 2	Output of round 1	82.12%	89.71%	90.64%
Round 3	Output of round 2	82.34%	90.75%	90.69%
Round 4	Output of round 3	81.91%	90.21%	90.27%
U-Net + CutMix				
Round 1	Weak labels	83.05%	91.19%	90.51%
Round 2	Output of round 1	83.58%	91.20%	91.12%
Round 3	Output of round 2	**83.77%**	91.23%	**91.29%**
Round 4	Output of round 3	83.64%	**91.75%**	90.62%

we are unable to further leverage recursive training. Designing such a prediction refinement step will be the topic of future work.

5.5 Qualitative Results

We compare the free space estimates from weak labels with the predictions of our best model on test set samples on Fig. 5.

The ability of our learned model to generalize past some of the noise present in the weak labels that were used during training is clearly visible in the first two rows of Fig. 5. Indeed, the cars and side walks that were wrongly considered free space in the weak labels are correctly predicted by our trained model. In addition to its higher Precision, our model also has higher IoU and Recall, as illustrated by the near-absence of orange areas in its predictions.

The third row shows a more contrasted situation. Although our model is able to cover more free space, it still shows some signs of overfitting to noise in the weak labels. Shadows are especially problematic because they are likely to impact the superpixel segmentation that the weak labels are based on, resulting in missed free space areas such as the one present in front of the cyclist. Since this

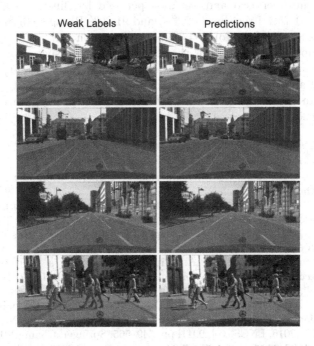

Fig. 5. Qualitative results from the test set obtained from a U-Net trained with Cut-Mix for 4 rounds. Predictions are color-coded using the ground truth: green and red respectively corresponds to correct and incorrect predictions, orange represents missing free space, and areas that are ignored at evaluation time are denoted in blue (see Sect. 4.1). (Color figure online)

effect happens fairly consistently over the training set, our model is incapable of completely addressing it.

Finally, the fourth row illustrates another partial failure of our model in a particularly crowded scene. Compared to the corresponding weak labels, the trained model correctly rejects pedestrians, but is unable to produce a clean segmentation around them and considers the pavement as occupied space. Although the prediction still contains errors, we note that red areas in our prediction are much more acceptable from a semantics point-of-view than the ones from the corresponding weak labels.

6   Conclusion

In this work, we investigate different weakly-supervised training strategies for teaching a neural network to predict free space from images taken with a single road-facing camera. Our models are trained using weak labels that are generated without human intervention, and we investigate the impact of recursive training with several data augmentation schemes. We show that the CutMix augmentation is particularly efficient for free space estimation, especially when combined with recursive training. We benchmark our results on the Cityscapes dataset and improve over unsupervised and weakly-supervised baselines, reaching 83.64% IoU (+2.3%), 91.75% Precision (+2.4%) and 91.29% Recall (+0.4%). Our best model obtains 88.8% of the IoU, 94.3% of the Precision and 93.1% of the Recall of the fully-supervised competitor that trains from expensive pixel-wise labels. Finally, we show that simple recursive training is limited in its ability to increase performances, and suggest directions to improve the approach. Future work will also investigate improvements to weak label generation and applications to more general segmentation scenarios.

References

1. Torchvision: Datasets, transforms and models specific to computer vision (2021). https://github.com/pytorch/vision
2. Badino, H., Franke, U., Pfeiffer, D.: The Stixel world - a compact medium level representation of the 3D-world. In: Denzler, J., Notni, G., Süße, H. (eds.) DAGM 2009. LNCS, vol. 5748, pp. 51–60. Springer, Heidelberg (2009). https://doi.org/10.1007/978-3-642-03798-6_6
3. Badrinarayanan, V., Kendall, A., Cipolla, R.: SegNet: a deep convolutional encoder-decoder architecture for image segmentation. IEEE Trans. Pattern Anal. Mach. Intell. **39**(12), 2481–2495 (2017)
4. Bearman, A., Russakovsky, O., Ferrari, V., Fei-Fei, L.: What's the point: semantic segmentation with point supervision. In: Leibe, B., Matas, J., Sebe, N., Welling, M. (eds.) ECCV 2016. LNCS, vol. 9911, pp. 549–565. Springer, Cham (2016). https://doi.org/10.1007/978-3-319-46478-7_34 http://www.eccv2016.org/
5. Chang, Y., Wang, Q., Hung, W., Piramuthu, R., Tsai, Y., Yang, M.: Mixup-CAM: weakly-supervised semantic segmentation via uncertainty regularization. In: 31st British Machine Vision Conference 2020, BMVC 2020, Virtual Event, UK, 7–10 September 2020. BMVA Press (2020). https://www.bmvc2020-conference.com/assets/papers/0367.pdf

6. Chiaroni, F., Rahal, M.C., Hueber, N., Dufaux, F.: Hallucinating a cleanly labeled augmented dataset from a noisy labeled dataset using GANs. In: 26th IEEE International Conference on Image Processing (ICIP), Taipei, Taiwan. IEEE, September 2019. https://hal.archives-ouvertes.fr/hal-02054836

7. Cordts, M., et al.: The cityscapes dataset. In: CVPR Workshop on the Future of Datasets in Vision, vol. 2 (2015)

8. Cordts, M., et al.: The stixel world: a medium-level representation of traffic scenes. Image Vis. Comput. **68** (2017). https://doi.org/10.1016/j.imavis.2017.01.009

9. Dai, J., He, K., Sun, J.: BoxSup: exploiting bounding boxes to supervise convolutional networks for semantic segmentation. In: Proceedings of the IEEE International Conference on Computer Vision, pp. 1635–1643 (2015)

10. Davison, A.J., Reid, I.D., Molton, N.D., Stasse, O.: MonoSLAM: real-time single camera SLAM. IEEE Trans. Pattern Anal. Mach. Intell. **29**(6), 1052–1067 (2007). https://doi.org/10.1109/TPAMI.2007.1049

11. Deng, J., Dong, W., Socher, R., Li, L., Kai, L., Li, F.-F.: ImageNet: a large-scale hierarchical image database. In: 2009 IEEE Conference on Computer Vision and Pattern Recognition, pp. 248–255 (2009). https://doi.org/10.1109/CVPR.2009.5206848

12. Durand, T., Mordan, T., Thome, N., Cord, M.: WILDCAT: weakly supervised learning of deep convnets for image classification, pointwise localization and segmentation. In: 2017 IEEE Conference on Computer Vision and Pattern Recognition (CVPR), pp. 5957–5966 (2017). https://doi.org/10.1109/CVPR.2017.631

13. Engel, J., Schöps, T., Cremers, D.: LSD-SLAM: large-scale direct monocular SLAM. In: Fleet, D., Pajdla, T., Schiele, B., Tuytelaars, T. (eds.) ECCV 2014. LNCS, vol. 8690, pp. 834–849. Springer, Cham (2014). https://doi.org/10.1007/978-3-319-10605-2_54

14. Harakeh, A., Asmar, D., Shammas, E.: Identifying good training data for self-supervised free space estimation. In: Proceedings of the IEEE Conference on Computer Vision and Pattern Recognition (CVPR), June 2016

15. He, K., Zhang, X., Ren, S., Sun, J.: Deep residual learning for image recognition. In: Proceedings of the IEEE Conference on Computer Vision and Pattern Recognition, pp. 770–778 (2016)

16. Hoffman, J., Wang, D., Yu, F., Darrell, T.: FCNs in the wild: pixel-level adversarial and constraint-based adaptation. CoRR abs/1612.02649 (2016). http://arxiv.org/abs/1612.02649

17. Isensee, F., et al.: NNU-Net: self-adapting framework for U-Net-based medical image segmentation. CoRR abs/1809.10486 (2018). http://arxiv.org/abs/1809.10486

18. Janai, J., Güney, F., Behl, A., Geiger, A.: Computer vision for autonomous vehicles: problems, datasets and state-of-the-art. ArXiv abs/1704.05519 (2020)

19. Jégou, S., Drozdzal, M., Vázquez, D., Romero, A., Bengio, Y.: The one hundred layers tiramisu: fully convolutional densenets for semantic segmentation. In: 2017 IEEE Conference on Computer Vision and Pattern Recognition Workshops (CVPRW), pp. 1175–1183 (2017)

20. Kervadec, H., Dolz, J., Wang, S., Granger, E., ben Ayed, I.: Bounding boxes for weakly supervised segmentation: global constraints get close to full supervision. In: Medical Imaging with Deep Learning (2020). https://openreview.net/forum?id=VOQMC3rZtL

21. Khoreva, A., Benenson, R., Hosang, J., Hein, M., Schiele, B.: Simple does it: weakly supervised instance and semantic segmentation. In: 2017 IEEE Conference on Computer Vision and Pattern Recognition (CVPR), pp. 1665–1674 (2017). https://doi.org/10.1109/CVPR.2017.181

22. Kingma, D.P., Ba, J.: Adam: a method for stochastic optimization. CoRR abs/1412.6980 (2015)

23. Labayrade, R., Aubert, D., Tarel, J.P.: Real time obstacle detection in stereovision on non flat road geometry through "v-disparity" representation. In: Intelligent Vehicle Symposium 2002, vol. 2, pp. 646–651. IEEE (2002)

24. Laddha, A., Kocamaz, M.K., Navarro-Serment, L.E., Hebert, M.: Map-supervised road detection. In: 2016 IEEE Intelligent Vehicles Symposium (IV), pp. 118–123 (2016). https://doi.org/10.1109/IVS.2016.7535374

25. Li, M., Soltanolkotabi, M., Oymak, S.: Gradient descent with early stopping is provably robust to label noise for overparameterized neural networks. In: International Conference on Artificial Intelligence and Statistics, pp. 4313–4324. PMLR (2020)

26. Lin, D., Dai, J., Jia, J., He, K., Sun, J.: ScribbleSup: scribble-supervised convolutional networks for semantic segmentation. In: 2016 IEEE Conference on Computer Vision and Pattern Recognition (CVPR), pp. 3159–3167 (2016). https://doi.org/10.1109/CVPR.2016.344

27. Lin, T.-Y., et al.: Microsoft COCO: common objects in context. In: Fleet, D., Pajdla, T., Schiele, B., Tuytelaars, T. (eds.) ECCV 2014. LNCS, vol. 8693, pp. 740–755. Springer, Cham (2014). https://doi.org/10.1007/978-3-319-10602-1_48

28. Long, J., Shelhamer, E., Darrell, T.: Fully convolutional networks for semantic segmentation. In: Proceedings of the IEEE Conference on Computer Vision and Pattern Recognition, pp. 3431–3440 (2015)

29. Lu, Z., Fu, Z., Xiang, T., Han, P., Wang, L., Gao, X.: Learning from weak and noisy labels for semantic segmentation. IEEE Trans. Pattern Anal. Mach. Intell. **39**, 486–500, March 2017. https://doi.org/10.1109/TPAMI.2016.2552172

30. Mairal, J., Elad, M., Sapiro, G.: Sparse representation for color image restoration. Trans. Img. Proc. **17**(1), 53–69 (2008). https://doi.org/10.1109/TIP.2007.911828

31. Mayr, J., Unger, C., Tombari, F.: Self-supervised learning of the drivable area for autonomous vehicles. In: 2018 IEEE/RSJ International Conference on Intelligent Robots and Systems (IROS), pp. 362–369. IEEE (2018)

32. Milletari, F., Navab, N., Ahmadi, S.: V-Net: fully convolutional neural networks for volumetric medical image segmentation. In: 2016 Fourth International Conference on 3D Vision (3DV), pp. 565–571 (2016). https://doi.org/10.1109/3DV.2016.79

33. Newcombe, R., Lovegrove, S., Davison, A.: DTAM: dense tracking and mapping in real-time, pp. 2320–2327, November 2011. https://doi.org/10.1109/ICCV.2011.6126513

34. Oktay, O., et al.: Attention U-Net: learning where to look for the pancreas, March 2018

35. Oliveira, G.L., Burgard, W., Brox, T.: Efficient deep models for monocular road segmentation. In: 2016 IEEE/RSJ International Conference on Intelligent Robots and Systems (IROS), pp. 4885–4891 (2016). https://doi.org/10.1109/IROS.2016.7759717

36. Paszke, A., et al.: PyTorch: an imperative style, high-performance deep learning library. In: Wallach, H., Larochelle, H., Beygelzimer, A., d'Alché-Buc, F., Fox, E., Garnett, R. (eds.) Advances in Neural Information Processing Systems, vol. 32, pp. 8024–8035. Curran Associates, Inc. (2019). http://papers.neurips.cc/paper/9015-pytorch-an-imperative-style-high-performance-deep-learning-library.pdf

37. Peng, J., Estrada, G., Pedersoli, M., Desrosiers, C.: Deep co-training for semi-supervised image segmentation (2019)
38. Pinheiro, P.O., Collobert, R.: From image-level to pixel-level labeling with convolutional networks. In: 2015 IEEE Conference on Computer Vision and Pattern Recognition (CVPR), pp. 1713–1721 (2015). https://doi.org/10.1109/CVPR.2015.7298780
39. Robinet, F., Demeules, A., Frank, R., Varisteas, G., Hundt, C.: Leveraging privileged information to limit distraction in end-to-end lane following. In: 2020 IEEE 17th Annual Consumer Communications Networking Conference (CCNC), pp. 1–6 (2020). https://doi.org/10.1109/CCNC46108.2020.9045110
40. Ronneberger, O., Fischer, P., Brox, T.: U-Net: convolutional networks for biomedical image segmentation. In: Navab, N., Hornegger, J., Wells, W.M., Frangi, A.F. (eds.) MICCAI 2015. LNCS, vol. 9351, pp. 234–241. Springer, Cham (2015). https://doi.org/10.1007/978-3-319-24574-4_28
41. Sukhbaatar, S., Bruna, J., Paluri, M., Bourdev, L., Fergus, R.: Training convolutional networks with noisy labels. In: 3rd International Conference on Learning Representations, ICLR 2015, Conference date: 07 May 2015 Through 09 May 2015, January 2015
42. Tsutsui, S., Kerola, T., Saito, S., Crandall, D.J.: Minimizing supervision for free-space segmentation. In: Proceedings of the IEEE Conference on Computer Vision and Pattern Recognition Workshops, pp. 988–997 (2018)
43. Tsutsui, S., Saito, S., Kerola, T.: Distantly supervised road segmentation. In: 2017 IEEE International Conference on Computer Vision Workshops (ICCVW), pp. 174–181 (2017)
44. Watson, J., Firman, M., Monszpart, A., Brostow, G.J.: Footprints and free space from a single color image. In: Computer Vision and Pattern Recognition (CVPR) (2020)
45. Xiao, L., Dai, B., Liu, D., Hu, T., Wu, T.: CRF based road detection with multisensor fusion. In: 2015 IEEE Intelligent Vehicles Symposium (IV), pp. 192–198 (2015). https://doi.org/10.1109/IVS.2015.7225685
46. Xie, W., Wei, Q., Li, Z., Zhang, H.: Learning effectively from noisy supervision for weakly supervised semantic segmentation. In: BMVC (2020)
47. Yakubovskiy, P.: Segmentation models (2019). https://github.com/qubvel/segmentation_models
48. Yao, J., Ramalingam, S., Taguchi, Y., Miki, Y., Urtasun, R.: Estimating drivable collision-free space from monocular video. In: 2015 IEEE Winter Conference on Applications of Computer Vision, pp. 420–427 (2015). https://doi.org/10.1109/WACV.2015.62
49. Yun, S., Han, D., Oh, S.J., Chun, S., Choe, J., Yoo, Y.: CutMix: regularization strategy to train strong classifiers with localizable features. In: 2019 IEEE/CVF International Conference on Computer Vision (ICCV), pp. 6022–6031 (2019)
50. Zhang, H., Cisse, M., Dauphin, Y.N., Lopez-Paz, D.: Mixup: beyond empirical risk minimization. In: International Conference on Learning Representations (2018)
51. Zhao, H., Shi, J., Qi, X., Wang, X., Jia, J.: Pyramid scene parsing network. In: 2017 IEEE Conference on Computer Vision and Pattern Recognition (CVPR), pp. 6230–6239 (2017). https://doi.org/10.1109/CVPR.2017.660

Self-labeling of Fully Mediating
Representations by Graph Alignment

Martijn Oldenhof$^{(\boxtimes)}$ ⓘD, Adam Arany, Yves Moreau, and Jaak Simm

ESAT - STADIUS, KU Leuven, 3001 Leuven, Belgium
{martijn.oldenhof,adam.arany,yves.moreau,jaak.simm}@esat.kuleuven.be

Abstract. To be able to predict a molecular graph structure (W) given a 2D image of a chemical compound (U) is a challenging problem in machine learning. We are interested to learn $f : U \rightarrow W$ where we have a fully mediating representation V such that f factors into $U \rightarrow V \rightarrow W$. However, observing V requires detailed and expensive labels. We propose **graph aligning** approach that generates rich or detailed labels given normal labels W. In this paper we investigate the scenario of domain adaptation from the source domain where we have access to the expensive labels V to the target domain where only normal labels W are available. Focusing on the problem of predicting chemical compound graphs from 2D images the fully mediating layer is represented using the planar embedding of the chemical graph structure we are predicting. The empirical results show that, using only 4000 data points, we obtain up to 4x improvement of performance after domain adaptation to target domain compared to pretrained model only on the source domain. After domain adaptation, the model is even able to detect atom types that were never observed in the original source domain. Finally, on the Maybridge data set the proposed self-labeling approach reached higher performance than the current state of the art.

1 Introduction

Chemical compounds are often represented by a graph representation of their chemical structure. These graph representations are actually a simplification of the chemical compound as it loses some information about the electronic structure of the molecule. However, in the field of drug discovery this graph representation is often used as valuable input for machine learning pipelines. Examples of formats describing the graph representation of a chemical compounds are SMILES [36] and MOLfile [5]. However, especially in patents but also in scientific literature the chemical compound is only described using an image format. Automatically recognizing the chemical structures on these images is valuable for machine learning approaches to be able to process these sources of chemical compounds.

Learning to recognize a graph structure from 2D images of chemical compounds seems like a fairly simple task for humans. However, for machine learning models it seems that generalization to new domains of images (e.g. different line

© Springer Nature Switzerland AG 2022
L. A. Leiva et al. (Eds.): BNAIC/Benelearn 2021, CCIS 1530, pp. 46–65, 2022.
https://doi.org/10.1007/978-3-030-93842-0_3

width, font face) [21] is not happening naturally. When we humans see an image with a graph structure that we do not recognize completely, we start reasoning and analyzing the part of the graph we are not sure about. We humans automatically align the graph part we recognized on the image with the complete graph including the unrecognized part of the graph. One way to finish our graph prediction is to guess the unknown nodes or edges after which we check for correctness. If the graph prediction was correct we know that this guess was most probably correct and we could try to apply this new knowledge to other images.

To be able to do this reasoning on for example images using graph alignment in machine learning we need a detailed (on pixel level) representation. Therefore we assume a fully mediated model [2] where we are interested to learn $f : U \to W$ having a fully mediating representation V such that f factors into $U \to V \to W$, which is visualized in Fig. 1. Thus, in order to predict W from U we first need to pass the fully mediating layer, no side paths are allowed. When a fully mediating representation is used some assumptions [23,25,26] are made about the mechanism of the underlying process. This mechanistic prior restricts the space of possible models to all the models that follow the mechanistic assumption. We hypothesize that the use of this richer representation (fully mediating representation) enables for a better generalization. Additionally, as an interesting side effect, we observe that the mechanistic assumption allows for a better interpretability of the underlying model.

In the case of optical graph recognition of chemical compounds from 2D images, the fully mediating layer is represented using the planar embedding of the chemical graph structure we are predicting. In order to learn the planar embedding of a chemical graph structure, we start from a model described in Oldenhof et al. [21] which has two steps: an image segmentation and an image classification step. To train this model, **pixel-wise** annotations are needed for every image describing precise locations of nodes and edges in the graph (planar embedding) which we will call rich or detailed labels in our setup (V). However, these rich labels are not always available and implies a manual process where intermediate organic chemistry knowledge is required. In the more common cases, data sets only contain 2D images of chemical compounds (U in Fig. 1) and on the other side the final output in SMILES [36] or MOLfile [5] format (W in Fig. 1). These formats describe the graph structure of the chemical compound but not the particular planar embedding of this graph structure (V in Fig. 1) in the context of the image. To solve this problem, we propose a **graph aligning** approach[1] that generates rich labels V given normal labels W. This method would enable learning of the fully mediating representations given only normal labels W. In the Figs. 7, 8 and 9 in Appendix A.4 examples of U, V and W are shown.

In Sect. 4 we empirically evaluate our domain adaption method. We observe that compared to the non-adapted model we drastically increase accuracy even on atoms and bond that were not present in source domain.

---

[1] Code available: https://github.com/biolearning-stadius/chemgrapher-self-rich-lab eling.

Key Contributions: (1) we propose a novel rich labeling framework by introducing the use of a fully mediating layer, (2) in the case of graph recognition
we show that the rich labeling can be performed by graph alignment, (3) we
show it enables data efficient domain adaption and (4) reaches state-of-the-art
performance on Maybridge compound data set.

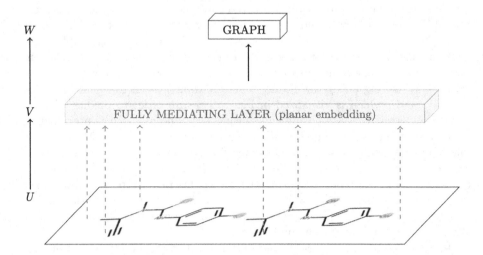

Fig. 1. We are interested to learn $f : U \rightarrow W$ having a fully mediating representation
V such that f factors into $U \rightarrow V \rightarrow W$. In the case of optical graph recognition of
chemical compounds from 2D images, the fully mediating layer is represented using
the planar embedding of the chemical graph structure we are predicting.

2   Related Work

Structural Scene Representation and Visual Reasoning. Our work has
similarities with research done on structural scene representation and visual reasoning [11,19,41]. The disentanglement of the reasoning and the representation
described in Yi et al. [41] enables the model to solve complex reasoning tasks.
In our work the complex reasoning task would be graph alignment which is
disentangled from the optical graph recognition.

Slot Attention. Our method is related with a method called slot attention [17]
where the Hungarian algorithm [16] is incorporated in a model for object detection. This Hungarian algorithm is limited to only sets while in our case we need
to map more complicated structures composed of different atoms connected with
different bond for which we need graph alignment in order to adapt iteratively
a model to a new target domain.

Image to Graph Methods. In the field of computational chemistry there are several tools available [7,18,20–22,33,34] to convert an 2D image of a chemical compound to a SMILES [36] format or similar which in fact represents a graph structure of a chemical compound. Also for road extraction from satellite images there are several methods available [3,8,12]

Graph Matching. In computer vision graph alignment is usually known as graph matching. It can be useful to (1) locate objects from features [10], (2) to transfer knowledge [42] and (3) to find matches in database [13]. Also for comparing social networks graph matching can be very important to allow to uncover identities of communities [14]. In chemistry, comparing graphs can be helpful to identify identical chemicals, substructures or maximum common part of chemicals. In the work of Willett et al. [37] an overview is presented about the use of similarity searches in chemical databases.

Domain Adaptation. In the work of Kouw and Loog [15] a comprehensive overview is given for domain adaptation methods when labels for the target domain are not available. Our method has some similarities with semi-supervised iterative self-labeling [4,27] approaches where predictions on a data set of a new domain of a pre-trained model are used as pseudo-labels and used to retrain the model again iteratively until convergence. In the work of Das and Lee [6] even a graph matching loss is first used to learn a domain invariant representation for source and target domain after which the use of pseudo-labels show a significant improvement of performance. In our work the graph matching is used for a different purpose as opposed to the work of Das and Lee [6]. Graph matching is used in our work to generate rich labels given the 'normal' labels we have from the target domain. This is where our method also differs from other semi-supervised methods for domain adaptation when no target label information at all is assumed and no distinction is made between rich and 'normal' labels.

Weak Supervision. In our setup we use the term 'rich' or 'detailed' labels to differentiate from the normal labels. We would like to contrast these 'rich' labels with the term 'strong labels' used in the setting of weak supervision. For example, in the machine learning task of image segmentation pixel-wise labels are needed which are expensive and often not readily available. Therefore, weak supervision methods have been developed to address this issue. Weak supervision can be used to help image segmentation by only using image labels (no pixel-wise labels) [35,38]. A more general framework was presented in Xu et al. [39] to be able to learn semantic segmentation from a variety of types of weak labels (*e.g.*, image tags, bounding boxes and partial labels). Another approach is to augment the strong labeled data set using weakly labeled data [40]. However, the main difference with all of the methods mentioned above is that our method does not work on weak labels because our end goal is different. The main goal of our machine learning approach is to help to predict 'normal' labels by using rich labels.

Front Door Criterion. Our framework exploits fully mediating variables. A variable is called a mediator when it meets several conditions regarding the relationship with other variables as described in Baron and Kenny [2]. Another perspective of the mediating relationship is given by Pearl [23, 26], Pearl et al. [25] who introduce the front door criterion where the mediator actually enables to estimate unbiased causal effects. A more formal interpretation of these causal effects is presented in Pearl [24]. In order to use a mediating model the mediator needs to be identified or assumed first, which is not always straightforward. In our setup (see Fig. 1), the assumption means that the relation between input $u \in U$ and planar embedding $v \in V$ is a map and as well as the relation between v and the final graph $w \in W$. Furthermore, we assume no side paths from u to w.

3   Self-labeling of Fully Mediating Representations

Our goal is to learn $f : U \to W$ assuming a fully mediating representation V such that f factors into $U \to V \to W$. In order to learn the first part of f ($U \to V$) we need labels for V which are expensive in the case of optical graph recognition of chemical compounds from 2D images where V is represented as the planar embedding of the chemical graph structure. Our method tries to address this issue by iteratively updating the model using self-labeled labels for V by graph aligning the graph predictions using the model from previous iteration with the given true graphs (labels W).

3.1   Graph Alignment

A possible and often used closeness score to compare graphs is the **graph edit distance** [29]: given 2 graphs, not necessarily of equal size and a set of operations, that are $\mathcal{O} = \{\text{vertex/edge/label   insertion/deletion/substitution}\}$, and a cost function $c : \mathcal{O} \mapsto \mathbb{R}$, so we find the cheapest sequence of operations that convert $\mathcal{G}_1$ into $\mathcal{G}_2$, which translates to an optimization problem:

$$\min_{\{e_i\}_{i=1}^k \in \mathcal{O}^k : \mathcal{G}_2 = (e_k \circ \dots \circ e_1) \times \mathcal{G}_1} \sum_{i=1}^k c(e_k),$$

Although there are some efficient algorithms available [30–32] in order to compute the graph edit distance, it remains a computational hard problem.

Closely related with the concept of graph edit distance we introduce for our method the map $E(v)$ which gives the allowed operations on a given graph v given a specific constraint. This constraint is a parameter which can be tuned for a specific data set or problem domain. Examples of such constraints are maximum 2 node substitutions or maximum 1 edge substitution as shown in Fig. 2.

3.2   Method

Let us now say we have a trained neural network model for $f : U \to V$, a projection (not trainable) $\phi : V \to W$, a pair (u, w) of input $u \in U$ and normal label $w \in W$ and we would like to infer rich label $v \in V$ from the given datapoint

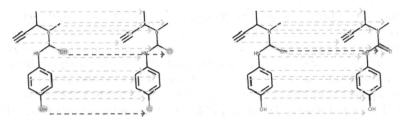

(a) Example of 2 chemical compounds with graph edit distance of 2 node substitutions. (b) Example of 2 chemical compound with graph edit distance of 1 edge substitution.

Fig. 2. Two examples of chemical compounds graphs with their graph edit distance. The nodes of the graphs are first aligned before computing the graph edit distance. The node alignments are marked with the gray dashed arrows. The differences after graph alignment are highlighted and the substitutions are marked with the red dashed arrows. (Color figure online)

(u, w). In the setting of chemical structure recognition the projection $\phi : V \to W$ is straightforward (U implies W) and a few examples are shown in Appendix A.4. We also assume the map $E(v)$ which gives all allowed graph edits for the graph v. Let $\hat{v} = f(u)$ be the predicted rich label from the model, then we define a term correcting edit as

Definition 1. *Edit e is a **correcting edit** if when e is applied to the prediction $\hat{v}$ and then projected to the W space the resulting graph is the true graph w (up to isomorphism), i.e.,*

$$\phi(e \times \hat{v}) \cong w,$$

where $\times$ is the application of edit to the planar embedded graph $\hat{v}$.

Notice that for a given $\hat{v}$ and w there can be multiple edits that are **correcting edits** which create a dilemma of choosing the best **correcting edit**. Therefore, we make the following assumption:

Assumption 1. *The probability that a correcting edit e results in the true underlying rich label v is monotonely decreasing with respect to the size of edit e (i.e., $|e|$).*

In other words, if we take two correcting edits e_1, e_2 then we assume the following:

$$|e_1| < |e_2| \quad \Rightarrow \quad P(e_1 \times \hat{v} = v) > P(e_2 \times \hat{v} = v)$$

The assumption is based on the fact the *probability of any individual mistake in a graph* by the model is low. This is because if the probability of a mistake would be high the model would not be able to produce a graph with a total of 1–2 edit distance. Thus, the graphs with few edits have low mistake probability and for them the Assumption 1 is valid.

Then we use the following optimisation problem to find the best correcting edit e to convert $\hat{v}$ to rich label v for input u:

$$\mathcal{E}^* = \underset{e \in E(\hat{v})}{\arg\min} |e| \quad \text{such that} \quad \phi(e \times \hat{v}) \cong w,$$

where arg min returns the set of minimal solutions or the empty set if no solutions exist.

There are three possible outcomes of last mentioned optimization problem: (1) no solution is found, (2) a single e is found or (3) multiple equal size e are found. In the optimal case (2) a single e is found so we can label a new v for our given datapoint (u, v). In the case of (1) when no solution is found, no new v is labeled. In the last case (3) when multiple equal size solutions are found there are four options we could do. First (3.1), we could discard the solutions and not label u. Second (3.2), we could take e that results in the highest likelihood for $e \times \hat{v}$ based on the model f. Third (3.3), a solution e is picked uniformly randomly in order to generate the rich label v. Fourth (3.4), pick e randomly according to the likelihood of $e \times \hat{v}$ in the model f.

This process is repeated for every datapoint (u, w) we have available from the target domain. Thus, several new labels v are found for different datapoints. Once all datapoints are processed these new rich labeled datapoints are added to the training data set after upsampling and our model can be retrained. Upsampling is recommended especially in the case when a low number of normal labelled data points are available compared to the original training dataset. In Sect. 4 different upsampling strategies will be evaluated. After this, a new iteration begins and all available datapoints (u, v) are again processed to find even more new rich labels v and we can retrain the model again. This iterative process can be repeated until convergence (see Algorithm 1).

Algorithm 1: Iterative algorithm for Self-Labeling of Fully Mediating Representations

---

Data:

Target domain data $\mathbf{L} = \{(u_i^t, w_i^t)\}_{i=1}^n$

Source domain data $\mathbf{S} = \{(u_j^s, v_j^s)\}_{j=1}^m$ (rich labels)

Result: $f : U \to V$

repeat

> // Inferring rich labels for target data
> $\mathbf{T} = [];$
> **for** (u, w) **in** $\mathbf{L}$ **do**
>> $\hat{v} \leftarrow f(u);$
>> $\mathcal{E}^* \leftarrow \underset{e \in E(\hat{v})}{\arg\min} |e|$ such that $\phi(e \times \hat{v}) \cong w;$
>> **if** $\mathcal{E}^*$ *is a not empty* **then**
>>> $e \leftarrow \text{choose}(\mathcal{E}^*);$
>>> $v \leftarrow e \times \hat{v};$
>>> $\text{appendRichLabels}(\mathbf{T}, (u, v));$
>> **end**
> **end**
> $\mathbf{T} \leftarrow \text{UpSample}(\mathbf{T});$
> $f \leftarrow \text{RetrainModel}(\mathbf{S}, \mathbf{T});$

until $\text{Converged}(f);$

---

4   Experiments

For the experiments we focus on the problem of predicting chemical compound graphs from 2D images where the fully mediating layer is represented using the planar embedding of the chemical graph structure we are predicting. In order to measure empirically the performance of our method of self-labeling fully mediating representations we perform three steps. (1) We pre-train (training details in Appendix A.2) a ChemGrapher [21] model (summarized in Appendix A.1) wherefore, corresponding to the pipeline described in the work of Oldenhof et al. [21], we sample around 130K chemical compounds from ChEMBL [9] in SMILES format and artificially generate, using an RDKit fork [1], a rich labeled dataset with 2D images of chemical compounds. (2) Secondly, we test the baseline performance of this pre-trained model on two different test sets from two different target domains than the source domain of the pre-trained model. (3) Thirdly, we apply our domain adaptation method and measure performance again on the two target domains.

For the first target domain we take a data set from the work from Staker et al. [33], which we will call Indigo data set. For the second target domain we take the data set which was published by the developers of MolRec [18] which we will call the Maybridge data set. Both data sets provide 2D images from a chemical compound together with corresponding identifier of a the chemical compound like SMILES [36] or MOLfile [5]. These identifiers describe the graph structure of the chemical compound however they do not provide the planar embedding of the graph (e.g. no information about the pixel coordinates of every node or edge in the image). Visually we can also observe that the Maybridge dataset contains images where the style is closer related to the training images style used for the pre-trained model compared with the images in Indigo dataset where the style of images is quite different. Therefore we expect a significant worse starting performance of the pre-trained model on the Indigo dataset compared with the Maybridge dataset.

Table 1. Summary of datasets from the 2 different target domains

Dataset	Orig. size	# samples to be considered for self-rich-labeling	# test samples
Indigo	50,000	4,000	1,000
Maybridge	5,740	4,000	1,000

From both data sets we randomly sample 5,000 datapoints which are split in 4,000 datapoints used for our method and 1,000 datapoints to measure performance on (summarized in Table 1). When processing the 4,000 datapoints our method will be able to generate rich labels for the datapoints where the graph prediction could be graph aligned with the true graph. As the number of rich labeled datapoints this way is maximum 4,000 we will upsample them (x number of copies) before adding them to the training data set. In our experiments we differentiate between two strategies of upsampling. One way is to upsample all the rich labeled data points equally from the target domain to a fixed number, for example 20,000. Another way is to take into account, while upsampling, the number of atom types that are rich labeled and make sure that the rare atom types are upsampled to a specific threshold.

One important tuning parameter in our method is the number of allowed operations. For our experiments we will try two different values for this parameter. Firstly, we set this parameter to zero meaning we do not allow any operation for graph alignment. We will call this **exact graph alignment**. Secondly, we allow a maximum of 2 node substitutions or a maximum of 1 edge substitution for graph alignment, which we will call **correcting graph alignment**.

In total we will measure the performance of 4 variations of our method (varying allowed operations and upsampling strategy) on both data sets. The performance we will measure is the accuracy of $U \rightarrow W$ as we only have access to the normal labels of target domain. However, we assume that if the final graph prediction is correct (W) it is highly likely that also the planar embedding (V) is correct. As our method is an iterative method we will report results for every iteration starting with the initial performance before applying our method. The results of these experiments are summarized in Fig. 3. We observe that all variations of our method are able to improve performance on target domain compared with initial pre-trained model on source domain. On the Indigo data set the best variation is even able to obtain 4x improvement. The best variation of our method on the Indigo data set was using **correcting graph alignment** without upsampling of rare atom types while on the Maybridge data set the best variation was also using **correcting graph alignment** but with upsampling of rare atom types. Some of the underperforming variations of our method were stopped early in order to save computational resources.

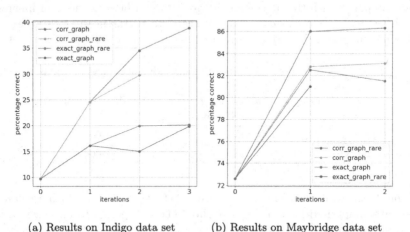

(a) Results on Indigo data set   (b) Results on Maybridge data set

Fig. 3. Comparison performance of methods on Indigo and Maybridge data set. Self-labeling by **correcting graph alignment** is clearly better performing than when **exact graph alignment** is used. Sometimes upsampling of rare atoms to a specific threshold (note postfix_*rare*) before retraining of model can boost performance. Performance on target domain at iteration 0 is the performance of pre-trained (on source domain) ChemGrapher before domain adaptation.

We choose the best variation of our method for every data set and analyze the performance on different atom and bond types per iteration. We measure for every atom or bond type the percentage of graphs predicted correctly from the total number of graphs containing that specific atom or bond type per iteration, which is visualized in Fig. 4. Most of the performances of the different atom and bond types increase per iteration for both data sets even when initial performance was 0%.

The atom types where initial performance was 0% are atom types never seen before in source domain. For example in the Indigo data set there are compounds with atom labels like R1, R2 and R3 representing R-groups which were not present in the original data set from the source domain. For illustration purposes we visualize in Fig. 5 the segmentation step which forms part of the graph recognition model used in this study. In the initial segmentation from the pre-trained model we can clearly see that the model confuses the R-group atoms with the oxygen atom type and the hydrogen atom type. After applying our method the model is able to make correct predictions. In the same Fig. 5 we also observe that in the Indigo data set carbon sometimes also is represented using a C which was never the case in the original data set. The initial segmentation mainly confuses these carbon atom types with the oxygen atom type. After applying our method the model again makes the correct prediction.

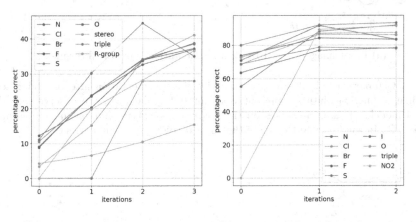

(a) Results on Indigo data set   (b) Results on Maybridge dataset

Fig. 4. We take the best performing methods and analyze their performance on different atom and bond types per iteration. We observe that for some atom types the method is able to increase performance even though initial performance was 0%. This is the case in for example R-groups in Indigo data set or superatom NO_2 in Maybridge data set.

Similarly, the superatom NO_2 present in the Maybridge data set was never observed in the source domain. However, again after applying our method the model is able to detect superatom NO_2 correctly. We illustrate the segmentation step of the graph recognition model in Fig. 6 for an example image taken from the Maybridge data set. We observe that in the initial segmentation the pre-trained model confuses NO_2 with nitrogen atom and also oxygen atom which chemically is not the correct prediction. In the final segmentation after applying two iterations of our method the newly trained model is able to make the correct prediction.

Additionally Fig. 5 and Fig. 6 also show an interesting side effect when using a fully mediating representation. Consider a classical model where input is an image and output is SMILES. When the output prediction of the model is incorrect it is not clear in which part of the image the mistake was made but in the case of having available the planar embedding (mediation representation) the expert can see where and how the mistakes happened. This makes the model more interpretable.

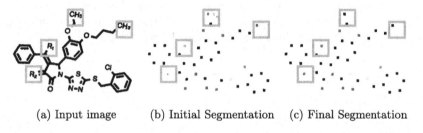

(a) Input image   (b) Initial Segmentation   (c) Final Segmentation

Fig. 5. Comparison initial segmentation with final segmentation after applying self-labeling of fully mediating representations for Indigo data set. We observe that the initial model is making mistakes on the R-group atom type and carbon represented with a 'C'. In the final model we see that now predictions are all correct.

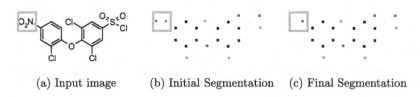

(a) Input image   (b) Initial Segmentation   (c) Final Segmentation

Fig. 6. Comparison initial segmentation with final segmentation after applying self-labeling of fully mediating representations for Maybridge data set. The initial model predicts the superatom NO_2 as two separate atoms O and N which is chemically not correct. The final model makes the correct prediction.

Finally we compare in Table 2 the resulting best performance of the model after applying our method on the Maybridge data set with several other methods available. We observe that our approach enables to reach higher performance than the current state of the art. For the freely available tools OSRA [7] and Molvec [28] we measured the performance using the same randomly 1000 data-points from the Maybridge dataset. For MolRec [18] this was not possible but we report for information the performance on the total Maybride dataset as reported in the work of M. Sadawi et al. [18]. Finally for ChemGrapher [21] we measured performance using three different training datasets. Firstly, we measure the performance when we only have access to the source domain (generated using RDKit [1]). Secondly, we measure performance using the same training dataset from source domain but adding upsampled (100 copies) 20 handpicked manually rich labeled datapoints from the target Maybridge domain (as was done in the work of Oldenhof et al. [21]). Finally, instead of manually rich label-ing datapoints, we process the 4,000 datapoints from Maybridge target domain where our method will be able to generate rich labels for the datapoints where the graph prediction could be graph aligned with the true graph, after which these rich labeled datapoints are added to the training dataset.

Table 2. Comparison performance on Maybridge data set. We observe that our app-roach enables to reach higher performance than the current state of the art. Most of the tools available for chemical graph recognition are rule based approaches for which a training dataset is not relevant.

Method	Training dataset		Accuracy
	Source domain	Target domain	
OSRA (v2.1.0) [7]	N/A	N/A	80.4%
Molvec (v0.9.8) [28]	N/A	N/A	78.4%
ChemGrapher [21]	130K images	N/A	72.6%
ChemGrapher [21] (using manually rich-labeling)	130K images	40 manually handpicked and rich-labeled images (upsampled)	81.6%
Proposed domain adaptation	130K images	4,000 non-rich labeled	**86.3%**
MolRec [18]	N/A	N/A	83.8% from [18]

5   Conclusion

Machine learning models often are faced with the problem to not generalize well to a new domain. This is also the case for chemical graph recognition from images. We have shown that fully mediating layers can be exploited in machine learning models to adapt in data efficient way to new domains, without the need of rich expensive labels as they can be generated using our method. In the case of chemical graph recognition we empirically show that our method is able to adapt to a new domain of chemical compounds, with **previously unobserved** atom or bond types. Our rich-labeling method required only 4,000 normal labeled points in the target domain to go from 10% accuracy to 39%, i.e., almost 4x improvement in the difficult Indigo data set. Using more normal labeled points and more iterations would most probably give a higher resulting accuracy. Furthermore, on Maybridge data set, again using only 4,000 images, we reached high accuracy obtaining better performance than the current state of the art.

Effective tools of chemical structure recognition from images enable access to the knowledge in chemical literature which is currently only available through expensive chemistry databases. We believe it as an important step towards open pharmaceutical science.

It would be interesting to apply this method to other contexts where the output of a machine learning model could be represented with a graph structure. For example, the case of structural scene representation, where a scene could be represented using a graph where every vertex could represent an object and every edge would represent the relations between the objects (e.g. side-by-side, on-top-of, under). This structural scene could be in form of 2D images or it could be even generalized to 3D models, where point clouds are available and one is interested to transform them into 3D graphs of connected parts.

Acknowledgments. MO, AA, YM, and JS are funded by (1) Research Council KU Leuven: C14/18/092 SymBioSys3; CELSA-HIDUCTION, (2) Innovative Medicines Initiative: MELLODDY, (3) Flemish Government (ELIXIR Belgium, IWT: PhD grants, FWO 06260) and (4) Impulsfonds AI: VR 2019 2203 DOC.0318/1QUATER Kenniscentrum Data en Maatschappij. Computational resources and services used in this work were provided by the VSC (Flemish Supercomputer Center), funded by the Research Foundation - Flanders (FWO) and the Flemish Government - department EWI. We also gratefully acknowledge the support of NVIDIA Corporation with the donation of the Titan Xp GPU used for this research.

A   Appendix

A.1   Architecture Summary of Graph Recognition Tool

Every iteration of our method we need to train the graph recognition tool described in Oldenhof et al. [21]. This graph recognition tool is built using a combination of different convolutional neural networks. The first part is a semantic segmentation network to pixel-wise predict every atom, bond and charge type. The second part consists of three classification networks to classify every segment predicted by the semantic segmentation network. After the first step of the ChemGrapher model [21], the segmentation network (Table 3), the predicted segments are processed so that for every segment the center of mass is calculated. These centers of mass would be the atom/bond/charge candidates to be classified by the classification networks (Table 4).

Table 3. Summary of the layers of the segmentation network

Layer	Kernel	Nonlinearity	Padding	Dilation
conv1	3×3	ReLU	1	No dilation
conv2	3×3	ReLU	2	2
conv3	3×3	ReLU	4	4
conv4	3×3	ReLU	8	8
conv5	3×3	ReLU	8	8
conv6	3×3	ReLU	4	4
conv7	3×3	ReLU	2	2
conv8	3×3	ReLU	1	No dilation
Last	1×1	None	No padding	No dilation

Table 4. Different layers in the classification network

Layer	Kernel	Nonlinearity	Padding	Dilation
Depthconv1	3×3	ReLU	1	No dilation
conv2	3×3	ReLU	2	2
conv3	3×3	ReLU	4	4
conv4	3×3	ReLU	8	8
conv5	3×3	ReLU	1	No dilation
Global maxpool	Input size	None	No padding	No dilation
Last	1×1	None	No padding	No dilation

A.2   Training Details for Graph Recognition Tool

Training details of the graph recognition tool for every iteration of our method are summarized in Table 5. The input images used for training of the different networks are a mix if images from source domain and upsampled rich labeled images from target domain. For pretraining of the ChemGrapher model only images from source domain were used. The training was performed using a compute node with 2 NVIDIA v100 GPUs with 32 GB of memory.

Table 5. Training details for different networks

Network	#input images		#epochs	Walltime	Minibatch size	Learning rate
	Source domain	Target domain (upsampled)				
Segm. network	114K	20K	5	24 h	8	0.001
Atom clas.	12.4K	2.6K	2	8 h	16	0.001
Charge clas.	12.4K	2.6K	2	8 h	16	0.001
Bond clas.	4.4K	2.1K	2	4 h	64	0.001

A.3   Computational Cost per Rich-Labeling Iteration

In the following Table 6 the computational cost for 1 rich-labeling iteration is summarized including all steps: (re)training, predicting and graph aligning rich-labeling.

Table 6. Computational costs per rich-labeling iteration

	Training	Predict	Graph aligning	
Hardware	2 NVIDIA v100 GPUs	1 NVIDIA v100 GPU	Intel Xeon Gold 6240 2.6 GHz	
Dataset	Source+Target domain	Indigo/Maybride	Indigo	Maybridge
#datapoints	See Table 5	4,000	4,000	4,000
Walltime	~44 h (details Table 5)	~2 h	~40 min	~3 min

A.4   Examples of Cases Where Graph Alignment Fails

We would like to showcase some examples where the constrained (max 2 node substitutions or max 1 edge substitution) graph alignment fails. At the same time it is important to note that our proposed domain adaptation method is an iterative method, so if a graph alignment fails in a previous iteration it could succeed in a next one when the new model makes a new graph prediction closer to the true graph.

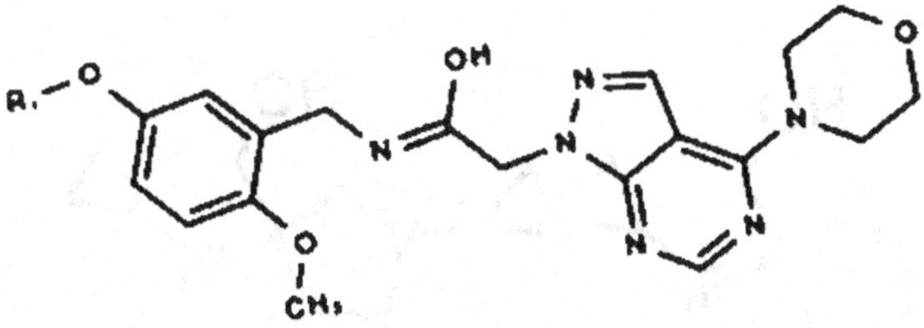

(a) Input Image(U)

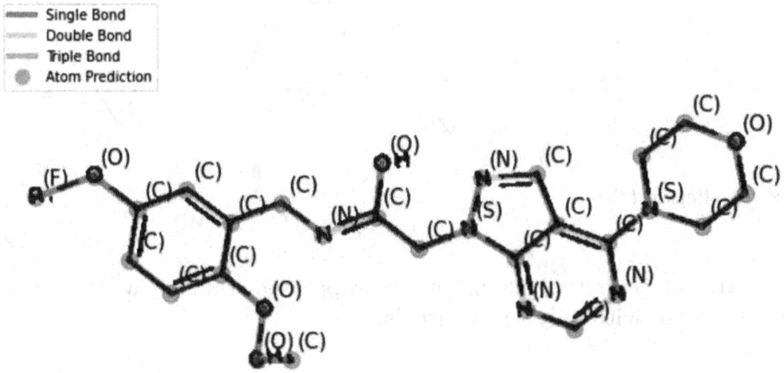

(b) Planar embedding prediction (V')

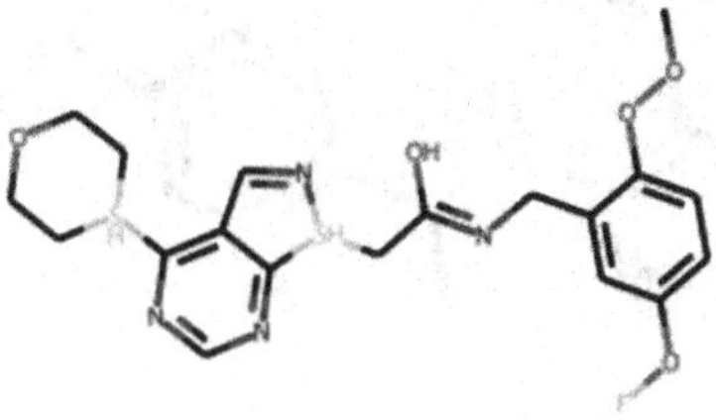

(c) Graph Prediction (W')

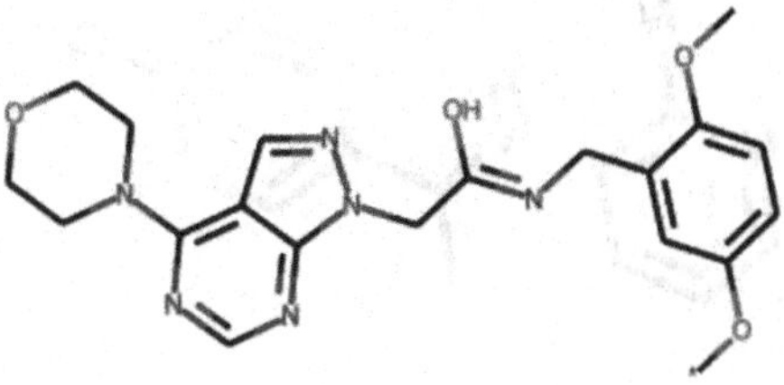

(d) True Graph (W)

Fig. 7. Example 1: It is clear that to align the graph prediction W' with the true graph W more than 2 node substitutions are needed. So no rich labeling is possible for this example in this iteration.

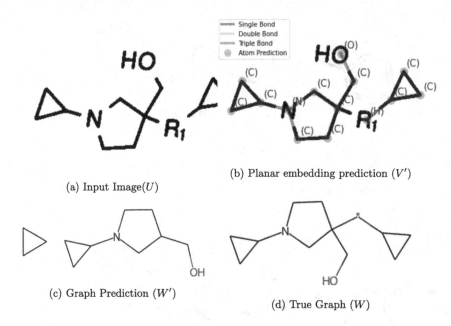

(a) Input Image(U)

(b) Planar embedding prediction (V')

(c) Graph Prediction (W')

(d) True Graph (W)

Fig. 8. Example 2: It is clear that alignment of the graph prediction W' with the true graph W can not be solved with only substitutions.

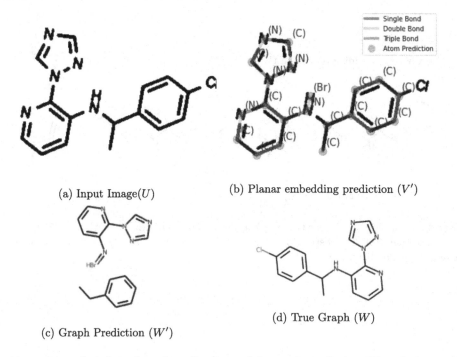

(a) Input Image(U)

(b) Planar embedding prediction (V')

(c) Graph Prediction (W')

(d) True Graph (W)

Fig. 9. Example 3: It is clear that alignment of the graph prediction W' with the true graph W can not be solved with only substitutions.

References

1. Fork of the official sources for the RDKit library (2020). https://github.com/biolearning-stadius/rdkit. Accessed 12 Nov 2020
2. Baron, R.M., Kenny, D.A.: The moderator-mediator variable distinction in social psychological research: conceptual, strategic, and statistical considerations. J. Pers. Soc. Psychol. **51**(6), 1173 (1986). https://doi.org/10.1037/0022-3514.51.6.1173
3. Belli, D., Kipf, T.: Image-conditioned graph generation for road network extraction. arXiv preprint arXiv:1910.14388 (2019)
4. Bruzzone, L., Marconcini, M.: Domain adaptation problems: a DASVM classification technique and a circular validation strategy. IEEE Trans. Pattern Anal. Mach. Intell. **32**(5), 770–787 (2009). https://doi.org/10.1109/TPAMI.2009.57
5. Dalby, A., et al.: Description of several chemical structure file formats used by computer programs developed at Molecular Design Limited. J. Chem. Inf. Comput. Sci. **32**(3), 244–255 (1992). https://doi.org/10.1021/ci00007a012
6. Das, D., Lee, C.S.G.: Graph matching and pseudo-label guided deep unsupervised domain adaptation. In: Kůrková, V., Manolopoulos, Y., Hammer, B., Iliadis, L., Maglogiannis, I. (eds.) ICANN 2018. LNCS, vol. 11141, pp. 342–352. Springer, Cham (2018). https://doi.org/10.1007/978-3-030-01424-7_34
7. Filippov, I.V., Nicklaus, M.C.: Optical structure recognition software to recover chemical information: OSRA, an open source solution. J. Chem. Inf. Model. **49**(3), 740–743 (2009). https://doi.org/10.1021/ci800067r
8. Gao, L., Song, W., Dai, J., Chen, Y.: Road extraction from high-resolution remote sensing imagery using refined deep residual convolutional neural network. Remote Sens. **11**(5), 552 (2019). https://doi.org/10.3390/rs10091461
9. Gaulton, A., et al.: The ChEMBL database in 2017. Nucleic Acids Res. **45**(D1), D945–D954 (2017). https://doi.org/10.1093/nar/gkw1074
10. Gold, S., Rangarajan, A.: Graduated assignment graph matching. In: Proceedings of International Conference on Neural Networks (ICNN 1996), vol. 3, pp. 1474–1479. IEEE (1996). https://doi.org/10.1109/34.491619
11. Han, C., Mao, J., Gan, C., Tenenbaum, J., Wu, J.: Visual concept-metaconcept learning. In: Advances in Neural Information Processing Systems, pp. 5001–5012 (2019)
12. Henry, C., Azimi, S.M., Merkle, N.: Road segmentation in SAR satellite images with deep fully convolutional neural networks. IEEE Geosci. Remote Sens. Lett. **15**(12), 1867–1871 (2018). https://doi.org/10.1109/LGRS.2018.2864342
13. Kisku, D.R., Rattani, A., Grosso, E., Tistarelli, M.: Face identification by sift-based complete graph topology. In: 2007 IEEE Workshop on Automatic Identification Advanced Technologies, pp. 63–68. IEEE (2007). https://doi.org/10.1109/AUTOID.2007.380594
14. Kong, X., Zhang, J., Yu, P.S.: Inferring anchor links across multiple heterogeneous social networks. In: Proceedings of the 22nd ACM International Conference on Information & Knowledge Management, pp. 179–188 (2013). https://doi.org/10.1145/2505515.2505531
15. Kouw, W.M., Loog, M.: A review of domain adaptation without target labels. IEEE Trans. Pattern Anal. Mach. Intell. **43**(3), 766–785 (2019). https://doi.org/10.1109/TPAMI.2019.2945942
16. Kuhn, H.W.: The Hungarian method for the assignment problem. Naval Res. Logist. Q. **2**(1–2), 83–97 (1955). https://doi.org/10.1002/nav.3800020109

17. Locatello, F., et al.: Object-centric learning with slot attention. arXiv preprint arXiv:2006.15055 (2020)

18. Sadawi, N.M., Sexton, A., Sorge, V.: Chemical structure recognition: a rule based approach. In: Proceedings of SPIE, vol. 8297, p. 32, January 2012. https://doi.org/10.1117/12.912185

19. Mao, J., Gan, C., Kohli, P., Tenenbaum, J.B., Wu, J.: The neuro-symbolic concept learner: interpreting scenes, words, and sentences from natural supervision. arXiv preprint arXiv:1904.12584 (2019)

20. McDaniel, J.R., Balmuth, J.R.: Kekule: OCR-optical chemical (structure) recognition. J. Chem. Inf. Comput. Sci. **32**(4), 373–378 (1992). https://doi.org/10.1021/ci00008a018

21. Oldenhof, M., Arany, A., Moreau, Y., Simm, J.: ChemGrapher: optical graph recognition of chemical compounds by deep learning. J. Chem. Inf. Model. **60**(10), 4506–4517 (2020). https://doi.org/10.1021/acs.jcim.0c00459

22. Park, J., Rosania, G., Shedden, K.A., Nguyen, M., Lyu, N., Saitou, K.: Automated extraction of chemical structure information from digital raster images. Chem. Cent. J. **3** (2009). Article number: 4. https://doi.org/10.1186/1752-153X-3-4

23. Pearl, J.: Causal diagrams for empirical research. Biometrika **82**(4), 669–688 (1995). https://doi.org/10.1093/biomet/82.4.669

24. Pearl, J.: Direct and indirect effects. In: Proceedings of the Seventeenth Conference on Uncertainty in Artificial Intelligence, pp. 411–420 (2001)

25. Pearl, J.: Causality. Cambridge University Press, Cambridge (2009)

26. Pearl, J., et al.: Models, Reasoning and Inference. Cambridge University Press, Cambridge (2000)

27. Pérez, Ó., Sánchez-Montañés, M.: A new learning strategy for classification problems with different training and test distributions. In: Sandoval, F., Prieto, A., Cabestany, J., Graña, M. (eds.) IWANN 2007. LNCS, vol. 4507, pp. 178–185. Springer, Heidelberg (2007). https://doi.org/10.1007/978-3-540-73007-1_22

28. Peryea, T., Katzel, D., Zhao, T., Southall, N., Nguyen, D.T.: MOLVEC: open source library for chemical structure recognition. In: Abstracts of Papers of the American Chemical Society, vol. 258. American Chemical Society, Washington, DC (2019)

29. Sanfeliu, A., Fu, K.S.: A distance measure between attributed relational graphs for pattern recognition. IEEE Trans. Syst. Man Cybern. **3**, 353–362 (1983). https://doi.org/10.1109/TSMC.1983.6313167

30. Serratosa, F.: Fast computation of bipartite graph matching. Pattern Recogn. Lett. **45**, 244–250 (2014). https://doi.org/10.1016/j.patrec.2014.04.015

31. Serratosa, F.: Computation of graph edit distance: reasoning about optimality and speed-up. Image Vis. Comput. **40**, 38–48 (2015). https://doi.org/10.1016/j.imavis.2015.06.005

32. Serratosa, F.: Speeding up fast bipartite graph matching through a new cost matrix. Int. J. Pattern Recogn. Artif. Intell. **29**(02), 1550010 (2015). https://doi.org/10.1142/S021800141550010X

33. Staker, J., Marshall, K., Abel, R., McQuaw, C.M.: Molecular structure extraction from documents using deep learning. J. Chem. Inf. Model. **59**(3), 1017–1029 (2019). https://doi.org/10.1021/acs.jcim.8b00669. ISSN: 1549-9596

34. Valko, A.T., Johnson, A.P.: CLiDE Pro: the latest generation of CLiDE, a tool for optical chemical structure recognition. J. Chem. Inf. Model. **49**(4), 780–787 (2009). https://doi.org/10.1021/ci800449t

35. Vezhnevets, A., Ferrari, V., Buhmann, J.M.: Weakly supervised structured output learning for semantic segmentation. In: 2012 IEEE Conference on Computer Vision and Pattern Recognition, pp. 845–852. IEEE (2012). https://doi.org/10.1109/CVPR.2012.6247757

36. Weininger, D.: SMILES, a chemical language and information system. 1. Introduction to methodology and encoding rules. J. Chem. Inf. Comput. Sci. **28**(1), 31–36 (1988). https://doi.org/10.1021/ci00057a005

37. Willett, P., Barnard, J.M., Downs, G.M.: Chemical similarity searching. Chem. Inf. Comput. Sci. **38**(6), 983–996 (1998). https://doi.org/10.1021/ci9800211

38. Xu, J., Schwing, A.G., Urtasun, R.: Tell me what you see and i will show you where it is. In: Proceedings of the IEEE Conference on Computer Vision and Pattern Recognition, pp. 3190–3197 (2014)

39. Xu, J., Schwing, A.G., Urtasun, R.: Learning to segment under various forms of weak supervision. In: Proceedings of the IEEE Conference on Computer Vision and Pattern Recognition, pp. 3781–3790 (2015)

40. Xu, Z., Huang, S., Zhang, Y., Tao, D.: Augmenting strong supervision using web data for fine-grained categorization. In: Proceedings of the IEEE International Conference on Computer Vision, pp. 2524–2532 (2015)

41. Yi, K., Wu, J., Gan, C., Torralba, A., Kohli, P., Tenenbaum, J.: Neural-symbolic VQA: disentangling reasoning from vision and language understanding. In: Advances in Neural Information Processing Systems, pp. 1031–1042 (2018)

42. Zhang, H., Xiao, J., Quan, L.: Supervised label transfer for semantic segmentation of street scenes. In: Daniilidis, K., Maragos, P., Paragios, N. (eds.) ECCV 2010. LNCS, vol. 6315, pp. 561–574. Springer, Heidelberg (2010). https://doi.org/10.1007/978-3-642-15555-0_41

Recognizing Objects

Task Independent Capsule-Based Agents for Deep Q-Learning

Akash Singh[✉], Tom De Schepper, Kevin Mets, Peter Hellinckx,
José Oramas, and Steven Latré

imec IDLab, University of Antwerpen, Antwerpen, Belgium
akash.singh@uantwerpen.be
https://www.uantwerpen.be/en/

Abstract. In recent years, Capsule Networks (CapsNets) have achieved
promising results in tasks such as object recognition thanks to their
invariance characteristics towards pose and lighting. They have been proposed as an alternative to relational insensitive and translation invariant
Convolutional Neural Networks (CNN). It has been empirically proven
that CapsNets are capable of achieving competitive performance while
requiring significantly fewer parameters. This is a desirable characteristic
for Deep reinforcement learning which is known to be sample-inefficient
during training. In this paper, we propose DCapsQN, a task-independent
CapsNets-based architecture in the deep reinforcement learning setting.
We experiment in the model-free reinforcement learning setting, more
specifically in Deep Q-Learning using the Atari suite as the testbed of
our analysis. To the best of our knowledge, this work constitutes the first
CapsNets-based deep reinforcement learning architecture to learn state-
action value functions without the need for task-specific adaptation. Our
results show that, in this setting, DCapsQN requires 92% fewer parameters than the baseline. Moreover, despite their smaller size, the DCapsQN
provides significant boosts in performance (score), ranging between 10%–
77% while further stabilising the Deep Q-Learning. This is supported by
our empirical results which shows that DCapsQN agents outperform the
benchmark Double-DQN agent, with Prioritized experience replay, in
eight out of the nine selected environments.

Keywords: Deep reinforcement learning · Capsule networks · Deep
Q-learning

1 Introduction

Reinforcement Learning (RL) is an experience-based learning paradigm, where
the agent interacts with the environment by performing an action and learns how
to maximize its cumulative reward based on the returned rewards. The learning is
based on trial and error and often requires a large amount of data for Deep Reinforcement Learning (DRL). In recent years, with advancements in Deep Learning (DL), Convolutional Neural Networks (CNNs) have made breakthroughs in

© Springer Nature Switzerland AG 2022
L. A. Leiva et al. (Eds.): BNAIC/Benelearn 2021, CCIS 1530, pp. 69–85, 2022.
https://doi.org/10.1007/978-3-030-93842-0_4

multiple machine learning tasks like natural language processing and computer vision [12,14]. The field of DRL has benefited from the remarkable flexibility and advancement of DL as well. CNNs have remarkable flexibility to learn features for the agent to learn a proper policy or value function. Having scalar nature, CNNs have additive nature in neurons at any given layer, they are ambivalent to spatial relationships within their kernel of previous layers [15]. Thus despite their good performance, they have an inherent weakness of limited modelling capabilities for spatial relationships between the learned features [25,29]. For example, for the task of recognizing faces in images, CNNs are capable of learning the regions that resemble a nose or a mouth. However, when recognizing a face, at test time, they have the weakness of focusing on the occurrence of these "facial parts" and completely ignore the spatial arrangement in which these should occur in order to effectively represent a face.

Capsule Networks (CapsNets) were designed to mimic human vision [9,25]. They address the inherent limitation of CNNs, while significantly decreasing the required number of parameters. CapsNets aim to preserve the spatial information (pose and precise location) and attributes (length, thickness etc.) by encoding features in vectors rather than scalar values. Under this formulation, the magnitude of the vector represents the probability of the existence of the entity it is representing. CapsNets in DL require less training data, which is a desirable attribute within a DRL setting. The architectural design of CapsNets profits from *dynamic routing*. Routing by agreement is a novel dynamic routing technique, it plays a key role in preserving spatial information. The architectural overview of capsules draws inspiration from the Multi-Layer Perceptron architecture. This architecture with *routing by agreement* is designed to preserve part-whole relationships (locations, orientations, etc.) between various entities levels which may be a complete entity or part-of an entity. For example, the relative positions of a nose and a mouth on a face in a portrait. [25] used the magnitude of a vector from the last layer of CapsNets for classification in supervised deep learning.

Reinforcement learning approaches such as DQN strive to estimate the action-value function [18,19]. Traditionally for vision-based tasks, an agent's architecture uses CNNs and fully connected layers to approximate the optimal action-value function. The CNN-based architecture of the agent in various deep reinforcement learning algorithms [19,26,28] are inspired from [11]. The agent learns on raw sensory input that uses CNNs to mimic the effects of receptive fields [19]. While the magnitude of the vector in CapsNets is a good surrogate for multi-class classification, it is not a good candidate for estimating the state-action value function in DRL.

Here we propose DCapsQN, an architecture suitable for an agent to learn value functions based on part-whole relationships. We demonstrate how part-whole relationships assist in value function estimation and that Q-estimates from them are much more self-coherent. Owing to a large number of atari environments and their experimental/computational costs, we limit our experiments to a diverse subset of environments with different natures and tasks.

Across multiple environments, the proposed agent uses 92% fewer parameters and improves 10%–77% on performance (score) compared to the baseline.

The main contributions of this paper are:

1. Introducing DCapsQN, a task-agnostic CapsNets-based architecture.
2. Presenting the first CapsNets based architecture study on the atari bench-mark.
3. Comparing DCapsQN to the traditional CNN-based architecture of DeepQN, showing a reduction in the number of trainable parameters.

2 Background

2.1 Capsule Networks

Computer graphics employ *Hierarchical Modeling* for building complex objects by placing simpler objects and their known relations [7]. The idea of CapsNets is to achieve the capabilities of inverse hierarchical modelling to better understand the scene where lower level capsules represents simpler entities and higher level capsule represent the complex. The concepts of capsule (Fig. 1) and CapsNets (Fig. 2) were introduced in [25] to retain the spatial relationship between complex and simple entities [9,25].

CapsNets architecture is inspired from Multi-Layer Perceptron architecture, where a capsule replaces a neuron in a layer. Capsule [25], as a fundamental unit of CapsNets, can be defined as a group of neurons where the activities of the neurons within a capsule represent the various properties like pose (position, size, orientation) (Fig. 1). Capsule encodes an entity as a vector where its magnitude represents the probability of entity occurrence and its orientation represents attributes of the entity (Fig. 1). The magnitude of the vector output is always bound between 0 and 1.

We arrange capsules in 2 levels, in lower level l they are called primary capsules and upper-level $l + 1$ they are called secondary capsules.

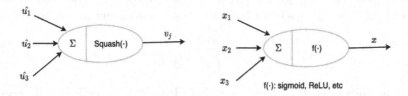

Fig. 1. The similarity between a capsule and a neuron [16].

Primary Capsules: Following the first convolutional layer, the primary capsule (*PrimaryCaps*) is responsible for transforming scalar values into a vector. A capsule in Fig. 2 refers to a group of convolutional layers. It is the first layer where the process of inverse hierarchical modelling takes place. The capsule here reshapes the feature maps outputs of convolutional layers to output vectors.

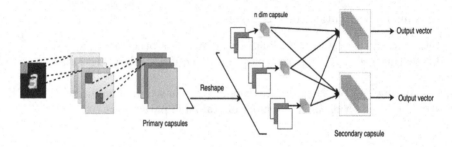

Fig. 2. The figure shows fundamental Capsule network architecture.

Secondary Capsules: Following PrimaryCaps is Secondary Capsules (*SecondaryCaps*). They receive an input vector from PrimaryCaps. The weight matrix $\mathbf{W}_{ij}$ transforms the output vector of a PrimaryCaps to serve as input to SecondaryCaps.

$$\hat{u}_{j|i} = W_{ij}u_i \tag{1}$$

Routing by Agreement: Routing by agreement is a dynamic routing technique introduced in [25]. Pooling operations statically forward the relevant information from the previous layer to the following layer and in this process, it loses information. Contrary to statically connected pooling layers, dynamic routing during the forward pass redirects the output from PrimaryCaps to the most relevant parent in SecondaryCaps. Each capsule i (where $1 \leq i \leq N$) in a layer l has vector u_i to encode spatial information. The output of PrimaryCaps u_i of the ith layer acts as input to all capsules in layer $l + 1$ of SecondaryCaps.

The *Coupling coefficient* c_{ij} is iteratively determined through routing by agreement. It represents the agreement of a capsule of layer l with $l + 1$. If the agreement is high, the coupling coefficient for child-parent will increase, otherwise, it would decrease. The coupling coefficient plays a role in the child-parent relationship to form a parse tree-like structure in CapsNets. The weighted sum (s_j) from all PrimaryCaps contributes to forming the output of SecondaryCaps.

$$s_j = \sum_{i=1}^{N} c_{ij}\hat{u}_{j|i} \tag{2}$$

The magnitude of the output vector from PrimaryCaps is limited between 0 and 1 by using a *squashing function*. The magnitude of the vector represents the probability of the existence of an entity represented by a capsule.

$$\mathbf{v}_j = \frac{\|\mathbf{s}_j\|^2}{1 + \|\mathbf{s}_j\|^2} \frac{\mathbf{s}_j}{\|\mathbf{s}_j\|} \tag{3}$$

The squashing function makes sure to limit the length while still retaining the positional information.

2.2   Deep Reinforcement Learning

We study the utility of CapsNets-based representations in Double DQN using prioritised experience replay. The method uses *proportional prioritization* of prioritised experience replay.

The Q-learning algorithm is a temporal difference learning algorithm. To update the value estimate of a state-action pair, the temporal difference (TD) error is computed at each time step. Deep Q-learning was first introduced by [18] to approximate Q-values for high dimensional sensory input. Deep Q-learning is known to be unstable and it overestimates the Q-values. To remedy this [28] proposed Double DQN. They decoupled the networks for selecting and evaluating an action separately. The agent generally selects an action using ϵ-greedy policy. Under the ϵ-greedy policy, agents can take a random action with ϵ probability or select an action with 1-ϵ probability maximising $Q(s, a)$.

An *Experience replay* is used to store the agent's interaction with the environment at each time step [18]. This buffer is used to sample batches of experience during training. [26] proposed a new experience replay design called prioritised experience replay (PER), where the most important experiences were replayed to the agent. The importance or priority of experience was calculated using the TD error. With the design choice, [26] were able to empirically show that experience replay became more efficient and effective, which led to even better and faster learning of an agent. The agent performed better compared to the previous state-of-the-art DQN.

3   Related Work

On account of the drawbacks of CNNs, [25] introduced the idea of CapsNets, but most of the published research on CapsNets is currently focused in the field of deep learning. [5, 21, 23, 24] extend the work of [25] by proposing new capsule-based architectures. [23] proposes a DenseNet-like skip connection where the standard convolution component in the CapsNet is replaced with a hierarchical architecture. The resulting architecture outperforms the original CapsNets on datasets like SmallNORB and Cifar-10. [24] remove the margin loss to show that unsupervised training of sparse capsules can potentially lead to deeper architectures while achieving higher accuracy. [5] proposes a novel routing algorithm based on eigen-decomposition of votes. This leads to a higher convergence speed of the new architecture compared to original CapsNets. [1-3] and [15] investigate the performance of CapsNets in medical applications like brain tumour classification, COVID cases classification, Alzheimer disease detection and Lung segmentation. [30] study 3D-capsules for pose estimation. The work exploits the structural relations among local parts for pose estimation. [10] propose dual attention mechanism capsule network for higher accuracy and faster training.

While CapsNets have gained popularity in standard deep learning approaches, their study within a Deep Reinforcement Learning (DRL) context has received significantly less attention. [4] tries integrating CapsNets with Deep-Q Learning.

They showed that CapsNets-based agents underperform with respect to their baseline. The experiments were done on FlashRL with environments like Flappy Bird, Deep Line wars etc. The architecture takes 84×84 input which propagates to output $n \times 16$ vector from last capsule layer. n being number of actions. The architecture proposed by [4], employs the magnitude of the vector output from the last capsule layer for action-value estimation. The authors [4], do not take into consideration that magnitude of the vector from a capsule is not a good fit for action-value estimation. While the value function could have any negative or positive value, the magnitude of the vector output from CapsNets is bounded between zero and one (Eq. 3).

[20] combines CapsNets with A2C, but limits the scope of the study to only maze navigation in the ViZDoom environment. The ViZDoom environment only [13] provides tasks like move-and-shoot and maze navigation. Unlike the ViZDoom, the atari benchmark offers a more diverse, challenging and conceivable tasks in learning, modelling, and planning. Inspired from previous studies [18,19,28], we choose a widely accepted Atari benchmark [6] to empirically show the advantage of our framework in task-agnosticism and parameter reduction. The study proposes a generalised CapsNets-based agent to learn a state-action value function with no task-specific adjustments. Our DCapsQN, to the best of our knowledge, is the first generalised, task agnostic framework to learn state-action value functions to solve nine diverse atari tasks in addition to maze traversals.

4 Methodology

In this section, we introduce the agents and the environment used as a testbed for the analysis. We employ the atari suite for our experiments as it provides a variety of environments with respect to input space, action space and rewards.

Baseline Agent. For the baseline, we choose Double-DQN with prioritised experience replay [26,28]. The first layer in this architecture is a convolutional layer composed of 32, 8×8 convolution kernels with a stride of 4. This first layer feeds a second convolutional layer of 64, 4×4 kernels with a stride of 2. The third layer receives input from the second and has 64, 3×3 kernels with a stride of 1. The last convolutional layer of this set is connected to two FC layers. The first FC layer is composed of 512 neurons while the second FC layer is composed of a number of neurons equal to the output value estimates for the actions of interest. ReLU acts as the activation function for all the layers except the last FC layer. The architectural design of the CapsNets-based agent is depicted in Fig. 3 (bottom).

DCapsQN Agent. In a DRL agent, CNNs learn relevant visual features with respect to the task at hand while the FC layers aim at learning valuable combinations of these features and map them to value functions related to the actions of interest. In this regard, the FC layers learn the value function based on the features generated by CNNs. We explore the application and utility of CapsNets-based representations with Double DQN. The architectural design of the

DCapsQN depicted in Fig. 3 (top), takes inspiration from [25, 28] to learn part-whole relationship between visual entities in input state.

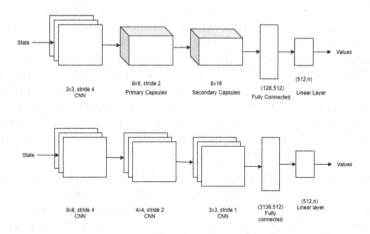

Fig. 3. DCapsQN (top) and Double-DQN (bottom) architecture.

A convolutional layer acts as the first layer, as shown in Fig. 3. The Convolution layer has 16, 3×3 convolution kernels with a stride of 4 and ReLU activation. This layer detects features from states and serves as an input to the Primary capsule layer. We have 49 capsules in the Primary capsule layer. A Primary capsule layer, here is a collection of convolutional capsules. A single convolution capsule comprises of a group of convolution layers with 9×9 kernel and with a stride of 2. Each capsule in the PrimaryCaps receives the input of all convolutional layers. Each primary capsule outputs an 8-dimensional vector. The output from the Primary capsule serves as input to the Secondary capsule layer. The Secondary capsule layer has 8 capsules with each Secondary capsule producing a 16-dimensional vector as output. Each of the Secondary capsules receives the input from all Primary capsules. The connection between the PrimaryCaps layer and the SecondaryCaps is controlled by *dynamic routing*. In our study, we followed the *routing by agreement* algorithm [25] where each child chooses its parent based on the cosine similarity between its transformed vector output and the vector output of its candidate parent. The dynamic routing between layers utilizes the vector output from capsules to preserve hierarchical relations in a state. Three routing iterations are used between capsule layers in order to find optimal weights for relations between layers.

Environment. The Arcade Learning Environment (ALE) [6] is a popular benchmark composed of a collection of Atari 2600 games. It provides a challenging and diverse set of tasks with respect to visual input, rewards returned by the environment, action space and difficulty. [17] integrate around 40 techniques from a dozen papers in order to determine the difficulty level of the games that are part of the benchmark.

Atari offers 57 environments, to compare the performance of our DCapsQN agent with respect to the baseline agent, we choose a subset of the environments that are diversified in terms of visual input (simple, complex), reward (sparse, dense), action space (3, 4, 6, 8, 18) and difficulty score [17]. Across various tasks, both agents are tasked with collecting the maximum reward. The environment gets reset the moment when the agents use all of their lives.

The input states are composed of simple states such as Pong, Boxing to fairly complex input states like Fishing Derby or Alien. The tasks are also diversified with respect to rewards offered by the environments. The agents are evaluated with dense rewards environments like Breakout, Pong and sparse rewards environments like Fishing Derby. Further, we the select the tasks that lay in difficulty spectrum of −2 to 10. Higher the difficulty score, lower was the performance of most able techniques considered in [17].

Training Protocol. With Atari, we restrict the training of both agents to only 20 million steps. The DCapsQN-based agent uses a batch size of 128 and a Learning rate of 0.00015 with RMSprop optimizer and Prioritised experience replay with alpha = 0.5 and beta with linear annealing from 0.4 to 1. The other hyper-parameters such as discount rate, the size of the experience replay memory, target network updates are the same as [26]. Baseline agents use the same hyper-parameters as described in [26]. An epsilon-greedy action selection method is employed to balance our exploration and exploitation. Both Double DQN and DCapsQN based agents randomly explore for the first 50000 steps and then linearly decrease the probability to randomly select an action for the next 1e6 steps. At end of 20 million steps, there still remains an exploration probability of 0.01. The evaluation section compares the cumulative reward collected by agents in all tasks. The average is calculated from 4 randomly initialized agents.

Evaluation Protocol. For evaluation, we refer to [26,28]. We evaluate both agents every 1 million steps and average over 100 episodes. The other hyper-parameters are the same as Double-DQN [28].

5   Analysis

In any given task an agent collects rewards to maximize its performance. The cumulative reward collected by an agent is the attribute that links to the agent's success in a given task. Apart from the cumulative rewards, to better understand the CapsNets-based representation in DRL environments, we try to get a deeper insight regarding the agents' performance under different attributes, e.g. input states, rewards and action space, of the environments.

5.1   Cumulative Reward and Parameters

Our DCapsQN agent (Sect. 4) has around 92% lower number of trainable parameters compared to baseline. To highlight the difference, Table 1 presents a comparison of trainable parameters of both agents under different environments.

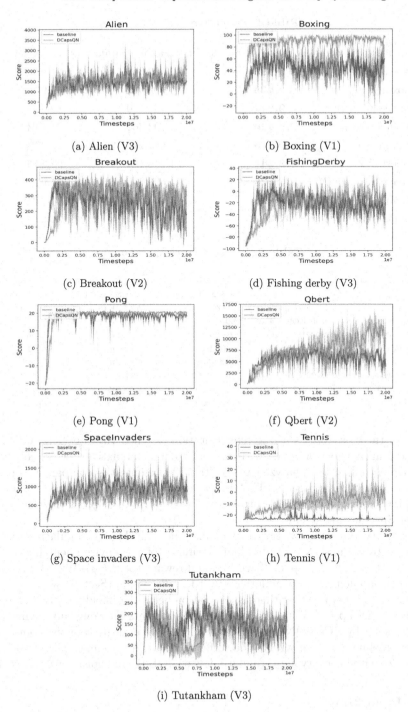

Fig. 4. Average score collected by the agents in the respective environment. The agents follow an epsilon greedy policy. The shaded area represents the ± standard deviation over 4 runs.

Table 1. Parameters comparison.

Environment name	DCapsQN parameters	Baseline parameters	Difference
Alien (V3)	**136,426**	1,693,362	91.94%
Boxing (V1)	**136,426**	1,693,362	91.94%
Breakout (V2)	**129,244**	1,686,180	92.33%
Fishing Derby (V3)	**136,426**	1,693,362	91.94%
Pong (V1)	**130,270**	1,687,206	92.27%
Qbert (V2)	**129,244**	1,686,180	92.33%
Space Invaders (V3)	**136,426**	1,693,362	91.94%
Tennis (V1)	**130,270**	1,687,206	92.27%
Tutankham (V3)	**131,296**	1,688,232	92.22%

Table 2. Performance comparison

Environment name	Difficulty	Actions	DCapsQN score ± S.D	Baseline score ± S.D	Performance
Alien (V3)	–	18	**1678.20** ± 261	1503.79 ± 351	11.60%
Boxing (V1)	−2.11368712	18	**92.87** ± 6	58.74 ± 18	58.10%
Breakout (V2)	−0.44196066	4	**259.4** ± 59	191.1 ± 87	35.74%
Fishing Derby (V3)	1.28989165	18	**−11.99** ± 14	−27.19 ± 14	55.90%
Pong (V1)	−0.04440702	3	**20.15** ± 0.8	18.25 ± 1.7	10.41%
Qbert (V2)	1.39864132	6	**9942.95** ± 1918	5616.26 ± 1349	77.03%
Space Invaders (V3)	0.16420283	6	787.64 ± 172	**924.11** ± 232	−14.76%
Tennis (V1)	10.48605210	18	**−7.138** ± 6	−23.645 ± 0.98	69.79%
Tutankham (V3)	1.98175005	8	**148.75** ± 37	129.20 ± 61	15.13%

To show the effectiveness of the representations learned via CapsNets, we compare the agents' performance with respect to the cumulative reward collected by them in all of the analyzed tasks. Table 2 presents the comparison of the performance of both agents. Though DCapsQN agents have a lower number of training parameters, they outperform baseline in all selected environments except SpaceInvaders.

Further in our study, we try to rationalise about the higher cumulative reward collected by DCapsQN on individual attributes of the environment like input state (Sect. 5.2), action space (Sect. 5.3) and reward (Sect. 5.4). We also discuss, how they supplement to cumulative reward in discussion (Sect. 6.2).

It is also observable that there is co-relation between difficulty score and average score of DCapsQN. With low difficulty environments like Pong and Boxing, the average score by DCapsQN is more stable and has lower degree of noise compared to the baseline. However with higher difficulty score environment like Tennis or Qbert, we witness a very high standard deviation (S.D) and noisier average score.

5.2 Input State

In this section, we reason how the input state of an environment (Fig. 5) is an influencing factor for DCapsQN agent. The CapsNets architecture focuses on

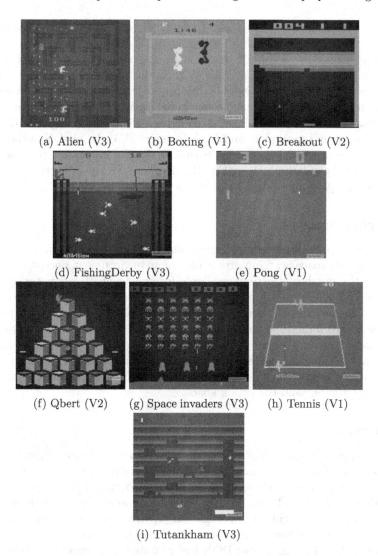

Fig. 5. State input of various Atari environments.

recognising simple and complex entities. As shown in Fig. 5 we can organize the environments in terms of a number of entities and their visual attributes. Pong, Boxing, Tennis are one of the visually simple environments with low number of entities, referring to them as *V1*. Breakout and QBert are more complex than V1, referred to as *V2*. But V2 is simpler compared to Alien, SpaceInvaders, Tutankham and Fishing Derby of *V3*.

It is observable that in the simpler input state of V1, a DCapsQN agent performs excellently. The performance could be highly attributed to the very simple input state. In these environments, there are clear separate entities such as players, ball in the input state. The DCapsQN agent's learning curve is swifter compared to the baseline Double DQN (Fig. 6). With comparably complex V2, the convergence of the DCapsQN-based agent is slower yet they outperform the Double DQN based baseline as well. With added visual complexities and an increase in the number of observable objects, we can observe that convergence slows down further. The same can be concluded for V3. The principle that DCapsQN focuses highly on entities further strengthen when comparing the difference in performance in Tennis (V1) and SpaceInvaders (V3). DCapsQN outperforms the baseline agent which struggles to learn with simpler input state that has clear separate entities in Tennis (V1) (Fig. 4h). However DCapsQN struggles where there are multiple copies of the same entities in SpaceInvaders (V3) (Fig. 4g).

5.3   Action Space

The atari suite provides a variety of environments with respect to action space as well. The action space is an important part of an environment since it is directly related to the number of actions available for the agent. A larger action space expresses a higher degree of freedom for an agent to choose an action from. For our study, we started with a small action space of 3 and 4, in Pong and Breakout, respectively. From there, we go to the largest action space available in atari, i.e. 18, in Alien, Boxing, Fishing Derby and Tennis. As can be noticed in Table 1, apart from the expected increase in the number of parameters introduced by the fully connected layers, there does not seem to be a direct correlation between an agent's performance and the action space.

5.4   Reward

In RL, the agent interacts with the environment to get a reward signal and the next state. With the goal of maximising the cumulative rewards, the reward as part of the environment governs how well an agent comprehends the input state. The environments in ALE can broadly be classified into dense rewards or sparse rewards environments. For our investigation, we diversify our environments with some dense reward environments such as Alien and some marginally sparse environments such as Fishing Derby. DQN suffers from poor sample efficiency when rewards are very sparse in an environment [8]. There is a relation between reward density and convergence of an agent to a value function. In the dense reward environment Alien, it takes around 3 million steps for a DCapsQN based agent to outperform the baseline while in Fishing Derby, it takes around 13 million (Fig. 4).

6   Discussion

6.1   Training

DQN [19] based algorithms use their own estimates to update their value. In order to analyze and gain insight into the potential of part-whole relations based representations, we plot and compare the loss (Fig. 7) and value estimates (Fig. 6) of both agents while training.

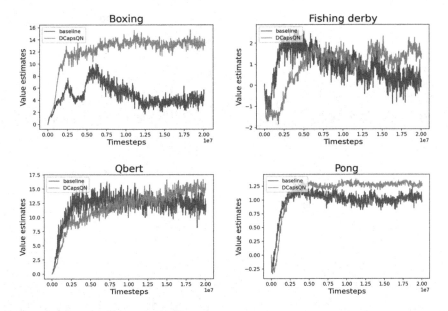

Fig. 6. Value estimates comparison of agents in various environments. It is noticeable that the baseline is more volatile compared to DCapsQN.

Figure 6 compares the value estimates over time from DCapsQN and the baseline. Value functions estimate how good it is to perform a given action in a given state. The notion of "how good" here is defined in terms of future rewards or expected return [27]. A high oscillation of value estimates in consecutive steps translates to a high uncertainty of future rewards. We can observe the difference in magnitude and higher oscillation in consecutive steps between baseline and DCapsQN. We hypothesize that vectored representations in CapsNets further help in stabilizing the change in value function of Double DQN. The hypothesis is further supported by comparing the loss (Fig. 7) of DCapsQN and the baseline. The losses in DCapsQN are comparatively smaller in magnitude compared to those from the baseline agents. This can be attributed to a lower change in weights because the target is often very close to the agent's current estimate. The low magnitude of loss in DCapsQN also indicates that CapsNets do not start representing new entities.

6.2 Environment

While we rationalize the better performance of DCapsQN based agents, there is not a single most powerful component that directly contributes to it. It is the combination of all three elements i.e. action space, reward and input state.

It is noticeable the performance of the agent in the environment Tennis is similar to Boxing although they both have a different difficulty level. The leading performance of DCapsQN based agents in both environments can be attributed

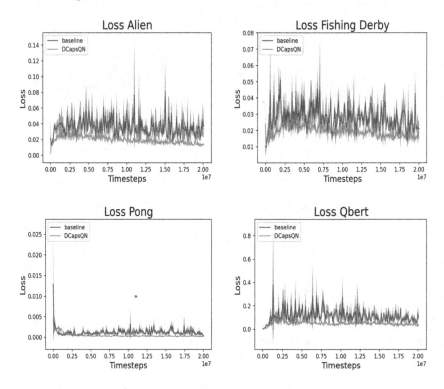

Fig. 7. Training loss comparison of agents in various environments. The shaded area represents the ± standard deviation over 4 runs.

to very simple visual input and high action space. If compared to the difference in the convergence of agents in Alien (a maze traversal environment and with a highly dense reward) with Tutankham, which is maze traversal but with a comparatively sparse reward environment. We notice that the combination of reward and action space contributed more to the performance, compared to the visual input state.

Human perception suffers from crowding, The DCapsQN based agent seems to a show similar phenomenon in SpaceInvaders. The low performance could be attributed to the combination of crowding and low action space, where there are multiple instances of the same part and whole objects in the input state [22,25].

7   Conclusion

The paper introduced DCapsQN, a CapsNets-based agent for DRL. We empirically show how CapsNets-based architectures perform well with Double DQN. The DCapsQN architecture uses fewer parameters while still outperforming the baseline agent in terms of cumulative reward collected by an agent in a given task. In contrast to previous research [4] where the agent did not converge, DCapsQN converges to find a value function.

The presented architecture was found to be the best performing in terms of design and capabilities in the environments. The outcome confirms the initial hypothesis that the value function is learned by the fully connected layers while CapsNets learns to better represent input states.

Based on observations made in this work, we consider that transfer learning of representations learned via CapsNets could be an interesting direction for future research. Once learned part-complex objects, the agent would only need to converge to find the value function. Although our evaluation covered a variety of tasks and reward systems, it would be useful to investigate the performance of the agents in other tasks, domains and within other settings like continuous action spaces.

Acknowledgement. This research received funding from the Flemish Government under the "Onderzoeksprogramma Artificiële Intelligentie (AI) Vlaanderen" programme.

References

1. Afshar, P., Heidarian, S., Naderkhani, F., Oikonomou, A., Plataniotis, K.N., Mohammadi, A.: COVID-CAPS: a capsule network-based framework for identification of COVID-19 cases from X-ray images. Pattern Recogn. Lett. **138**, 638–643 (2020)
2. Afshar, P., Plataniotis, K.N., Mohammadi, A.: Capsule networks for brain tumor classification based on MRI images and course tumor boundaries. In: ICASSP 2019–2019 IEEE International Conference on Acoustics, Speech and Signal Processing (ICASSP), pp. 1368–1372, November 2019
3. Allioui, H., Sadgal, M., Elfazziki, A.: Deep MRI segmentation: a convolutional method applied to Alzheimer disease detection. Int. J. Adv. Comput. Sci. Appl. **10**(11) (2019). https://doi.org/10.14569/IJACSA.2019.0101151
4. Andersen, P.A.: Deep reinforcement learning using capsules in advanced game environments. arXiv:1801.09597 [cs, stat], January 2018
5. Bahadori, M.T.: Spectral capsule networks, p. 5 (2018). https://openreview.net/forum?id=HJuMvYPaM
6. Bellemare, M.G., Naddaf, Y., Veness, J., Bowling, M.: The arcade learning environment: an evaluation platform for general agents. J. Artif. Intell. Res. **47**, 253–279 (2013). https://doi.org/10.1613/jair.3912
7. Eck, D.J.: Introduction to Computer Graphics (2016)
8. Gou, S.Z., Liu, Y.: DQN with model-based exploration: efficient learning on environments with sparse rewards. arXiv:1903.09295 [cs, stat], March 2019
9. Hinton, G., Sabour, S., Frosst, N.: Matrix capsules with EM routing. In: International Conference on Learning Representations (2018). https://openreview.net/forum?id=HJWLfGWRb
10. Huang, W., Zhou, F.: DA-CapsNet: dual attention mechanism capsule network. Sci. Rep. **10**(1), 1–13 (2020)

11. Hubel, D.H., Wiesel, T.N.: Shape and arrangement of columns in cat's striate cortex. J. Physiol. **165**(3), 559–568 (1963). https://doi.org/10.1113/jphysiol.1963.sp007079

12. Kalchbrenner, N., Grefenstette, E., Blunsom, P.: A convolutional neural network for modelling sentences. In: Proceedings of the 52nd Annual Meeting of the Association for Computational Linguistics (Volume 1: Long Papers), pp. 655–665. Association for Computational Linguistics, Baltimore (2014). https://doi.org/10.3115/v1/P14-1062

13. Kempka, M., Wydmuch, M., Runc, G., Toczek, J., Jaśkowski, W.: ViZDoom: a doom-based AI research platform for visual reinforcement learning. In: 2016 IEEE Conference on Computational Intelligence and Games (CIG), pp. 1–8. IEEE (2016)

14. Krizhevsky, A., Sutskever, I., Hinton, G.E.: ImageNet classification with deep convolutional neural networks. Commun. ACM **60**(6), 84–90 (2017). https://doi.org/10.1145/3065386

15. LaLonde, R., Bagci, U.: Capsules for object segmentation. arXiv:1804.04241 [cs, stat], April 2018

16. Liao, H.: CapsNet-Tensorflow (2018). https://github.com/naturomics/CapsNet-Tensorflow/blob/master/imgs/capsuleVSneuron.png

17. Martnez-Plumed, F., Hernandez-Orallo, J.: AI results for the Atari 2600 games: difficulty and discrimination using IRT. In: Evaluating General-Purpose AI, p. 6 (2017)

18. Mnih, V., et al.: Playing Atari with deep reinforcement learning. arXiv:1312.5602 [cs], December 2013

19. Mnih, V., et al.: Human-level control through deep reinforcement learning. Nature **518**(7540), 529–533 (2015). https://doi.org/10.1038/nature14236

20. Molnar, T., Culurciello, E.: Capsule network performance with autonomous navigation. Int. J. Artif. Intell. Appl. **11**(1), 1–15 (2020). https://doi.org/10.5121/ijaia.2020.11101

21. Pan, C., Velipasalar, S.: PT-CapsNet: a novel prediction-tuning capsule network suitable for deeper architectures. In: Proceedings of the IEEE/CVF International Conference on Computer Vision, pp. 11996–12005 (2021)

22. Pelli, D.G.: Crowding: a cortical constraint on object recognition. Curr. Opin. Neurobiol. **18**(4), 445–451 (2008). https://doi.org/10.1016/j.conb.2008.09.008

23. Phaye, S.S.R., Sikka, A., Dhall, A., Bathula, D.: Dense and diverse capsule networks: making the capsules learn better. arXiv:1805.04001 [cs], May 2018

24. Rawlinson, D., Ahmed, A., Kowadlo, G.: Sparse unsupervised capsules generalize better. arXiv:1804.06094 [cs], April 2018

25. Sabour, S., Frosst, N., Hinton, G.E.: Dynamic routing between capsules. In: Guyon, I., et al. (eds.) Advances in Neural Information Processing Systems, vol. 30, pp. 3856–3866. Curran Associates, Inc. (2017). http://papers.nips.cc/paper/6975-dynamic-routing-between-capsules.pdf

26. Schaul, T., Quan, J., Antonoglou, I., Silver, D.: Prioritized experience replay. In: Bengio, Y., LeCun, Y. (eds.) 4th International Conference on Learning Representations, ICLR 2016, San Juan, Puerto Rico, 2–4 May 2016, Conference Track Proceedings (2016). http://arxiv.org/abs/1511.05952

27. Sutton, R.S., Barto, A.G.: Reinforcement Learning: An Introduction. MIT Press, Cambridge (2018)

28. van Hasselt, H., Guez, A., Silver, D.: Deep reinforcement learning with double Q-learning. arXiv:1509.06461 [cs], December 2015

29. Wen, X., Han, Z., Liu, X., Liu, Y.S.: Point2SpatialCapsule: aggregating features and spatial relationships of local regions on point clouds using spatial-aware capsules. IEEE Trans. Image Process. **29**, 8855–8869 (2020)
30. Wu, Y., Ma, S., Zhang, D., Sun, J.: 3D capsule hand pose estimation network based on structural relationship information. Symmetry **12**(10) (2020). https://doi.org/10.3390/sym12101636. https://www.mdpi.com/2073-8994/12/10/1636

Object Detection with Semi-supervised Adversarial Domain Adaptation for Real-Time Edge Devices

Mattias Billast[✉], Tom De Schepper, Kevin Mets, Peter Hellinckx, José Oramas, and Steven Latré

IDLab, Department of Computer Science, University of Antwerp - imec, Sint-Pietersvliet 7, 2000 Antwerp, Belgium
mattias.billast@uantwerpen.be

Abstract. Object detection on real-time edge devices for new applications with no or a limited amount of annotated labels is difficult. Where traditional data-hungry methods fail, transfer learning can provide a solution by transferring knowledge from a source domain to the target application domain. We explore domain adaptation techniques on a one-stage detection architecture, i.e. YOLOv3, which enables use on edge devices. Existing methods in domain adaptation with deep learning for object detection, use two-stage detectors like Faster-RCNN with adversarial adaptation. By using a one-stage detector, the speed increases by a factor of eight. With our proposed method, we reduce by 28% the changes in performance introduced by the gap between the source and target domains.

Keywords: Domain adaptation · Object detection · Adversarial learning

1 Introduction

Object detection and classification are amongst the main tasks addressed by computer vision [30]. They are used in a wide variety of application domains like autonomous driving, robotics, medical imaging, tracking of various subjects, counting, manufacturing, etc. In general, deep learning techniques are applied which require significant amounts of examples. The performance of deep neural networks with abundantly available labels surpasses other techniques. Examples of such use cases are car detection and classification of written characters [11,15].

Most of these deep neural networks also require a GPU which provides the necessary computing power. Hence, the main obstacles for the adoption of these supervised machine learning approaches in new applications remain the lack of (labeled) data and the needed computing power for inference. This last factor clearly limits their use in edge devices. Often, there already exist application domains with similar properties and labeled data which can be used as a starting point, i.e. the source domain. Ideally, the knowledge from the source domain can

© Springer Nature Switzerland AG 2022
L. A. Leiva et al. (Eds.): BNAIC/Benelearn 2021, CCIS 1530, pp. 86–102, 2022.
https://doi.org/10.1007/978-3-030-93842-0_5

be transferred to the new application domain, the target domain. New application domains often do not have enough labels. Examples of these include the detection of animals other than a cat or dog, autonomous vehicles other than cars, and even detecting the same subject in another environment/dataset can cause the source model to have a significant drop in performance. Therefore, an automated framework to adapt a source model to a target domain with only a few target labels can prevent the time- and cost-consuming task of labelling a large dataset.

Existing methods [3,9] for domain adaptation rely on creating domain-invariance between source and target domain. This can be done by adversarially changing the feature encodings from convolutional layers or creating synthetic images which close the gap between the two domains. These techniques will be discussed in detail in Sect. 2. Regarding domain adaptation for the object detection task, most efforts from the literature are based on the Faster-RCNN detector [9]. Faster-RCNN is a good choice for applications with sufficient computational power or when no real-time inference is needed.

This is even more critical given the increasing number of new use cases where computations are expected to take place in real-time on-site, instead of on a remote cloud server [31]. With limited resources and/or the need for a real-time application, faster frameworks like one-stage detectors provide opportunities to meet the demand. By using a one-stage network, e.g. YOLOv3 [22], as the backbone network to perform object detection, the use of edge devices in real-time is made possible. This is mainly due to the inference speed advantage of YOLO over Faster-RCNN [23].

A good application example is an autonomous vessel that needs real-time tracking of the vessels in the near distance with the computational power on-board. Maritime vessels scan the whole environment with a radar once or twice every second [2]. This is sufficient due to their low speed. To make the step towards autonomous vessels, a camera and/or LiDar sensor needs to be added to be able to make navigation decisions with a more comprehensive understanding of the environment. If a camera can locate and classify objects in the water with the computation power on-board, in synchronization with the radar, then this could constitute a leap forward for the maritime industry.

Taking the previous application setting into account, in this paper we present a transfer learning technique based on feature adaptation that uses the labeled data in a source domain to improve the performance in a target domain with no or limited labeled data. This effectively increases the overall generalization and robustness of the source model. The performance is compared against other transfer learning techniques like cycleGAN image adaptation [33] and combining feature adaptation with image adaptation. To validate the different transfer learning techniques, two experiments are set up. First, the different techniques are used to transfer knowledge from one dataset to another when detecting the same subject (i.e. cars). The two datasets used in are COCO2017 [18] and KITTI [7]. Second, the techniques are used to detect similar classes from the same dataset, i.e. learning to properly detect a lion by transferring the obtained knowledge from detecting a tiger. The dataset used for this task is OpenImages. In both cases, there are 30 labelled target images available to fine-tune the source model. With feature adaptation, there is a 5 to 9% improvement of the mean Average Precision (mAP) compared to the fine-tuned source model.

To summarize, we propose domain adaptation techniques based on feature alignment and synthetic image alignment with fast real-time object detection models that enable use on the edge with limited labeled data.

2   Related Work

The proposed method lies at the intersection of object detection and domain adaptation. As such, we will position our system with respect to efforts addressing those tasks.

2.1   Object Detection

To perform object detection, the subject first has to be localised and then classified. There are two main categories for object detection models, i.e. traditional models without deep learning and models with deep learning.

Engineered Features. SIFT [20] detects objects in the image by matching local features which are scale- and orientation-invariant. SURF [1] uses a similar feature descriptor as SIFT but speeds up the process significantly by the integral image for image convolutions and simplifying the overall method. Other feature descriptors such as Haar-like features [16], HOG [5], and ORB [24] perform similarly. They all have their advantages depending on shape, colour, texture, and illumination. On the one hand, these methods have the advantage of being relatively lightweight, they are outperformed by their counterparts based on deep neural networks. This discourage their use in critical applications.

Learning-Based Representations. With the advent of big data and increased computational power, representation learning methods got a lot of interest. Moreover, in computer vision, all the current State Of The Art (SOTA) methods are based on deep convolutional neural networks [13]. Their success is attributed to the large number of parameters present in Deep Neural Networks (DNN), which can be used to model all the possible variations of how an object is depicted. Faster-RCNN [23] is a very commonly used two-stage model which uses a Region Proposal Network (RPN). This is based on the feature encodings after multiple convolutional layers to first propose possible bounding boxes to focus on. In the next step, these region proposals are used to locate the best proposals and classify the object. To speed up the whole process, there are one-stage models such as YOLO [21] and SSD [19] without the RPN, making it more a regression/classification model. YOLOv3 [22] improves YOLO with bounding boxes at three different scales by using a similar idea as a Feature Pyramid Network [17] and with increased frames per second (fps). There is a small drop in performance from a two-stage to a one-stage model but the gained speed enables to detect objects in real-time, even with less computational power.

2.2 Domain Adaptation

The focus of this paper is to improve object detection performance when operating on setting with no or limited annotated data is available. While there are different options to apply transfer learning, they all involve domain-invariance between source and target domain [8,9,29,32,33]. A possible method is to map extracted features, which are the input to the domain classifier, from source to target domain or the other way around [32]. Another option is to change the style of an image synthetically from source to target domain or vice-versa. This mapping is primarily done by a Generative Adversarial Network (GAN) [8]. Recent SOTA combines both techniques, i.e. creating domain-invariant features which are based on source images translated to target images.

Real-to-sim domain adaptation [32] adapts the real images to synthetic images to make the robot feel at home for its navigation task. They use a cycle-GAN [33] and shift loss for more consistent subsequent frames. The previous method translates every synthetic frame to the realistic style during the training of navigation policies. Although effective, this approach still adds an adaptation step before each training iteration, which can slow down the whole learning pipeline. Instead of using a GAN to upsample the image to perform domain adaptation, it is also possible to change the extracted features to another domain without upsampling. In French et al. [6] self-ensembling is used with a student-teacher method to achieve SOTA results on different visual domain adaptation benchmarks for classification. Adversarial Discriminative Domain Adaptation (ADDA) [29] generalizes the model from the source to the target domain by changing the feature encodings in the layer before the output layer. The main method used throughout this paper is based on ADDA and will be further explained in Sect. 3. More recently, the strong-weak alignment method [25] adapts global and local features adversarially with a domain classifier to again create domain-invariance. Selective Cross-Domain Alignment [34] uses a similar idea but focuses on discriminative regions of the image representations to perform adaptations. The main ideas are "where to look" and "how to align". Diversify and match [12] obtains better generalization to other domains by diversifying the labeled data and then matching the features adversarially to make them close to domain-invariant. FRCNN in the wild [3] uses the representation from the RPN to get instance-level invariance and the image representation to get image-level invariance. Hsu et al. [9] combine techniques from ADDA and image-adaptation, using a cycleGAN, to improve generalization to a target domain.

All the methods listed above use a two-stage detector, mostly Faster-RCNN. These two-stage detectors reduce halfway the changes in performance introduced by the domain gap between the model trained on source data and target data (oracle). To the best of our knowledge, these unsupervised domain adaptation approaches have not been tested on one-stage detectors like YOLO which would significantly improve the fps and could enable use on edge devices.

3   Proposed Method

We hypothesize that a model trained on a large labelled dataset can be transferred to a new environment by adversarial training on- or offline. This hypothesis is based on the success of the transfer learning techniques mentioned in Sect. 2.2. We test this hypothesis by using the principle of adversarial feature manipulation for domain adaptation. Adversarial Discriminative Domain Adaptation [29] is a method to acquire a classification model for a target domain which only has unlabelled samples. This method consists of the following steps (see Fig. 1): First, an initial classification model is trained on a large dataset of labelled data sampled from the source domain. Then, a domain discriminator and another classification and detection model, i.e. the target model, are trained alternately. The input of the discriminator is the feature encoding just before the last YOLO-layer, computed by alternately encoding the source and target images. After training, the discriminator should not be able to distinguish the extracted feature encodings from source and target domain. This can be done by using an inverted-label GAN loss, with the following loss function for the domain discriminator:

$$L_{disc} = -(1 - Y)log(1 - D(E(I))) - Ylog(D(E(I))), \qquad (1)$$

where Y represent the domain label, $E(I)$ the encoded feature from image I, and $D(X)$ the prediction of the domain classifier with feature X as input. The discriminator is trained by minimizing L_{disc}, while the encoder is trained by minimizing the binary cross-entropy loss of the detector and maximizing L_{disc}.

Finally, the target encoder is evaluated by feeding target samples which are mapped to an approximately domain-invariant feature space and afterwards classified by the source classifier.

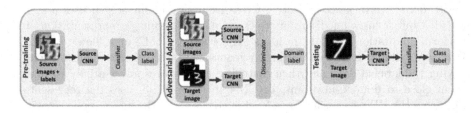

Fig. 1. Adversarial Discriminative Domain Adaptation (figure adapted from [29]) consists of three steps: 1. Pretraining the source model. 2. While freezing the source encoder, adversarially training target encoder and domain discriminator to obtain feature encodings that fool the domain discriminator. 3. Evaluate performance by combining target encoder and source classifier.

3.1   Adversarial Domain Adaptation for Object Detection

The focus in this paper is not only a classification task but also a localization aspect, i.e. object detection. Although different, the principle of ADDA in an object detection setting remains the same by mapping the feature encodings to a shared feature space between domains. As mentioned in Sect. 2, the application of ADDA for object detection has been studied in several manners in conjunction with a Faster-RCNN network and has shown promising results. For successful domain adaptation with a one-stage detector like YOLOv3 [22], an extra step is needed to align the domain-invariant features with the source output layer, i.e. a detection and classification YOLO-layer. This can be done by training on a small target dataset for a couple of epochs. Consequently, there is no mismatch between encoding and output layer. The feature encodings will be slightly shifted to the target domain which can cause a decrease in performance in the source domain, yet enhance its performance on the target domain.

Applying ADDA in the context of the object detection task consists, mainly, of three steps (see Fig. 2):

First, the source model needs to be fine-tuned on the large source dataset.

Second, (a) as an intermediate improvement step, it is possible to use a cycle-GAN [33] to create synthetic images from the source dataset that are more similar to the target images. This is achieved by using cycle consistency loss, which enables the use of unpaired data. Two generators map domain A to B and vice versa. The principle here is that by applying both generators sequentially, the output image should be the same as the input image. The comparison between input and output is the basis for the generator loss function. In between generators, domain classifiers differentiate between synthetic and real images. The generators are thus trained by minimizing generator loss and maximizing discriminator loss. In this way, we create an intermediate domain that is closer to the target domain, and makes it easier to close the domain gap with domain adaptation. These synthetic images substitute the original source dataset and do not alter the structure of the adversarial feature adaptation algorithm.

(b) Training a domain classifier alternately on source and target images to distinguish between them and adapt the feature maps with an inverted-label GAN loss [29]. This loss is used to achieve domain-invariant features in order to fool the discriminator. Important for this step is that the discriminator is pre-trained, otherwise, it may take a longer training time to show significant improvement, if any. The quality of the domain-invariant features depends on the quality of the domain classifier.

Third, the target model is fine-tuned with a small number of target images. For our experiments, we use 30 randomly chosen target images as the small fine-tuning dataset. More details will be presented in Sect. 5.2.

4   Implementation Details

In our experiments we considering the YOLOv3 [22] detector with Darknet-53 feature extractor which has 53 convolutional layers. The input images are resized to 640×320 pixels and training is done with a batch size of 16. These features form the basis for the detection, classification and localization with the final YOLO-layer. Due to a feature pyramid network (FPN) [17], it is possible

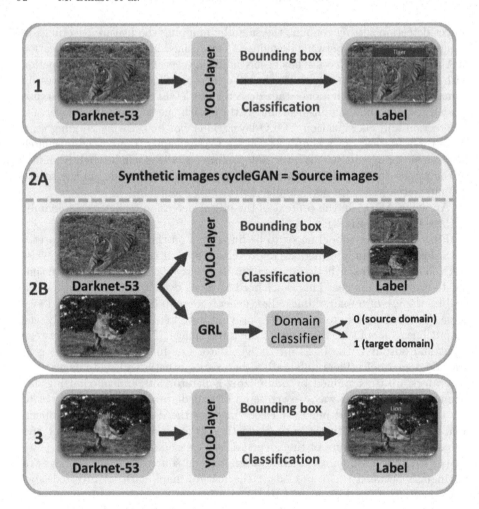

Fig. 2. Inspired by ADDA [29], our domain adaptation algorithm for one-stage object detection also consists of three steps: 1. Pre-training on source images. 2a. An intermediate improvement step of the model is replacing the source domain images with synthetic images generated from a cycleGAN. These generated images create an intermediate domain, which is closer to the target domain. 2b. Adversarially train Darknet-53 encoder and domain discriminator for obtaining domain-invariant features. Note that, the difference with ADDA here is that the source and target encoder have shared weights which improves generalization to both domains. 3. Fine-tuning the model on a small target dataset.

to predict objects more accurately at different scales because of the up- and downsampling steps with skip connections between layers with equal feature size. These skip connections combine low-resolution complex features with simple high-resolution features. The FPN of YOLOv3 consists of three different scaling stages and can thus predict for 3 different image sizes.

The domain classifier is a feed-forward model with 5 convolutional layers and a sigmoid classification layer at the end.

All models are trained on an Nvidia Tesla V100-SXM3-32 GB GPU. For the training of the Darknet-53 network, binary cross-entropy is used as the loss function. Stochastic gradient descent with Nesterov momentum $\beta = 0.937$ optimizes training. The initial learning rate is $\alpha = 1e-2$ and the final learning rate is $\alpha_f = 5e-4$ where the learning is rate is defined by a cosine curve.

$$\alpha_{current} = \alpha_f + \frac{1}{2}(\alpha - \alpha_f)(1 + cos(\frac{epoch_{current}}{epoch_{max}}\pi)) \tag{2}$$

The discriminator is trained on batches of 16 images utilizing an Adam optimizer with $\beta_1 = 0.5$ and $\beta_2 = 0.999$ to decrease the binary cross-entropy loss function. The domain classifier is more difficult to train. Its learning rate is changed depending on the problem and domain gap. We empirically determined the interval of the learning rate as $\alpha = 2e-8 - e-10$. The learning rate for the experiments is optimized with a hyperparameter sweep.

5   Evaluation

5.1   Datasets

We evaluate our method in the following datasets:

COCO2017 (COCO) [18] is a large dataset that consists of 80 labeled classes. In this study, only the car class is considered. From these examples, 8000 images are used for training and 4000 for testing.

KITTI Object Detection Benchmark (KITTI) [7] is a large annotated dataset with 15000 images captured from a car-mounted camera. We used 5400 images for training and 1300 for testing.

OpenImages (OI) [14] is a dataset of 9M images annotated with image-level labels, object bounding boxes, object segmentation masks, visual relationships, and localized narratives. For the transfer learning task covered in this research, we chose two similar classes, i.e. Tiger and Lion. Each class has approximately 1000 samples after cleaning up the data.

Cityscapes (CS) [4] is a dataset that consists of 6 labeled classes from urban street scenes. 2976 images are used for training and 500 for testing. For domain adaptation benchmarks, Cityscapes also has foggy Cityscapes dataset which consists of the same images synthetically augmented with a fog using depth images to blur distant objects [26].

5.2   Experiments

To validate the proposed adversarial feature adaptation method when integrated with single-stage detectors, we test our approach on two simple domain adaptation problems with datasets that look similar, i.e. a smaller domain gap.

Concretely, we look at the COCO dataset versus the KITTI dataset with the focus on the car class. This exhaustively studied case can be a stepping stone towards other autonomous means of transportation. We will adopt the Mean Average Precision (mAP), at 0.5 Intersection over Union (IoU), precision, and recall as performance metrics. In addition, we report the framerate, i.e. the number of frames processed per second (fps), as an indicator of the computation costs during inference.

Inference Speed. The framerate is only dependent on the type of detector that is used as a backbone. The YOLOv3 detector achieves a framerate of 156 fps on an Nvidia Tesla V100-SXM3-32 GB GPU and 1.83 fps on a 2.7 GHz vCPU. In comparison, the Faster-RCNN with VGG-16 [28] achieves a framerate of 17 and 0.24 fps on the same GPU and vCPU, respectively. The latter is more representative for edge devices.

These results stress the need for good object detection performance with one-stage detectors since this speed-up can determine the feasibility of an application or not. For example, in the marine sector, a lot of research is done on autonomous vessels, with an operating speed from 5 to 15 km/h. To navigate autonomously, they need to detect nearby objects in the waterway. Importantly, these vessels should be able to scan the environment frequently, around one or two times per second, which is sufficient at these low speeds [2]. Comparable new applications will thus benefit from a fast domain adaptation pipeline.

Object Detection Performance with Domain Adaptation. To measure the performance of the method, we compare the mAP, precision, and recall of each transfer learning technique to a target domain with two models trained on target data. We compare with the following two models:

Base (no TL): the vanilla YOLOv3 model trained on 30 annotated target images without transfer learning. *Oracle*: the YOLOv3 detector trained on the full annotated target dataset.

Table 1. Performance baselines on COCO and KITTI focused on the car class

Fine-tuned on	KITTI			COCO		
Tested on	mAP	P	R	mAP	P	R
COCO	0.744	0.623	0.785	0.704	0.666	0.713
KITTI (Base)	0.728	0.733	0.718	0.318	0.464	0.367
KITTI (Oracle)	0.974	0.936	0.961	0.22	0.822	0.166

Table 1 shows the results for the *Base* and *Oracle* models evaluated on the validation sets of the COCO and KITTI datasets. Several observations can be made in Table 1. First, and as expected, the models trained on images with the same distribution as the validation images have the highest performance.

Second, a model fine-tuned on a larger dataset (*Oracle*) performs better than one trained on a smaller dataset (*Base*). However, it seems that this gain in performance comes a the cost of lower generalization towards other datasets, e.g. cross-dataset evaluation.

Taking the observations from above into account, we expect the performance of the models with transfer learning to lie somewhere in between *Base* and *Oracle*.

Measuring the Effect of Domain Adaption. We designed two experiments to measure the effect that domain adaptation has on performance.

On the first experiment we apply domain adaptation to train a model from COCO to KITTI dataset, with the focus on the car class. This experiments will focus on modelling intra-class variations introduced by the domain shift.

On the second experiment, we apply domain adaptation to train a model for a Lion class starting from the Tiger class. Both classes are extracted from the OpenImages dataset. Here, transfer learning is performed between two similar, yet different, classes. This experiment aims at assessing the effect of domain shift caused by inter-class variations [10].

For both experiments, we limit ourselves to only consider 30 labelled target images. In future work, the minimum number of needed labelled target images to achieve improvements will be investigated.

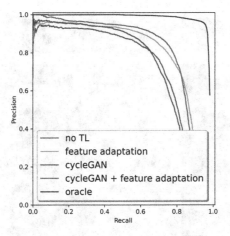

Fig. 3. Precision and Recall curves for the different transfer learning methods (trained on the COCO dataset) and the oracle model, evaluated on the KITTI dataset.

Table 2. Performance domain adaptation techniques from COCO to KITTI tested on both COCO and KITTI validation sets.

Method	KITTI			COCO		
	mAP	P	R	mAP	P	R
No TL (*Base*)	0.728	0.733	0.718	0.318	0.464	0.367
Feature adaptation	0.796	0.824	**0.727**	0.584	0.729	0.54
CycleGAN	0.733	0.81	0.653	0.421	0.664	0.378
CycleGAN + feature adaptation	**0.797**	**0.876**	0.714	0.519	0.826	0.411

Tables 2 and 3 show the results for experiments one and two, respectively.

In general, it can be noted that combining feature adaptation with synthetic data augmentation from a cycleGAN gives the best results (mAP) for both experiments in their respective target domains, i.e. KITTI-cars and Lion. The models for KITTI-cars and Lion improve 5% and 10%, respectively, compared to their *Base* performance. If we define the domain performance gap as the difference in mAP between *Base* and *Oracle*, then the gap is closed by 28%, from 0.728 to 0.797 with an *Oracle* of 0.974 mAP. The precision improves significantly by adding the synthetic images while maintaining a similar recall. Figure 3 further confirms the fact that the combination of feature adaptation together with

Fig. 4. The ground truth is shown above the line and predictions on images from the KITTI dataset, generated by the different models, under the line. The models from top to bottom are: no TL (Base) (R1), feature adaptation (R2), cycleGAN (R3), feature adaptation with cycleGAN (R4), and Oracle (R5).

Table 3. Performance domain adaptation techniques from Tiger to Lion tested on both Tiger and Lion validation sets.

Method	Lion			Tiger		
	mAP	P	R	mAP	P	R
No TL	0.727	0.919	0.609	0.797	0.915	0.607
Feature adaptation	0.764	0.855	**0.715**	0.908	0.881	0.906
CycleGAN	0.747	**0.99**	0.661	0.947	0.967	0.836
CycleGAN + feature adaptation	**0.768**	0.922	0.711	0.926	0.896	0.906

synthetic images from a cycleGAN has the best performance out of the domain adaptation techniques. It also shows that using synthetic images has an advantage regarding precision while maintaining a similar recall. As hypothesized earlier, we observe that the *Oracle* model outperforms the transfer learning techniques.

The focus is on the car experiment, as the KITTI and COCO dataset sizes are large compared to the OI datasets of the Tiger and Lion classes. This means that more labelled source domain images are present for training, and the evaluation results are more accurate representations of the models' performance on the target domain, as an outlier will have less impact on the overall performance. Although smaller, the Tiger to Lion domain adaptation still shows the increased performance with adversarial learning in an inter-class setting.

Figure 4 shows qualitative detection results. More specifically, it shows predictions of the different models on the KITTI validation dataset. The different baselines include: *Base* (no TL) (R1), a feature adaptation model (R2), a model trained on cycleGAN synthetic images (R3), a feature adaptation model with cycleGAN synthetic images (R4), and *Oracle* (R5). The target models are designed for the target dataset. Remarkably, applying transfer learning techniques improves the generalization back to the source domain. This is in contrast to no transfer learning (no TL) with a model only fine-tuned on 30 labelled target images starting from the source model. The domain-invariant features and the intermediate domain dataset generated from a cycleGAN play the most important factors for this result.

Use of Intermediate Domain from a CycleGAN. Figure 5 shows the result of using a cycleGAN to generate the synthetic images in an intermediate domain between source and target domain. It is clear that after the transformation from tiger to lion, the tiger stripes have vanished and that the colour changed from orange to tawny yellow. There is a blurring effect that can have a negative effect on performance but this is likely caused by the small size of the Lion dataset. The transformation from COCO to KITTI mostly changed the background as the COCO dataset contains more urban-based images while the KITTI dataset depicts cars more in or around a forest. That is why the generated images contain fake trees in the background, even in the reflection of the car window.

Effect on the Domain-Shift. The accuracy of the domain classifier, before and after adversarial training on the image encoder, can also provide some insight on the observed performance. Before any adversarial training of the feature encodings, the pre-trained domain classifier can predict with approximately 55% accuracy, in both experiments, what the domain of the tested feature encodings is. After adversarial training, this drops to 50%. The similarity between datasets causes a very low accuracy of 55%. Still, the feature encoder manages to extract useful information from the domain classifier to compensate for the subtle differences between datasets.

To follow up on this observation, we conducted an additional experiment focused on the ships class. More specifically, where the source dataset is the Seaships dataset [27] and the target dataset is a self-annotated dataset from videos recorded on a cargo ship on inland waterways. The main difference between those two datasets is the point-of-view, on-board versus on-shore. Because of this significant difference, the discriminator model performs very well and has an accuracy of 95+%. Because of this large domain gap, the adversarial model is not able to manipulate the encoded feature spaces toward each other. This shows the limitations of using *only* adversarial training. More pre-processing steps are needed than only a Cycle-GAN to close the domain gap for effective adversarial learning.

Unsupervised Setting. In Table 4 a comparison is made between existing methods and the methods explained and tested in this paper in an unsupervised manner to adapt from the Cityscapes to the foggy Cityscapes dataset. The difference with the experiments above is that this time, there is not a last fine-tuning step with a small target dataset. In Table 4, it is clear to see that the methods with feature adaptation in combination with YOLO do not improve the results. Using a CycleGAN to create synthetic images works well. As the foggy Cityscapes itself is a synthetic dataset, it is not surprising that training on synthetic images from a CycleGAN generates a good result.

The other methods all also use some kind of adversarial feature adaptation, the main difference is the object detection architecture. In Faster-RCNN, there is

Table 4. Performance domain adaptation techniques from Cityscapes to foggy Cityscapes, tested on the foggy Cityscapes validation set.

Method	Car	Truck	Bus	Train	Motorcycle	Bicycle	mAP
FRCNN in the wild [3]	40.5	22.1	35.3	20.2	20.0	27.1	27.6
Diversify and match [12]	44.3	27.2	38.4	34.5	28.4	32.2	34.6
Strong-weak align [25]	43.5	24.5	36.2	32.6	30.0	35.3	34.3
Progressive DA [9]	54.4	24.3	44.1	25.8	29.1	35.9	36.9
Feature adaptation	45.9	26.9	22.1	4.77	12.3	21.8	22.3
CycleGAN	68.7	41.8	40.1	17.9	16.7	30	35.9
CycleGAN + feature adaptation	37	27.5	30.4	14.2	7.46	16	22.1

Fig. 5. These four columns of images show the transformations, by using a cycleGAN, of the source domain images to generate synthetic images, which try to match the target domain distribution. The source image is shown in the first and third column in both examples (Tiger from Open Images, and car from COCO), and the generated output which tries to mimic the target images is shown in the second and fourth column (fake Lion from Open Images, and fake car from KITTI). In the Tiger to Lion example, the generated output is blurred, yet tiger stripes have vanished and the colour changed from orange to tawny yellow. In the car example, the environment changes from urban to woodland. (Color figure online)

a Region Proposal Network (RPN) which already gives a good idea where objects of interest are while filtering out the background. Our theory is that performing adversarial feature adaptation on these region proposals is much more specific and accurate domain adaptation. This understanding can be the key for future work to understand how to replace this RPN in YOLO to have fast, accurate and specific domain adaptation without the need for a small target dataset. The previous semi-supervised experiments are still valid as they improve the baseline model significantly.

Summarizing. To summarize, this one-stage object detection model enables near real-time use on edge devices with 2 fps on a 2.7 GHz vCPU. The domain performance gap is reduced by 28% (difference between mAP of *Base* and *Oracle*) on the COCO (source) and KITTI (target) datasets. The synthetic images from a cycleGAN to replace the source images have a positive effect on the precision and mAP of the model and form a good option to boost performance. The algorithm works both for inter- and intra-class domain adaptation.

6   Conclusion

We presented a method that enables object detection with a limited amount of labels on edge devices in near real-time. The main advantages are three-fold. First, the use of only a limited annotated target dataset, the amount of labels needed depends on the desired trade-off between cost and performance. Second, by using a one-stage detector, the proposed system achieves an increased object detection speed approximately eight times faster. This enables the possibility to use edge devices, such as a 2.7 GHz CPU which reaches almost 2 fps. Third, a reduction of 30% in the changes in performance introduced by the domain gap. Moreover, we observed a significant increase in performance for inter- and intra class domain adaptation. In the unsupervised setting, we saw that finding an alternative for the RPN, implemented in the Faster-RCNN model, for the YOLO model can accelerate the adversarial training to achieve specific, accurate and fast domain adaptation. There are also some disadvantages of using this method: On the one hand, a two-stage detector like Faster-RCNN closes the domain gap more. In Hsu et al. [9] the domain gap is closed by 56% where the target domain is Cityscapes [4] and the source domain is KITTI, also focused on the car class. On the other hand, a source domain with abundantly available data is needed that resembles the target domain. In our experiment, these source domains are the Tiger class and COCO. When the gap is too large between source (Seaships) and target domain (self-annotated vessel dataset), using only adversarial training methods fall short and additional pre-processing is needed to close the domain gap before using this algorithm.

References

1. Bay, H., Ess, A., Tuytelaars, T., Van Gool, L.: Speeded-up robust features (SURF). Comput. Vis. Image Underst. **110**(3), 346–359 (2008). https://doi.org/10.1016/j.cviu.2007.09.014, https://www.sciencedirect.com/science/article/pii/S1077314207001555

2. Bole, A., Wall, A., Norris, A.: Chapter 1 - basic radar principles. In: Bole, A., Wall, A., Norris, A. (eds.) Radar and ARPA Manual, 3rd edn., pp. 1–28. Butterworth-Heinemann, Oxford (2014). https://doi.org/10.1016/B978-0-08-097752-2.00001-5, https://www.sciencedirect.com/science/article/pii/B9780080977522000015

3. Chen, Y., Li, W., Sakaridis, C., Dai, D., Van Gool, L.: Domain adaptive faster r-CNN for object detection in the wild. In: Proceedings of the IEEE Conference on Computer Vision and Pattern Recognition (CVPR), June 2018

4. Cordts, M., et al.: The cityscapes dataset for semantic urban scene understanding. In: Proceedings of the IEEE Conference on Computer Vision and Pattern Recognition (CVPR) (2016)

5. Dalal, N., Triggs, B.: Histograms of oriented gradients for human detection. In: 2005 IEEE Computer Society Conference on Computer Vision and Pattern Recognition (CVPR2005). vol. 1, pp. 886–893 (2005). https://doi.org/10.1109/CVPR.2005.177

6. French, G., Mackiewicz, M., Fisher, M.H.: Self-ensembling for domain adaptation. CoRR abs/1706.05208 (2017), http://arxiv.org/abs/1706.05208

7. Geiger, A., Lenz, P., Urtasun, R.: Are we ready for autonomous driving? the KITTI vision benchmark suite. In: Conference on Computer Vision and Pattern Recognition (CVPR) (2012)

8. Goodfellow, I., et al.: Generative adversarial nets. Adv. Neural Inf. Process. Syst. **27** (2014)

9. Hsu, H.K., et al.: Progressive domain adaptation for object detection. In: Proceedings of the IEEE/CVF Conference on Computer Vision and Pattern Recognition (CVPR) Workshops, June 2019

10. Kang, G., Jiang, L., Yang, Y., Hauptmann, A.G.: Contrastive adaptation network for unsupervised domain adaptation. In: Proceedings of the IEEE/CVF Conference on Computer Vision and Pattern Recognition (CVPR), June 2019

11. Khirodkar, R., Yoo, D., Kitani, K.: Domain randomization for scene-specific car detection and pose estimation. In: 2019 IEEE Winter Conference on Applications of Computer Vision (WACV), pp. 1932–1940 (2019). https://doi.org/10.1109/WACV.2019.00210

12. Kim, T., Jeong, M., Kim, S., Choi, S., Kim, C.: Diversify and match: a domain adaptive representation learning paradigm for object detection. In: Proceedings of the IEEE/CVF Conference on Computer Vision and Pattern Recognition (CVPR), June 2019

13. Krizhevsky, A., Sutskever, I., Hinton, G.E.: Imagenet classification with deep convolutional neural networks. Adv. Neural Inf. Process. Syst. **25**, 1097–1105 (2012)

14. Kuznetsova, A., et al.: The open images dataset v4: Unified image classification, object detection, and visual relationship detection at scale. Int. J. Comput. Vis. **28**, 1956–1981 (2020)

15. LeCun, Y., et al.: Backpropagation applied to handwritten zip code recognition. Neural Comput. **1**(4), 541–551 (1989)

16. Lienhart, R., Maydt, J.: An extended set of haar-like features for rapid object detection. In: Proceedings of the International Conference on Image Processing, vol. 1, p. I (2002). https://doi.org/10.1109/ICIP.2002.1038171

17. Lin, T.Y., Dollar, P., Girshick, R., He, K., Hariharan, B., Belongie, S.: Feature pyramid networks for object detection. In: Proceedings of the IEEE Conference on Computer Vision and Pattern Recognition (CVPR), July 2017

18. Lin, T.Y., et al.: Microsoft coco: Common objects in context. In: Fleet, D., Pajdla, T., Schiele, B., Tuytelaars, T. (eds.) Computer Vision - ECCV 2014, pp. 740–755. Springer International Publishing, Cham (2014)

19. Liu, W.: SSD: single shot multibox detector. In: Leibe, B., Matas, J., Sebe, N., Welling, M. (eds.) ECCV 2016. LNCS, vol. 9905, pp. 21–37. Springer, Cham (2016). https://doi.org/10.1007/978-3-319-46448-0_2

20. Lowe, D.G.: Distinctive image features from scale-invariant keypoints. Int. J. Comput. vision **60**(2), 91–110 (2004)

21. Redmon, J., Divvala, S., Girshick, R., Farhadi, A.: You only look once: Unified, real-time object detection. In: Proceedings of the IEEE Conference on Computer Vision and Pattern Recognition (CVPR), June 2016

22. Redmon, J., Farhadi, A.: Yolov3: an incremental improvement. CoRR abs/1804.02767 (2018), http://arxiv.org/abs/1804.02767

23. Ren, S., He, K., Girshick, R., Sun, J.: Faster r-CNN: towards real-time object detection with region proposal networks. In: Advances in Neural Information Processing Syst. pp. 91–99 (2015)

24. Rublee, E., Rabaud, V., Konolige, K., Bradski, G.: Orb: An efficient alternative to sift or surf. In: 2011 International Conference on Computer Vision, pp. 2564–2571. IEEE (2011)

25. Saito, K., Ushiku, Y., Harada, T., Saenko, K.: Strong-weak distribution alignment for adaptive object detection. In: Proceedings of the IEEE/CVF Conference on Computer Vision and Pattern Recognition (CVPR), June 2019

26. Sakaridis, C., Dai, D., Van Gool, L.: Semantic foggy scene understanding with synthetic data. Int. J. Comput. Vis. **126**(9), 973–992 (2018)

27. Shao, Z., Wu, W., Wang, Z., Du, W., Li, C.: Seaships: a large-scale precisely annotated dataset for ship detection. IEEE Trans. Multimedia **20**(10), 2593–2604 (2018)

28. Simonyan, K., Zisserman, A.: Very deep convolutional networks for large-scale image recognition. arXiv preprint arXiv:1409.1556 (2014)

29. Tzeng, E., Hoffman, J., Saenko, K., Darrell, T.: Adversarial discriminative domain adaptation. CoRR abs/1702.05464 (2017), http://arxiv.org/abs/1702.05464

30. Voulodimos, A., Doulamis, N., Doulamis, A., Protopapadakis, E.: Deep learning for computer vision: a brief review. Comput. Intelli. Neurosci. 2018 (2018)

31. Wu, B., Iandola, F., Jin, P.H., Keutzer, K.: Squeezedet: unified, small, low power fully convolutional neural networks for real-time object detection for autonomous driving. In: Proceedings of the IEEE Conference on Computer Vision and Pattern Recognition (CVPR) Workshops, July 2017

32. Zhang, J., et al.: Vr-goggles for robots: real-to-sim domain adaptation for visual control. IEEE Robot. Autom. Lett. **4**(2), 1148–1155 (2019). https://doi.org/10.1109/LRA.2019.2894216

33. Zhu, J.Y., Park, T., Isola, P., Efros, A.A.: Unpaired image-to-image translation using cycle-consistent adversarial networks. In: Proceedings of the IEEE International Conference on Computer Vision (ICCV), October 2017

34. Zhu, X., Pang, J., Yang, C., Shi, J., Lin, D.: Adapting object detectors via selective cross-domain alignment. In: Proceedings of the IEEE/CVF Conference on Computer Vision and Pattern Recognition (CVPR), June 2019

Explaining Outcomes

Exploring Explainable AI in the Financial Sector: Perspectives of Banks and Supervisory Authorities

Ouren Kuiper[1]([⊠]) [iD], Martin van den Berg[1] [iD], Joost van der Burgt[2], and Stefan Leijnen[1]

[1] HU University of Applied Sciences Utrecht, Utrecht, Netherlands
{ouren.kuiper,martin.m.vandenberg,
stefan.leijnen}@hu.nl
[2] De Nederlandsche Bank, Amsterdam, Netherlands

Abstract. Explainable artificial intelligence (xAI) is seen as a solution to making AI systems less of a "black box". It is essential to ensure transparency, fairness, and accountability – which are especially paramount in the financial sector. The aim of this study was a preliminary investigation of the perspectives of supervisory authorities and regulated entities regarding the application of xAI in the financial sector. Three use cases (consumer credit, credit risk, and anti-money laundering) were examined using semi-structured interviews at three banks and two supervisory authorities in the Netherlands. We found that for the investigated use cases a disparity exists between supervisory authorities and banks regarding the desired scope of explainability of AI systems. We argue that the financial sector could benefit from clear differentiation between technical AI (model) explainability requirements and explainability requirements of the broader AI system in relation to applicable laws and regulations.

Keywords: Explainable AI · Artificial intelligence · Financial sector

1 Introduction

In recent years increasingly powerful, but often also increasingly complex, machine learning methods have become available and are used to greater extent in commercial contexts [1, 2]. Generally, this form of machine learning is referred to simply as "artificial intelligence" (AI). The increasing use of novel and hard-to-understand types of AI systems has sparked a discussion on the need for explainability of AI [3, 4]. Especially for high-risk use cases there is a realization, both scientifically and societal, that AI needs to be explainable to be understood. For instance, the upcoming EU legislature on AI [5] will require demonstrable transparency for which explainable AI will be essential. In the financial sector comprehensive understanding of the use of AI systems is even more crucial: both stipulated by a wide range of laws and regulations and because trust in financial institutions is of high importance [6]. Simultaneously, expectations of new AI systems are high in the financial sector, while regulators need

© Springer Nature Switzerland AG 2022
L. A. Leiva et al. (Eds.): BNAIC/Benelearn 2021, CCIS 1530, pp. 105–119, 2022.
https://doi.org/10.1007/978-3-030-93842-0_6

time to keep up with the speed of development [7]. Striking the right balance between performance and explainability can present a difficult dilemma for financial institutions.

The field of explainable AI (or 'xAI') studies how AI can be made explainable by making algorithms and their systems more transparent, often referred to as "opening the black box" [3]. An improved understanding of the working of these algorithms helps us to verify them, improve them, and implement them ethically. Most developments in xAI focus on either technical tools for model developers or approach explainability as a social or cognitive challenge [8, 9]. Other authors have stated that making models explainable should be foregone instead of using inherently interpretable models [10]. Given the attention transparency and explainability receive as a requirement for ethical AI, it is no surprise that many reports on the responsible use of AI have stressed the need for xAI [11]. Notably, the number of empirical studies that provide practical insights into how xAI is actually used in practice is very limited [12] which we believe represents a hiatus in the current literature.

Financial institutions, both large and SME, have begun to use AI, for instance in delivering instant responses to credit applications, claim settlement, and transaction monitoring [24, 25]. The World Economic Forum [16] notes that the opacity of AI systems poses a serious risk to the use of AI in the financial sector: lack of transparency can lead to loss of control by financial institutions and thereby damage consumer confidence and society. Given the crucial role of trust in the financial sector, explainability of the outcomes and functioning of AI systems is considered necessary [16]. Explainability is in fact one of the EU's key requirements for trustworthy AI [11]. With new EU AI legislation announced, explainability is expected to become even more important and necessary for some high-risk use cases such as consumer credit scoring [5].

Limited empirical descriptions on the challenges surrounding the application of xAI exist. In addition, only preliminary guidelines exist [17] on how to implement xAI, often based in theory and lacking empirical validation. In the future, a solid and practical framework could help organizations to better understand their obligations (regulatory and otherwise) regarding xAI and how to operationalize them. In the financial sector, such a framework could also help supervisory authorities to translate current regulations regarding transparency and the provision of information, to clear expectations regarding xAI to regulated entities. In lieu of such a framework, a starting point is to map what is currently expected of in terms of explainability of AI by banks and supervisory authorities.

The current exploratory study aims to identify what the differences are regarding the expectations of explainability of AI for supervisory authorities and regulated entities in the financial sector. Three use cases were examined in which AI is used at financial institutions in the Netherlands. Data were collected by means of semi-structured interviews with interviewees of both banks and supervisory authorities. This study is intended to add empirical data on how xAI is regarded and used in practice and as stepping stone towards a framework as described above. The main research question is: *What are the perspectives of supervisory authorities and regulated entities regarding the application of xAI in the financial sector?*

2   Theoretical Background

Explainable AI (xAI), also referred to as interpretable or understandable AI, aims to solve the "black box" problem in AI [18, 19]. A typical present-day AI system utilizes data (e.g., information on a person's financial situation) and produces an outcome (e.g., a risk of default indication). However, in such a system it is not always evident from the output how or why a certain outcome is reached based on the data. Especially when using more complex AI systems (e.g., using deep learning or random forest methods) the process from input to output is practically impossible to understand by humans even with full knowledge of the inner workings, weightings, and biases of the system. The term xAI encompasses a wide range of solutions that explain why or how an AI system arrives at outcomes or decisions [20]. One line of research focuses on technical tools to explore the relation between model input and output, such as SHAP [21] and LIME [22]. A critique on the xAI field expressed by various authors is that xAI is often not clearly defined and discussed without proper understanding of the surrounding concepts and the parties involved [19, 23]. As such, the exact scope of xAI is not always well-defined, as sometimes the term is used to focus on technical solutions directly relating to the model, but sometimes the system context is also taken into account.

Transparency is one of the central concepts of xAI. Importantly, the term is used in two distinguishable contexts or manners in the literature, which we differentiate by using *model transparency* and *process transparency*. Model transparency is the property of a model to be understood by a human as it is, in terms of its general working or design. The opposite of "black-boxness" is model transparency [3, 10]. This type of transparency is generally what model developers refer to and is highly related to the concept of interpretability [18, 24]. Process transparency is transparency of the use and development of an AI system; it relates to openness and not concealing information for stakeholders [24]. This form of transparency is generally what the colloquial meaning of transparency refers to. However, it is also the type of transparency that is meant in some of the literature on responsible use of AI when talking about "transparency" [10, 17].

Explainability means that an explanation of the operation and outcome of a system can be formulated in such a way that it can be sufficiently understood by the stakeholder [3]. The term "stakeholder" refers to the individual, party, or audience impacted by the functioning and/or outcomes of the AI system, requiring information in the form of an explanation. In a vacuum, i.e., without a stakeholder, an explanation cannot be said to do what is intended, namely making something understood by an individual [9]. We would argue that the core concept of explainable AI is *effectual* explanation. An effectual explanation is not only about providing the required information, but to do so in a manner that leads to stakeholder understanding [25], for instance by offering the right amount of detail or boundary conditions of a model [26]. In addition, explanations can be global or local [13, 14, 26]. That is, a global explanation reveals the inner workings of the entire AI system (potentially including a case at hand), a local explanation offers insight in a specific outcome.

We used the following definition of explainable AI in this study: *"Given a stake-holder, xAI is a set of capabilities that produces an explanation (in the form of details, reasons, or underlying causes) to make the functioning and/or results of an AI system sufficiently clear so that it is understandable to the stakeholder and addresses the stakeholder's concerns."* [15].

Various types of information that can be used as the basis for an explanation can be distinguished. A distinction that should be noted here is that of the of process-based versus outcome-based explanation [17]. A process-based explanation gives information on the governance of the AI system across its design and deployment; the explanation is about "the how". An outcome-based explanation gives information on what happened in the case of a particular decision; the explanation is about "the what". In addition, explanations can be said to be "global" (explaining the entire model) or "local" (explaining a specific outcome) [13, 14, 26]. Furthermore, xAI techniques to gain more information about the functioning of a model can be model-agnostic (and work on any model, e.g., SHAP [21]), or be model-specific.

As a basis for this study we established a list of types of information that can underpin an explanation (of an AI system) that are relevant in the financial sector. We based this list on literature on explainable AI (using snowball search and focusing on the most cited papers in the field) and adapted it to fit use cases in the financial sector [9, 13, 14, 17, 26]. It should be noted that we incorporated types of information that are related to process-based explanation (e.g. the process surrounding the AI system), and which might be omitted in some views of explainable AI, that are however relevant from a regulatory perspective on AI in finance.

- The reasons, details, or underlying causes of a particular outcome, both from a local and global perspective.
- The data and features used as input to determine a particular outcome, both from a local and global perspective.
- The data used to train and test the AI system.
- The performance and accuracy of the AI system.
- The principles, rules, and guidelines used to design and develop the AI system.
- The process that was used to design, develop, and test the AI system (considering aspects like compliance, fairness, privacy, performance, safety, and impact).
- The process of how feedback is processed.
- The process of how explainers are trained.
- The persons involved in design, development, and implementation of the AI system.
- The persons accountable for development and use of the AI system.

3   Research Method

3.1   Use Cases

To address our research question, we applied a qualitative research approach by means of a series of semi-structured interviews. Three types of use cases were examined. The two supervisory authorities took part in all three use cases, with each of the three banks partaking in two of the three use cases (due to constraints in availability of interviewees). The three use cases were: 1) consumer credit, 2) credit risk management, and 3) anti-money laundering. A brief outline of these use cases will now be given.

The use case on consumer credit considers a typical case for consumer credit and a mortgage lending case. Consumer credit is credit provided to a consumer, which can be used to purchase goods and services. Financial institutions that provide consumer credit in the Netherlands have the right and obligation to ensure that the borrower has the capacity to repay the loan. Credit risk management focusses on internal risk and/or capital requirement models (early warning systems and probability of defaults models) where AI systems can be used to improve or replace the currently used models. The use case on anti-money laundering (AML) concerned AI systems which are used to conduct suspicious activity monitoring and transaction monitoring.

3.2   Data Collection

The organizations involved in this study are two supervisory authorities (SAs) and three banks in the Netherlands. For reasons of anonymity these will be referred to as "SA", or "first SA", "second SA", "first bank", etc. depending on which interview took place first. The three banks belong to the major banks in the Netherlands, each with more than one million clients, and can be characterized as financial incumbents [27]. Semi-structured interviews were conducted with employees of these five organizations regarding the three use cases. For all interviews, use case experts (i.e., individuals that worked primarily on the use case at hand) were present. These experts either had a technical expertise (those directly involved with the development of the AI system) and/or a more supervising/governing role (such as compliance & risk officers and model owners).

At each interview at least two interviewees of that organization were present, and at most four (if the complexity of the use case required more diverse expertise in the interviewees). Interviews took between 1 and 1.5 h. In total 13 interviews took place, six with interviewees from supervisory authorities and seven with interviewees from banks (as one bank took part in an additional interview to fully cover all questions). In addition, the findings were refined in a plenary session in which at least one participant of all five organizations was present. As a starting point during the interviews, a list of questions was used to guide the discussion, but the conversation was permitted to develop naturally in the direction deemed most suitable by the interviewers and interviewees.

The interviews with the banks and supervisory authorities had a slightly different list of starting questions, as the SA interviewees did not have the same direct knowledge of a specific use case in contrast to the banks. The interviewees of the banks were asked questions about the following topics: the context of how AI is being used in the organization, the role of explainability in the AI development process, the workings of the use case at hand, the application of AI in the use case, the relevant stakeholders, and how the bank deals with explainability in this particular use case. Finally, the banks were asked what types of information that can serve as a basis for explanations (based on the list from Sect. 2) are considered relevant for supervisory authorities.

For the supervisory authorities, the focus of the interviews was on the boundaries of what they would allow in terms of AI and what their expectations of explainability were for that use case. The interviewees were asked questions concerning: their perception of the use of AI and xAI, applicable legislation around the use case, and the requirements for explainability from a supervisory perspective. In addition, they were asked what types of information (based on the list from Sect. 2) they consider relevant for their supervisory role for the use case at hand. The interviews with the two supervisory authorities were conducted with interviewees who were aware of the applicable prudential, integrity and conduct regulations relating to the use cases.

All interviews were conducted by two researchers of the HU University of Applied Sciences via Webex. During every interview, one of the researchers had the lead in asking questions while the other made notes used for later analysis. After the interviews, the interviewees verified the interview reports and supplemented information where needed.

3.3   Data Analysis

Data analysis was conducted based on the interview reports. As a first step we analyzed the interview reports and created a list of the main findings and conclusions per interview. These findings and conclusions were verified and supplemented by the interviewees. As a next step, we analyzed all interview reports and developed an overview of the main conclusions. These conclusions were discussed in a plenary session with participants of the supervisory authorities and banks. The output of this session was used to refine the conclusions.

4   Results

First, we discuss the most notable results per use case. Second, we discuss the overall findings.

4.1   Consumer Credit

The first bank provided a use case about mortgage lending (a type of consumer credit) in which an AI system was used to assess mortgages with traffic-light colors to support middle office employees. The AI system runs in parallel to other, more traditional systems in the mortgage approval and monitoring process (e.g. using business rules). The AI system uses a rather simple form of machine learning based on logistic regression and uses around 10 variables. It improves on a business rules system in that it uses historical data. Interestingly, relating to explainability the primary users of the AI system (the middle office employees) were by design not given detailed insight into the functioning and results of the AI system to prevent potential gaming of the system. Due to the relative interpretability of the model, explainability to other stakeholders was not considered to be a challenge beyond the previous systems.

The second bank also supplemented their traditional loan approval system for consumer credit with an AI system. The traditional system uses basic data, such as the data a client provides through the application process or data from credit bureaus. The new AI system is trained and continuously supplied with new transactional data. The combination of both models resulted in fewer defaults on loans. For this use-case, model developers are considered the most important stakeholders regarding explainability. It was stated that it would be possible from a technological point of view to explain the model to customers, although this requires a thorough understanding of which type of narratives would be comprehensible by different consumer groups. This might require an interactive process, which was indicated to present a challenging IT problem rather than a problem of getting the relevant information (and explanations) from the AI system.

One of the SAs monitors whether lenders (i.e. banks) comply with lending standards. The lending standards ("leennorm" in Dutch) follow straightforward rules limiting the amount that can be loaned depending on the financial situation of the lender and are the basis for valid loan approval. Regardless of what an AI system indicates, banks must (and do) conform to this lending standard in all cases. The interviewee of the SA indicated that this was the primary method by which the supervisory authority currently ensured a lending consumer was protected. An interesting point was raised that within the lending standards banks might use AI to find cases their traditional systems would not give a credit, but the AI determines as being profitable for the bank. However, this might not always be good for the consumer. Widespread adoption of AI models might thus require reevaluation of the lending standards.

In summary, for consumer credit, banks reported they use AI in conjunction to traditional ("business rules") systems. As a result of the lending standards, what is and isn't allowed for banks by supervisory authorities in terms of offering loans to consumers is currently clearly specified and understandable for both parties. As a result, in terms of explainability the lending standards are the basis (and thereby the explanation) for rejection of most loans of consumers. As for the edge cases where (within the lending standards) newer AI models might give a different recommendation compared to the traditional models of banks, explainable AI would be especially important to give insight into exactly what causes the deviation from traditional models. Due to the current simplicity of the utilized models, this is at the moment not yet a concern, as also stated by the interviewees. Interviewees at a bank indicated that automated explainability towards consumers (loan applicants) is in principle possible due to the high level of interpretability of the models. Currently, in most cases there is a human-in-the-loop (the advisor) who provides the customer with information and acts as a potential ethical safeguard.

4.2   Credit Risk Management

The AI system of the first bank in the credit risk management use case follows an AIRB (advanced internal rating-based) model for the bank's residential mortgage portfolio (a capital model). It predicts a probability of default for each mortgage customer and a prediction of loss-given-default for each customer. The model uses around 10–15 variables and is based on logistic regression. There is no interaction with any consumer based on the model, it is only used internally. The main stakeholders for explanations are the internal "first line" and the supervisory authority. More advanced AI is expected to potentially be able to lead to better performance, however, the interviewees reported apprehension to use more complex models due to the expected long and time-consuming process to get approval both internally and externally from supervisory authorities.

From the interview with the first SA, it became apparent that regulations such as capital requirements regulations (CRR [28]) heavily determine the boundaries for what type of AI systems can be used in this use case. Predominantly, logistic regression models are used across all financial institutions. Models that are more complex may not meet requirements like traceability and replicability. Another requirement for credit risk models is to demonstrate "experience" in applying a model. In practice, this means that the model must be used as a shadow model for at least three years before approval can be given. Banks are conducting plentiful research and pilots into AI in credit risk, but the regulations are a limiting factor for further implementation. Currently, AI in credit risk does not appear to lead to sufficient benefit compared to the challenge of getting its use approved within the current regulatory framework to make it worthwhile. It was indicated that the bank first to implement a new AI method must assume it takes at least a year and a half before approval is granted.

In summation, in credit risk management strict requirements are heavily embedded in regulations like CRR. Credit risk management forces 'transparent by design' models, therefore, xAI is less of an issue as AI models that are not inherently transparent are simply not used. Regulations/supervisory authorities are slow to change on credit risk, possibly to the more international nature and societal importance of regulation in this use case. Changing these regulations to allow for AI systems that are more complex will be an incremental process that takes time and trust in the safety of such systems.

4.3   Anti-money Laundering (AML)

For the first bank the use case of anti-money laundering (AML) involved an AI system developed to detect fraudulent activity in corresponding banking transactions. The AI system consists of two algorithms (models): a deduplication algorithm and a classification algorithm. As AML investigators check the flagged transactions, there is a human-in-the-loop. The AML investigator receives explanations (e.g., the most important features leading to a flagging) as part of the outcome of the AI system. The xAI tool SHAP [21] was used with output provided to the investigator. As such, the investigator can be said to be main stakeholder for explanation in this use case. Explanation, in a broader sense, to other stakeholders is done via technical documentation and various internal processes.

The use case of the second bank concerns machine learning (ML) used for transaction monitoring. In the past, transaction monitoring was only done rule-based. Currently, multiple ML models are used in conjunction with a rule-based methodology. For instance, there is a supervised AI model that is used as noise reduction (i.e. reduces false positives) on the output of the rule-based system. Furthermore, there is also a supervised model that gives customers scores based on suspicion of money laundering practices and an unsupervised anomaly detection AI model. The output of the models is intended for transaction monitoring analysts who have expertise in recognizing integrity risks. These analysts are generally not concerned with assessing the quality of model output, which is done by quality assurance analysts. The ML model output includes extensive information (which can be considered explanation) about suspicious situations, e.g., indicating the most relevant features, as opposed to rule-based systems. This explainability aspect of these (modern ML) models is thus an important part of the subsequent analysis done by the analyst. This analyst also uses a multitude of other data (sources) outside the detection models for further verification. The analyst can be seen as the human-in-the-loop in this use case, and as the most important stakeholder in need of explanation. Notably, results of the ML-models are improved over the traditional models: both fewer false positives and fewer false negatives (thus more suspicious transactions are reported).

Interviewees indicated that both internally for banks, but also for supervisory authorities, a change of mindset is required to transition from the traditional way of thinking in thresholds (contained in business rules), to more probabilistic thinking about the features of an AML case (contained in modern ML methods). With the latter, explanations can be more complex, but should not be of less quality.

The first SA, in the case of AML, is tasked with ensuring that banks comply with the Anti-Money Laundering and Anti-Terrorist Financing Act [29]. Currently, this SA does not impose any requirements on what type of AI system is used for AML as long as it can be properly explained both to the supervisory authority and internally. Exactly what sufficient explanation is for which type of AI system is not defined by the SA but assessed on a case-to-case basis, due to the highly varying contexts in which AI is used. For the time being, there is also no framework in which explainability is defined, which is directly applicable to this use case. In the context of controlled business operations, a bank must be able to explain how its systems work. If a bank cannot explain an AI system, both to the supervisory authority and internally, as there may be uncontrolled business operations the bank does not sufficiently manage its risks.

In summary, AML was indicated to be one of the use cases that can benefit most from AI in terms of improving results while also being the use case in which the supervisory authorities allow the most room for the use of novel AI methods. So far, the issue of explainability did not hinder the deployment of more complex AI systems in this use case. The internal AML analyst/investigator is viewed as the most important stakeholder regarding explanations by the banks. This investigator is trained to work with and understand model output, which can be seen as a form of, or bringing about of, explainability.

4.4   General

One of the main findings, reported throughout the interviews, is that explainable AI is high on the agenda of banks and supervisory authorities. Within banks, it either is or is planned to be an aspect of an ethical framework used within the organization. Such a framework generally builds on existing principles or procedures (not related to AI specifically), but there is a trend towards more unification of principles and a more explicit focus on AI. For supervisory authorities, explainability is not exclusively an ethical concern, as it is also relevant from a prudential and legal perspective (e.g., a prudential or legal framework such as CRR, lending standards, and the GDPR).

As such, explainability is relevant to a wide range of supervisory authorities in the financial sector among which the two in this study, but also including, e.g., data protection supervisory authorities.

The use of complex AI systems by banks is increasing although often still limited, mainly still using basic methods such as logistic regression. The use case of AML is a notable exception where more varied and advanced AI models are used. In the plenary session, the following reasons for the slow adoption of AI were mentioned: 1) The time needed to become familiar with and implement complex models and especially xAI methods (such as SHAP and LIME [21, 22]), which have emerged only in the last years. Deciding what xAI method to choose, and how to implement it, is a challenging process as xAI is still developing rapidly and in a short period new methods might make a current xAI method obsolete. 2) Uncertainty as to whether financial regulations (such as lending standards, CRR) or the supervisory authority would allow the use of novel AI. 3) Traditional models are deemed adequate for many use cases. 4) Internal hesitation to implement complex AI systems in customer facing applications. 5) AI systems that are more complex are difficult to maintain and monitor over time.

As for the types of information that can serve as the basis for explanations it could be noted that across all use cases the supervisory authorities indicated they are interested in the full range of types of information, while the interviewees from banks generally indicated only a subset per use case was relevant (see Table 1).

Table 1. Responses of SAs and banks on the importance of the types of information that can potentially underpin an explanation for supervisory authorities per use case. A plus-sign (+) indicates a positive, a minus-sign (−) a negative, and both (±) indicates a partial importance. Note that each of the three banks only partook in two use case interviews, and thus two banks responded per use case, except for the credit risk use case where only interviewees of one bank filled in this list.

	Consumer credit			Credit RIsk		AML		
	SAs	Bank	Bank	SAs	Bank	SAs	Bank	Bank
The reasons, details, or underlying causes of a particular outcome	+	−	+	+	−	+	−	+
The data and features used as input to determine a particular outcome	+	+	+	+	+	+	−	+
The data used to train and test the AI system	+	+	+	+	+	+	−	+
The performance and accuracy of the AI system	+	−	+	+	−	+	+	+
The principles, rules, and guidelines used to design and develop the AI system	+	+	+	+	+	+	+	+

(continued)

Table 1. (*continued*)

	Consumer credit			Credit RIsk		AML		
	SAs	Bank	Bank	SAs	Bank	SAs	Bank	Bank
The process that was used to design, develop, and test the AI system	+	+	+	+	+	+	+	+
The process of how feedback is processed	+	−	+	+	-	+	+	+
The process of how explainers are trained	+	+	+	+	+	+	−	+
The persons involved in design, development, and implementation of AI system	+	−	+	+	−	+	−	±
The persons accountable for development and use of the AI system	+	+	+	+	+	+	−	+

5 Discussion and Conclusions

The main finding of this study is that there appears to be a disparity between the supervisory authorities (SAs) and the banks regarding the desired scope of explainability required for the use of AI in finance. This is exemplified by responses by these two types of organization on what types of information are required by SAs in the various use cases (visible in Table 1). SAs indicate all types of information are relevant while banks indicate only a subset is relevant. Various laws and regulations already explicitly or implicitly impose requirements on the explainability of information systems, regardless of whether they are AI systems or other classes of systems. However, the use of AI systems brings with it a new type of ethical, social, and legal challenges in addition to the direct technical challenge of opening the black box of non-interpretable models [8, 9, 23, 30]. Therefore, it seems warranted to further explore how this disparity should be addressed.

The financial sector could perhaps benefit from clear differentiation between technical (model) explainability requirements and explainability requirements of business operations, applicable laws, and regulations on this topic of AI. A similar bifurcation as can be made for transparency (process transparency and model transparency [23]) might be useful for the xAI field: for instance, "AI model explainability" and "AI system explainability". The first of these relating to a set of techniques and methods that are directly used to better understand the AI model and how its input relates to its output. The second of these relating to the broader concept of explainability that views the AI model as embedded in a system or a set of systems or processes. Whether a black box houses a deterministic machine learning system, or whether a (larger) black box houses a complex system of processes and various agents interacting with an AI, both require explanation [25]. In the first case the questions will be more like "how does this input lead to this output", the opening of the traditional black box AI. However in the second case questions could be: "how is this process designed?" or "who is responsible for the data quality?".

Most interviewees, especially the technical (i.e. model developers) associated explainable AI with the technical tools that have been developed in the last few years, that focus on explaining the model in a low-level fashion. While technical tools, such as SHAP [21], give additional information about the operation of a model, they do not answer how such information in general is conveyed understandably to a stakeholder, by means of an explanation suited to that stakeholder [9]. Additionally, these tools are often post-hoc or after the fact [13]. Like requirements as privacy, security, and fairness, explainability should require attention from the onset of the design of an information system, "explainability by design" [31, 32].

It should be noted that several factors could have made the disparity (seen in Table 1) larger than it is in actuality. Firstly, the interviewees at the bank might not have the same understanding about the laws and regulations as interviewees from the SAs had. Another explanation for the disparity is that it is difficult to translate laws and regulations into precise requirements for information systems and AI systems in particular [33], thus for novel developments very broad ranges of requirements are assumed. The exact reason for the disparity found in this study is certainly a worthwhile topic of future research as well as for subsequent coordination and collaboration between supervisory authorities and regulated entities on topics such as transparency, explainability, and associated definitions.

The requirements regarding explainable AI reported in the interviews varied widely per use case and stakeholder. This limits the possibility of quickly creating a generic framework or checklist for AI in finance that covers all or most bases. Subsequent research could first explore a single use case to create a full picture of the explanation requirements and what information is relevant for which stakeholder given a range of possible AI models. Subsequently, mapping stakeholders to xAI methods [19, 21, 22] to see how they can be helped can be a valuable avenue of research that can produce practical instruments for the implementation of xAI.

This study has several limitations that should be noted. First, we only interviewed employees of a subset of the Dutch financial sector, three banks and two supervisory authorities. In addition, we only spoke to a total of 21 employees across the five organizations. Furthermore, we only touched the surface in the examination of the use cases with interviews as the main method to collect data. More in-depth studies are necessary to confirm and extend our findings and to determine whether our findings hold across different geographies.

We found banks are hesitant to put complex AI models into practice in their primary business processes for the lending and credit risk use cases. Interestingly, supervisory authorities indicated that they in principle do not restrict the use of specific types of AI systems. However, laws and regulations such as lending standards and CRR impose explainability requirements which limit the choice of AI methods beforehand. This might be a chicken-or-the-egg type problem, in which banks are unclear what regulators would precisely allow and therefore do not develop a certain AI solution (based on a certain model), while regulators wait for banks to put AI systems into practice before they can clearly say which type of model is allowed and which is not. To counteract this, in the plenary session it was proposed to increase communication between banks and SAs, also in the development process of new AI models.

Notably, in the consumer credit and AML use cases, the use of novel AI methods went hand in hand with the ability to leverage more (types) of data in addition to the ability to use historical data. This is a clear advantage of these novel AI methods over the traditional business rule systems and might explain the increased performance that was reported in these use cases.

The application of AI at banks for the three use cases is currently only focused on internal stakeholders, such as the investigators in the AML use case or the mid-office employees in the consumer credit use case. The fact that there is a human-in-the-loop was reported as a positive, as this offered an additional safeguard before action was taken based on the AI output. In the future, more familiarity with (fully) automated AI systems might lead to banks deploy more customer-oriented AI.

This is one of the first studies that provides practical insight in the application of xAI in the context of use cases and AI systems in the financial sector. It demonstrates that a wide range of aspects requires attention when designing and building AI systems, and that explainability cannot be considered as a merely technical challenge nor a one-size-fits-all solution. For financial law and policy makers, this research illustrates that financial laws and regulations have an impact on the design of information systems and in particular, AI systems.

In conclusion, there appears to be a disparity between the perspectives as provided by the interviewees of the banks and those of the supervisory authorities for the use cases investigated in this study. Namely, the supervisory authorities view explainability of AI in a wider fashion. Potentially, this can be reframed as the supervisory authorities requiring explanation of the AI model as embedded in a broader system, explicitly or implicitly part of financial laws and regulations. On the other hand, the regulated entities (i.e. the banks in this study) tended to view explainable AI more as a requirement of only the AI model. A clear differentiation between technical AI (model) explainability requirements and explainability requirements of the wider AI system in relation to applicable laws and regulations can potentially be of benefit to the financial sector and help in the communication between supervisory authorities and banks.

References

1. Schwab, K.: The Fourth Industrial Revolution, Random House LCC US (2017)
2. Zhang, D., et al.: The AI Index 2021 Annual Report. arXiv preprint arXiv:2103.06312 (2021)
3. Arrieta, A.B., et al.: Explainable artificial intelligence (XAI): concepts, taxonomies, opportunities and challenges toward responsible AI. Inf. Fusion **58**, 82–115 (2020)
4. Murdoch, W.J., Singh, C., Kumbier, K., Abbasi-Asl, R., Yu, B.: Definitions, methods, and applications in interpretable machine learning. Proc. Natl. Acad. Sci. **116**(44), pp. 22071–22080 (2019)

5. European Commission: Proposal for a regulation of the European Parliament and of the Council laying down harmonised rules on artificial intelligence (artificial intelligence act) and amending certain union legislative acts. https://eur-lex.europa.eu/legal-content/EN/TXT/?uri=CELEX:52021PC0206. Accessed 12 June 2021

6. Van der Cruijsen, C., De Haan, J., Roerink, R.: Financial Knowledge and Trust in Financial Institutions, Netherlands Central Bank, Research Department (2019)

7. Giudici, P., Hochreiter, R., Osterrieder, J., Papenbrock, J., Schwendner, P.: AI and financial technology. Front. Artif. Intell. **2**, 25 (2019)

8. Bauer, K., Hinz, O., Van der Aalst, W., Weinhardt, C.: Expl(AI)n it to me–explainable ai and information systems research. Bus. Inf. Syst. Eng. **63**(2) (2021)

9. Miller, T.: Explanation in artificial intelligence: Insights from the social sciences. Artif. Intell. **267**, 1–38 (2019)

10. Mueller, H., Ostmann, F.: AI transparency in financial services, The Alan Turing Institute. https://www.turing.ac.uk/news/ai-transparency-financial-services. Accessed 28 May 2021

11. The High-Level Expert Group on Artificial Intelligence, Ethics Guidelines for Trustworthy A, EU Document. https://ec.europa.eu/digital-single-market/en/news/ethics-guidelines-trustworthy-ai. Accessed 21 May 2021

12. Belle, V., Papantonis, I.: Principles and practice of explainable machine learning. Front. Big Data**4**, 688969 (2021). https://doi.org/10.3389/fdata.2021.688969

13. Adadi, A., Berrada, M.: Peeking inside the black-box: a survey on explainable artificial intelligence. IEEE Access **6**, 52138–52160 (2018)

14. Guidotti, R., Monreale, A., Ruggieri, S., Turini, F., Giannotti, F., Pedreschi, D.: A survey of methods for explaining black box models. ACM Comput. Surv. (CSUR) **51**(5), 1–42 (2018)

15. Van den Berg, M., Kuiper, O.X.: XAI in the financial sector. https://www.internationalhu.com/research/projects/explainable-ai-in-the-financial-sector. Accessed 08 Aug 2021

16. McWaters, R., Blake, M., Galaski, R.: Navigating uncharted waters: a roadmap to responsible innovation with AI in financial services. Part of the Future of Financial Services Series. World Economic Forum (2019)

17. ICO (Information Commissioner's Office) and Alan Turing Institute, Explaining decisions made with AI. https://ico.org.uk/for-organisations/guide-to-data-protection/key-data-protection-themes/explaining-decisions-made-with-ai/. Accessed 14 Apr 2021

18. Xie, N., Ras, G., Van Gerven, M., Doran, D.: Explainable deep learning: a field guide for the uninitiated. arXiv Preprint arXiv:2004.14545 (2020)

19. Lipton, Z.C.: The mythos of model Interpretability: in machine learning, the concept of interpretability is both important and slippery. Queue **16**(3), 31–57 (2018)

20. Schwalbe, G., Finzel, B.: AI method properties: a (Meta-)study (2021). X.ArXiv:2105.07190 *[Cs]*. http://arxiv.org/abs/2105.07190

21. Lundberg, S., Lee, S.I.: A unified approach to interpreting model predictions. arXiv preprint arXiv:1705.07874 (2017)

22. Ribeiro, M.T., Singh, S., Guestrin, C.: "Why should I trust you?" Explaining the predictions of any classifier. In: Proceedings of the 22nd ACM SIGKDD International Conference on Knowledge Discovery and Data Mining, pp. 1135–1144 (2016)

23. Gerlings, J., Shollo, A., Constantiou, I.: Reviewing the need for explainable artificial intelligence (xAI). In: Proceedings of the 54th Hawaii International Conference on System Sciences, pp. 1284–1293 (2021)

24. Confalonieri, R., Coba, L., Wagner, B., Besold, T.R.: A historical perspective of explainable artificial intelligence. Wiley Interdiscipl. Rev. Data Min. Knowl. Discov. **11**(1), e1391 (2021)

25. Xu, W.: Toward human-centered AI: a perspective from human-computer interaction. Interactions **26**(4), 42–46 (2019)

26. Mueller, S.T., Hoffman, R.R., Clancey, W., Emrey, A., Klein, G.: Explanation in human-AI systems: a literature meta-review, synopsis of key ideas and publications, and bibliography for explainable AI. arXiv preprint arXiv:1902.01876 (2019)
27. Zhang, B.Z., Ashta, A., Barton, M.E.: Do FinTech and financial incumbents have different experiences and perspectives on the adoption of artificial intelligence? Strateg. Chang. **30**(3), 223–234 (2021)
28. Joosen, B.P.: Regulatory capital requirements and bail in mechanisms. In: Haentjens, M., Wessels, B. (eds.) Research Handbook on Crisis Management in the Banking Sector. Edward Elgar Publishing (2015). https://www.elgaronline.com/view/edcoll/9781783474226/9781783474226.00022.xml
29. Anti-Money Laundering and Anti-Terrorist Financing Act (*Wet ter voorkoming van witwassen en financieren van terrorisme*). https://wetten.overheid.nl/BWBR0024282/2021-07-01. Accessed 10 Sep 2021
30. Dwivedi, Y.K., et al.: Artificial Intelligence (AI): multidisciplinary perspectives on emerging challenges, opportunities, and agenda for research, practice and policy. Int. J. Inf. Manag. **57**, 101994 (2019)
31. Leijnen, S., Aldewereld, H., Van Belkom, R., Bijvank, R., Ossewaarde, R.: An agile framework for trustworthy AI. In: NeHuAI@ ECAI, pp. 75–78 (2020)
32. Köhl, M.A., Baum, K., Langer, M., Oster, D., Speith, T., Bohlender, B.: Explainability as a non-functional requirement. In: 2019 IEEE 27th International Requirements Engineering Conference, pp. 363–368 (2019)
33. Siena, A., Mylopoulos, M., Perini, A., Susi A.: From laws to requirements. In: 2008 Requirements Engineering and Law, pp. 6–10 (2008)
34. Van der Burgt, J.: General principles for the use of AI in the financial sector. https://www.dnb.nl/actueel/algemeen-nieuws/dnbulletin-2019/dnb-komt-met-richtlijnen-voor-gebruik-kunstmatige-intelligentie/. Accessed 21 May 2021
35. Buckley, R.P., Zetzsche, D.A., Arner, D.W., Tang, B.W.: Regulating artificial intelligence in finance: putting the human in the loop. Sydney Law Rev. **43**(1), 43–81 (2021)
36. Rudin, C.: Stop explaining black box machine learning models for high stakes decisions and use interpretable models instead. Nat. Mach. Intell. **1**(5), 206–215 (2019)

The Effect of Noise Level on the Accuracy of Causal Discovery Methods with Additive Noise Models

Benjamin Kap[✉] [iD], Marharyta Aleksandrova[iD], and Thomas Engel[iD]

University of Luxembourg, 2, Avenue de l'Université,
4365 Esch-sur-Alzette, Luxembourg
{benjamin.kap,marharyta.aleksandrova,thomas.engel}@uni.lu

Abstract. In recent years a lot of research was conducted within the area of causal inference and causal learning. Many methods were developed to identify the cause-effect pairs. These methods also proved their ability to successfully determine the direction of causal relationships from observational real-world data. Yet in bivariate situations, causal discovery problems remain challenging. A class of methods, that also allows tackling the bivariate case, is based on Additive Noise Models (ANMs). Unfortunately, one aspect of these methods has not received much attention until now: *what is the impact of different noise levels on the ability of these methods to identify the direction of the causal relationship?* This work aims to bridge this gap with the help of an empirical study. We consider a bivariate case and two specific methods *Regression with Subsequent Independence Test* and *Identification using Conditional Variances*. We perform a set of experiments with an exhaustive range of ANMs where the additive noises' levels gradually change from 1% to 10000% of the causes' noise level (the latter remains fixed). Additionally, we consider several different types of distributions as well as linear and non-linear ANMs. The results of the experiments show that these causal discovery methods can fail to capture the true causal direction for some levels of noise.

Keywords: Causal learning · Additive noise models · Noise level

1 Introduction

Thanks to the technological and computational advances during the last decades, scientists were able to tackle successfully non-trivial problems from different research areas, with causality being a prominent example. One of the fundamental problems of causality theory is to determine the causal relationship between two or more variables. This problem is known as *causal discovery, causal identification* or *structure learning* [8,27]. For example, given altitude and temperature, we want to answer the question if the temperature has an effect on altitude, or if altitude has an effect on temperature. This is of particular interest since if such

© Springer Nature Switzerland AG 2022
L. A. Leiva et al. (Eds.): BNAIC/Benelearn 2021, CCIS 1530, pp. 120–140, 2022.
https://doi.org/10.1007/978-3-030-93842-0_7

a causal relationship is known then one can predict the effects on a system in case of an intervention or a perturbation.

Controlled experimentation, or A/B tests, are considered to be a golden standard for causal discovery [11,34]. In such experiments, there are two identical groups with only one variation. The only variable that is varied (intervened on) is the potential cause. This procedure allows estimating the causal effect of this variable in a given system. A/B tests are widely used in practical applications. For example, testing the efficacy of medications is usually done with A/B tests, see [32] for an example. In this case, the first group, also known as *control group*, receives no medication or a placebo, and the second group, known as *intervention group*, receives the real medication. The results show the true effect (if any) of the medication on human health. However, such tests are often too expensive, unethical, or even technically impossible to execute. For example, to test the effect of smoking on health with this approach, one needs two non-smoker groups. Next, the members of one group should be forced to smoke, and the others not do so. Therefore, it is of great interest to determine causal relationships from observational data only.

There exist many methods which are able to determine causal relationships from observational data. One particular group of such methods is based on *Additive Noise Models* (ANMs). These methods, as the name suggests, exploit the additivity of the random hidden noise. ANMs received a lot of attention as they are well established and yielded many good results [12]. Despite all the research in the past years, one small but nonetheless important aspect of causal discovery with ANMs has not received much attention: how do different noise *levels* of the additive noise impact the correctness of these methods? In the real world, it can occur that noise levels change drastically from cause to effect. It can happen, for example, if the data collection process has a lot of interference like in outer space.

In this work, we aim to bridge this research gap with an empirical study. For our analysis, we selected two specific methods: *Regression with Subsequent Independence Test (Resit)* [20] and *Identification using Conditional Variances (Uncertainty Scoring)* [17]. We chose Resit, as it is known to produce reliable results [15]. However, this method is not capable to identify the correct causal direction in the case both the cause and the noise are Gaussian. In fact, this case was only recently successfully tackled by the Uncertainty Scoring method. That is why we chose the latter one as well. We perform a set of experiments with an exhaustive range of ANMs where the additive noises' levels gradually change from 1% to 10000% of the causes' noise level (the latter remains fixed). We also consider several types of distributions as well as linear and non-linear data. The results of the experiments show that these causal discovery methods can fail to capture the true causal direction for some levels of noise.

This paper is organized as follows. In Sect. 2 we introduce related work. Next, in Sect. 3 we describe the chosen causal discovery methods. In Sect. 4 and Sect. 5 we discuss the experimental setup and the experimental results respectively. Lastly, in Sect. 6 we draw conclusions and present possible future work.

2   Related Work

Structure learning is the procedure of determining causal relationship directions from observational data only and representing these as a (causal) graph. The basic idea emerged from [33] as *path analysis*.

Judea Pearl presented in his work [8] a comprehensive theory of causality and unified the probabilistic, manipulative, counterfactual, and structural approaches to causation. From this work we have the following key point. If there is a statistical association, e.g. two variables X and Y are dependent, then one of the following is true: 1) there is a causal relationship, either X has an effect on Y or Y has an effect on X; 2) there is a common cause (*confounder*) that has an effect on both X and Y; 3) there is a possibly unobserved common effect of X and Y that is conditioned upon data acquisition (selection bias); or 4) there can be a combination of these. From there on, a lot of research has been conducted to develop theoretical approaches and methods for structure learning. In the rest of this section, we first introduce the common concept behind all these approaches, and then we present some major works related to additive noise models.

In general, all methods for structure learning exploit the complexity of the marginal and conditional probability distributions in some way, see [1–7,9,13,14,16,18–25,27–30,35]. Under certain assumptions, these methods are then able to solve the task of causal discovery. Let C denote the cause and E the effect. Then their joint density can be expressed with $p_{C,E}(c,e)$. This joint density can be factorized into either (1) $p_C(c) \cdot P_{E|C}(e|c)$ or (2) $p_E(e) \cdot P_{C|E}(c|e)$. The idea is then that (1) gives models of lower total complexity than (2) and this allows us to conclude the causal relationship direction. Intuitively, this makes sense, because the effect contains information from the cause but not vice-versa (of course, under the assumption that there are no cycles aka feedback loops). Therefore, (2) has at least as much complexity as (1). However, the definition of complexity is ambiguous. For example, one can say that "p_C *contains no information about* $P_{E|C}(e|c)$" and then draw partial conclusions about the causal direction in a given system. This complexity question is often colloquially referred to as *breaking the symmetry*, that is $p_C(c) \cdot P_{E|C}(e|c) \neq p_E(e) \cdot P_{C|E}(c|e)$.

As it was already mentioned, causal discovery based on ANMs was widely studied in the research literature. Silva et al. introduced in [26] a method for learning the structure of linear latent variable models. The main assumption in their work is that each variable is a linear function of its parents plus an additive error term of positive finite variance. Hoyer et al. generalized the linear framework of additive noise models to the nonlinear case [4]. Earlier works often assumed linear models for continuous variables. The authors showed that if data contains non-Gaussian variables, then this can help in distinguishing the causal directions and identifying the causal graph. Mooij et al. introduced Resit[1] method in [13]. This method is based on the idea of minimizing the statistical

---

[1] Resit method is described in Sect. 3.2.

dependence between the regressors and residuals[2]. The authors demonstrated that if the residuals are no longer dependent on the input, then regression can successfully model the causal dependence. This method does not need to assume a particular distribution of the noise because any form of regression can be used (e.g., Linear Regression), and it is well suited for the task of causal inference in additive noise models. Next, Mooij et al. introduced a method to determine the causal relationship in cyclic additive noise models and showed that such models are generally identifiable in the bivariate, Gaussian-noise case [14]. Their method works for continuous data and can be seen as a special case of nonlinear independent component analysis. Later, Peters and Bhlmann proved in [19] *full identifiability*[3] of linear Gaussian structural equation models if all the noise variables have the same variance. In the next work, Peters et al. proposed a method that can identify the directed acyclic graph from the distribution under mild conditions [20]. In contrast, previous methods assumed faithfulness and could only identify the Markov equivalence class of the graph[4]. Finally, the authors of [1,18] proved that linear Gaussian models with different error variance can be also identifiable. In their method, referred to as Uncertainty Scoring[5], this is done by ordering variables according to the law of total variances and then performing independence tests between them. Park extended this result to additive noise models in [17].

As we can see, many researchers contributed to the development of ANMs-based causal discovery methods and widened our understanding of their application cases. However, no previous research work analyzed how the level of noise variance relative to that of the cause variance can impact the accuracy of these methods. This question forms the basis of the current study.

3 Causal Discovery Methods

In this section, we introduce notations and then describe to two analyzed causal discovery methods: *Regression with Subsequent Independence Test (Resit)* [20], see Sect. 3.2, and *Identification using Conditional Variances (Uncertainty Scoring)* [17], see Sect. 3.3.

3.1 Notations

In the following text, we give a short definition of additive noise models for the bivariate case. For more details and multivariate cases, please refer to [4,20].

---

[2] The residuals are defined as the difference between the actual output and the predicted output.

[3] *Full identifiability* means that not only the skeleton of the causal graph is recoverable but also the arrows are.

[4] *Markov equivalence class* refers to the class of graphs in which all graphs have the same skeleton.

[5] Uncertainty Scoring method is described in Sect. 3.3.

Let $X, Y \in \mathbb{R}$ be the cause and the effect respectively. Let there also be m latent (hidden) causes $U = (U_1, \ldots, U_m) \in \mathbb{R}^m$. Then the causal relationship can be modeled as follows.

$$\begin{cases} Y = f(X, U_1, \cdots, U_m) \\ X \perp\!\!\!\perp U \end{cases}, \text{ with } X \sim p_X(x) \text{ and } U \sim p_U(u_1, \cdots, u_m),$$

where $f : \mathbb{R} \times \mathbb{R}^m \to \mathbb{R}$ is a linear or nonlinear function, and $p_X(x)$ and $p_U(u_1, \cdots, u_m)$ are the joint densities of the observed cause X and the latent causes U. We assume that there is no confounding, no selection bias, and no feedback loops between X and Y. In this case, X and U are independent, which is denoted by $X \perp\!\!\!\perp U$. Since the latent causes U are unobserved, their influence can be summarized with a single noise variable $N_y \in \mathbb{R}$, and the model can be rewritten as follows:

$$\begin{cases} Y = f(X, N_y) \\ X \perp\!\!\!\perp N_y \end{cases}, \text{ with } X \sim p_X(x) \text{ and } N_y \sim p_{N_y}(n_y).$$

In our experiments, we are considering both linear and nonlinear additive noise models:

$$Y = \beta X + N_y \text{ with } \beta \in \mathbb{R}, \text{ for the linear case}$$

and

$$Y = \beta X^\alpha + N_y \text{ with } \beta, \alpha \in \mathbb{R}, \text{ for the nonlinear case.}$$

Also, X and N_y can be drawn from one of the following three distributions: the normal distribution denoted by the calligraphic letter $\mathcal{N}$, the uniform distribution denoted by the calligraphic letter $\mathcal{U}$, or the Laplace distribution denoted by the calligraphic letter $\mathcal{L}$. For example, throughout this work "*X is drawn from a normal distribution*" is denoted by $X \sim \mathcal{N}$ or $X \sim \mathcal{N}(\mu_x, \sigma_x)$ with μ_x standing for the mean and σ_x for the standard deviation.

3.2   Regression with Subsequent Independence Test (Resit)

We implement Resit following Algorithm 1 from [15]. This algorithm requires the following inputs: X and Y, a regression method, and a score estimator $\hat{C} : \mathbb{R}^N \times \mathbb{R}^N \to \mathbb{R}$; it outputs *dir* (casual relationship **direction**). The idea is to regress Y on X, predict $\hat{Y}$, and then calculate residuals $Y_{res} = \hat{Y} - Y$. Y_{res} and X are then used to calculate $\hat{C}_{X \to Y}$, a score for the assumed case $X \to Y$. Similarly, to test the other causal direction ($Y \to X$), we regress X on Y, calculate residuals $X_{res} = \hat{X} - X$ and estimate $\hat{C}_{Y \to X}$. In our experiments, the generated data always follows $X \to Y$. This verifies the **assumption** that only one direction in our data is correct (and not both). Under this assumption, we can compare both scores directly to decide on the cause-effect direction, and we do not need to determine the value of α for the independence tests, see Eq. (1). Additionally, we can also use entropy estimators to estimate the score $\hat{C}$.

Algorithm 1. General procedure to decide whether $p(x, y)$ satisfies Additive Noise Model $X \to Y$ or $Y \to X$.

Input:
- I.i.d. sample data X and Y
- Regression method
- Score estimator $\hat{C} : \mathbb{R}^N \times \mathbb{R}^N \to \mathbb{R}$

Output:
- dir

1:   $reg_1 \leftarrow$ Regress Y on X
2:   $reg_2 \leftarrow$ Regress X on Y

3:   $Y_{res} \leftarrow reg_1.predict(X) - Y$
4:   $X_{res} \leftarrow reg_2.predict(Y) - X$

5:   $\hat{C}_{X \to Y} \leftarrow \hat{C}(X, Y_{res})$
6:   $\hat{C}_{Y \to X} \leftarrow \hat{C}(Y, X_{res})$

$$\mathbf{return}\ dir = \begin{cases} X \to Y & \text{if } \hat{C}_{X \to Y} < \hat{C}_{Y \to X}, \\ Y \to X & \text{if } \hat{C}_{X \to Y} > \hat{C}_{Y \to X}, \\ ? & \text{if } \hat{C}_{X \to Y} = \hat{C}_{Y \to X}. \end{cases} \tag{1}$$

In Algorithm 1, it is possible to split the data into training and test parts. In this case, the training data is used to fit the regression model and the test data is used to calculate the value of $\hat{C}$. This procedure is referred to as *decoupled estimation* [12]. The advantage of splitting the data lies in the reduction of the computational time for calculating independence estimates $\hat{C}$. However, in this work, we use *coupled estimation*. This means that the entire data-set is used for both the regression and the independence estimation steps. The latter approach tends to produce more accurate results for independence estimation.

In our work, we use Linear Regression as a regression algorithm. If an appropriate transformation of coordinates is applied, Linear regression can be used in the non-linear cases as well. In our experiments, we used six different independence tests and six different entropy measures for calculating $\hat{C}$. In general, for the independence tests we have:

$$\hat{C}(X_{Test}, Y_{res}) = I(X_{Test}, Y_{res}),$$

with $I(\cdot, \cdot)$ being any independence test. In the case of entropy estimators we have:

$$\hat{C}(X_{Test}, Y_{res}) = H(X_{Test}) + H(Y_{res}),$$

with $H(\cdot)$ being any entropy measure. The entropy-based estimator score is derived from Lemma 1 in [12].

The following estimators were used in this work. The implementation of estimators with numbers 2–12 was taken from the *information theoretical estimators* toolbox [31]. Here we briefly introduce every estimator. Mathematical formulas for each of them can be found in the Appendix.

1. *HSIC*: Hilbert-Schmidt Independence Criterion with RBF Kernel[6].
2. *HSIC_IC*: Hilbert-Schmidt Independence Criterion using incomplete Cholesky decomposition[7].
3. *HSIC_IC2*: Same as HSIC_IC but with lower precision.
4. *DISTCOV*: Distance covariance estimator using pairwise distances.
5. *DISTCORR*: Distance correlation estimator using pairwise distances. It is simply the standardized version of the distance covariance.
6. *HOEFFDING*: Hoeffding's Phi.
7. *SH_KNN*: Shannon differential entropy estimator using kNNs (k-nearest neighbors) where $k = 3$.
8. *SH_KNN_2*: Same as SH_KNN but with different search method.
9. *SH_KNN_3*: Same as SH_KNN but with $k = 5$.
10. *SH_MAXENT1*: Maximum entropy distribution-based Shannon entropy estimator.
11. *SH_MAXENT2*: Same as SH_MAXENT1 with minor changes.
12. *SH_SPACING_V*: Shannon entropy estimator using Vasicek's spacing method.

3.3   Identification Using Conditional Variances (Uncertainty Scoring)

The Uncertainty Scoring method is composed of Algorithm 2 and Algorithm 3 from [17]. It consists of two parts: 1) ordering and 2) conditional independence testing.

For the first step, ordering, we used *backward step-wise selection* (Algorithm 2), as it is more convenient for implementation. The algorithm starts with a set S which contains all variables represented as nodes in a causal graph. Next, we iterate over S, and for each node, we calculate its conditional variance given all other remaining nodes. Then, we select the node with the highest conditional variance, append it to the ordering π, and also remove it from the set S. With the updated set S, we repeat this process until S is empty. Lastly, the *reverse* of the ordering π is returned. The first node to be appended to the ordering is the last one in the ordering, which is reflected in the name *"backward step-wise selection"*.

In the second step, we perform uncertainty scoring using Algorithm 3. This algorithm iterates over the ordering π. For every node j, it performs conditional independence tests conditioning on every other node l appearing before the node j in the ordering π. If a node l is dependent on j, then it is added to the set of parents of j, denoted as $Pa(j)$. In this algorithm, the first node in the ordering never has parents, so the procedure starts with the second node. *Fisher's z-transform of the partial correlation,* is used for the conditional independence testing.

---

[6] Source: https://github.com/amber0309/HSIC.

[7] Low rank decomposition of Gram matrices, which permits an accurate approximation to HSIC as long as the kernel has a fast decaying spectrum.

Algorithm 2. Backward step-wise selection

Input: All variables from an ANM: $X = (x_1, x_2, \ldots, x_n)$
Output: Estimated ordering $\pi = (\pi_1, \pi_2, \ldots, \pi_n)$

1: Set $S = \{1, 2, \ldots, n\}$
2: List $\pi = [\ ]$
3: **for** $m = 1 \ldots n$ **do**
4:     **for** $j \in S$ **do**
5:         Estimate the conditional variance x_j given $\{x_1, \ldots, x_n\} \backslash x_j, \sigma^2_{j|S\backslash j}$
6:     **end**
7:     Append $\pi_m = argmax_j \sigma^2_{j|S\backslash j}$ to π
8:     Update $S = S \backslash \pi_m$
9: **end**
10: **return** Reversed list π

Algorithm 3. Uncertainty Scoring

Input: All variables from an ANM: $X = (x_1, x_2, \ldots, x_n)$
Output: Dictionary with estimated parents for all variables: $G = \{Pa(x_1) : [\ldots], Pa(x_2) : [\ldots], \ldots, Pa(x_n) : [\ldots]\}$

1: Get ordering from backward step-wise selection: $\pi = (\pi_1, \pi_2, \ldots, \pi_n)$
2: $G = \{\}$
3: **for** $m = 2 \ldots n$ **do**
4:     $Pa(\pi_m) = [\ ]$
5:     **for** $j = 1 \ldots m - 1$ **do**
6:         Conditional independence test between π_m and π_j given $\{\pi_1, \ldots, \pi_{m-1}\} \backslash \pi_j$
7:         If dependent, include π_j into $Pa(\pi_m)$
8:     **end**
9:     Insert $Pa(\pi_m)$ into G
10: **end**
11: **return** G

---

4 Experimental Setup

Generation of Synthetic Data. For all empirical tests, we assume X to be a cause of Y, that is $X \to Y$. In the sense of additive noise models, we use the following equations: $Y = X + N_y$ for the linear case, and $Y = X^3 + N_y$ for the non-linear case, where

$$X \sim \begin{cases} \mathcal{N}(0, 1) & \text{or} \\ \mathcal{U}(-1, 1) & \text{or} \\ \mathcal{L}(0, 1) \end{cases} \quad and \quad N_y \sim \begin{cases} \mathcal{N}(0, 1 \cdot i) & \text{or} \\ \mathcal{U}(-1 \cdot i, 1 \cdot i) & \text{or} \\ \mathcal{L}(0, 1 \cdot i) \end{cases}$$

with i being a scaling factor for the noise level in N_y. The goal is to analyze how different standard deviations (boundaries for the uniform case) in the noise term N_y relative to the standard deviations (or boundaries for the uniform case) in the X term impact the ANM methods.

To cover various dependencies between the distributions of X and N_y, we generate 199 different i factors:

$$i \in \{0.01, 0.02, \ldots, 1.00\} \cup \{1, 2, \ldots, 100\}.$$

For each i, every linear and non-linear combination with different distributions is tested. Totally, we have 18 combinations corresponding to the general structures $Y = X + N_y$ and $Y = X^3 + N_y$, where X and N_y are drawn from the three different distributions, $\mathcal{N}, \mathcal{U}$ or $\mathcal{L}$.

$$Y = X \sim \mathcal{N} + N_y \sim \mathcal{N},$$

$$Y = X \sim \mathcal{N} + N_y \sim \mathcal{U},$$

$$Y = X \sim \mathcal{N} + N_y \sim \mathcal{L},$$

$$\vdots$$

$$Y = X \sim \mathcal{L}^3 + N_y \sim \mathcal{L}.$$

Note that $\mathcal{L}^3$ here signifies the non-linear case $Y = X^3 + N_y$.

Evaluation. For each of the 18 combinations, we perform 100 tests. In every test, we generate 1000 new samples for X and N_y and attempt to identify the direction of the causal relationship[8] using one of the two algorithms presented in Sect. 3. Lastly, we simply calculate the fraction of successful tests and define this ratio as our accuracy measure.

5   Experimental Results

Since we used a large range for the values of i-factor, several different combinations of distributions, linear and non-linear data, we have too many results to show them all in detail in this paper. Therefore, we discuss several representative cases and provide a summary of all results. The latter shows for which values of i-factor the models are consistently identifiable. For the detailed analysis, we refer to the document [10]. Alternatively, all the results and source codes can be accessed from the relative repository[9].

5.1   Resit

We start with the analysis of Resit method. In this set of experiments, we are interested in which ranges of i-factor allow causal identifiability and how it is related to the functional model and the chosen independence estimator. Figure 1 shows the

---

[8] The true direction of the causal relationship is known as we generate synthetic data.
[9] https://gitlab.com/Shinkaiika/noise-level-causal-identification-additive-noise-models.

detailed results for the following 4 linear combinations and their nonlinear counterparts: $Y = \mathcal{N} + \mathcal{U}$, $Y = \mathcal{U} + \mathcal{N}$, $Y = \mathcal{U} + \mathcal{L}$, and $Y = \mathcal{L} + \mathcal{L}$. The y-axis shows the accuracy of causal discovery ($\frac{\#\text{successful tests}}{100}$), and the x-axis corresponds to i-factor. Different colors encode 12 estimators used in this work. The value of accuracy close to 0.5 means that Resit outputs the correct causal direction in only 50% of the tests thus indicating **unidentifiability.** The values close to 1 signify very good/consistent **identifiability**. In the following text, we analyze the results for individual models.

Figure 1a shows the linear model $Y = \mathcal{N} + \mathcal{U}$. We can see, that all estimators reach an accuracy close to 100% inside the interval $i \in [0.8; 5]$. However, for smaller or larger i-factors the accuracy of all estimators start to drop until they reach unidentifiability (~ 0.5). Not all estimators perform the same. For example, HISC with Incomplete Cholesky decomposition performs worse for decreasing i-factors compared to all other estimators. SH_SPACING_V performs the best among all estimators for this linear model. Figure 1b shows the non-linear model $Y = \mathcal{N}^3 + \mathcal{U}$. The non-linear version shows much better results. With $i \in [0.2; 100]$, we have accuracy close to 100% for all estimators. Only a few estimators drop towards unidentifiability for $i < 0.2$.

Figure 1c shows the linear model $Y = \mathcal{U} + \mathcal{N}$. For $i \in [0.1; 1]$ this model is identifiable. However, for larger values of i-factor, the accuracy of many estimators drop quickly. In this range, SH_SPACING_V remains above 90%, most other estimators drop between 60% and 80% but HSIC_IC and HSIC_IC2 drop to 50% accuracy demonstrating complete unidentifiability. Figure 1d shows the results for the non-linear version of this model. For $i \leq 1$, all estimators remain above 90% accuracy, with the exceptions now being HSIC_IC and HSIC_IC2. For i-factors larger than 1, estimators behave differently. SH_KNN, SH_KNN_2, SH_KNN_3, DISTCOV, DISCORR and HOEFFDING remain above 90% accuracy up to $i = 100$. SH_MAXENT1 remains between 80% and 90%, HSIC and SH_MAXENT2 between 60% and 80%, and HSIC_IC and HSIC_IC2 become unidentifiable.

Figure 1e shows the linear case $Y = \mathcal{U} + \mathcal{L}$ and Fig. 1f shows the non-linear case $Y = \mathcal{U}^3 + \mathcal{L}$. The demonstrated results are quite similar to the two cases discussed above. This indicates that models with the same type of distribution for X behave similarly.

Figure 1g shows the linear case $Y = \mathcal{L} + \mathcal{L}$. For $i \in [0.1; 10]$ most estimators are above 90%, except SH_KNN, SH_KNN_2 and SH_KNN_3 which are above 90% for $i \in [0.4; 2]$. For larger values of i-factor, all estimators drop quickly to unidentifiability. Finally, Fig. 1h shows the non-linear case $Y = \mathcal{L}^3 + \mathcal{L}$. Similarly to the model $Y = \mathcal{N}^3 + \mathcal{U}$ presented in Fig. 1b, this model demonstrates that non-linearity generally helps in identifying causal relationships. For $i \in [0.15; 100]$ all estimators are above 90% accuracy, often reaching 100%.

The experimental results for Resit with linear and non-linear models are summarized in Tables 1 and 2 respectively. The rows correspond to different estimators, and columns correspond to structural equation models. The values in the cells show

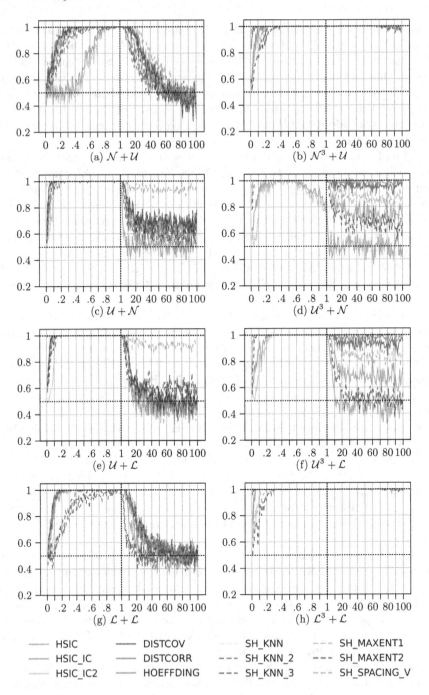

Fig. 1. Several selected detailed results for Resit. *x-axis shows the values of i-factor and y-axis shows the accuracy of causal identification.*

Table 1. Summary for Resit with linear models. The numbers reflect the ranges of i-factor that allow identifiability with accuracy around or above 90%.

Equation	$\mathcal{N}+\mathcal{N}$	$\mathcal{N}+\mathcal{U}$	$\mathcal{N}+\mathcal{L}$	$\mathcal{U}+\mathcal{N}$	$\mathcal{U}+\mathcal{U}$	$\mathcal{U}+\mathcal{L}$	$\mathcal{L}+\mathcal{N}$	$\mathcal{L}+\mathcal{U}$	$\mathcal{L}+\mathcal{L}$
HSIC		0.17–18	0.13–8	0.05–6	0.06–16	0.04–7	0.1–7	0.12–23	0.1–13
HSIC_IC		0.65–26	0.31–7	0.04–3	0.06–15	0.04–5	0.1–4	0.14–26	0.1–8
HSIC_IC2		0.7–26	0.33–7	0.1–3	0.14–15	0.11–5	0.1–4	0.14–26	0.12–8
DISTCOV		0.16–23	0.13–7	0.04–7	0.05–21	0.04–10	0.1–7	0.1–25	0.08–15
DISTCORR		0.16–23	0.13–7	0.04–7	0.05–21	0.04–10	0.1–7	0.1–25	0.08–15
HOEFFDING		0.16–25	0.13–8	0.04–7	0.05–21	0.04–8	0.1–7	0.1–25	0.1–10
SH_KNN		0.32–12	0.76–1	0.08–4	0.07–12	0.09–4	0.61–1	0.27–12	0.37–3
SH_KNN_2		0.32–12	0.76–1	0.08–4	0.07–12	0.09–4	0.61–1	0.27–12	0.37–3
SH_KNN_3		0.24–12	0.51–1	0.05–5	0.07–14	0.05–5	0.37–3	0.21–15	0.32–4
SH_MAXENT1		0.23–12	0.12–10	0.06–4	0.1–12	0.04–8	0.07–13	0.11–24	0.07–17
SH_MAXENT2		0.15–22	0.13–7	0.03–7	0.05–17	0.04–8	0.1–7	0.11–23	0.1–13
SH_SPACING_V		0.13–33	0.17–5	0.01–100	0.03–40	0.01–100	0.14–6	0.11–33	0.09–13

Table 2. Summary for Resit with non-linear data. The numbers reflect the ranges of i-factor that allow identifiability with accuracy around or above 90%.

Equation	$\mathcal{N}^3+\mathcal{N}$	$\mathcal{N}^3+\mathcal{U}$	$\mathcal{N}^3+\mathcal{L}$	$\mathcal{U}^3+\mathcal{N}$	$\mathcal{U}^3+\mathcal{U}$	$\mathcal{U}^3+\mathcal{L}$	$\mathcal{L}^3+\mathcal{N}$	$\mathcal{L}^3+\mathcal{U}$	$\mathcal{L}^3+\mathcal{L}$
HSIC	0.04–100	0.08–100	0.04–100	0.02–6	0.03–16	0.03–7	0.02–100	0.04–100	0.02–100
HSIC_IC	0.04–83	0.06–100	0.04–70	0.1–0.92	0.14–13	0.1–4	0.03–100	0.05–100	0.03–100
HSIC_IC2	0.08–83	0.08–100	0.09–70	0.12–0.91	0.17–13	0.17–4	0.7–100	0.07–100	0.09–100
DISTCOV	0.02–100	0.02–100	0.02–100	0.01–100	0.01–100	0.01–100	0.01–100	0.01–100	0.01–100
DISTCORR	0.02–100	0.02–100	0.02–100	0.01–100	0.01–100	0.01–100	0.01–100	0.01–100	0.01–100
HOEFFDING	0.01–100	0.01–100	0.01–100	0.01–100	0.01–100	0.01–100	0.01–100	0.01–100	0.01–100
SH_KNN	0.01–100	0.01–100	0.01–100	0.01–100	0.01–100	0.01–100	0.01–100	0.01–100	0.01–100
SH_KNN_2	0.01–100	0.01–100	0.01–100	0.01–100	0.01–100	0.01–100	0.01–100	0.01–100	0.01–100
SH_KNN_3	0.01–100	0.01–100	0.01–100	0.01–100	0.01–100	0.01–100	0.01–100	0.01–100	0.01–100
SH_MAXENT1	0.05–100	0.06–100	0.05–100	0.01–100	0.02–90	0.01–88	0.1–100	0.17–100	0.1–100
SH_MAXENT2	0.11–98	0.16–100	0.1–100	0.03–4	0.04–12	0.04–5	0.14–100	0.15–100	0.15–100
SH_SPACING_V	0.01–100	0.01–100	0.01–100	0.01–100	0.01–100	0.01–100	0.01–100	0.01–100	0.01–100

on what range of i a particular estimator *can* reach over 90% accuracy. Estimators have some variance in the results and thus on some intervals they fall below 90% accuracy. The limits in the cells were chosen as follows: the lower limit designates where an estimator reaches 90% or higher for the first time, and the upper limit designates for which value of i it was observed for the last time. In between, most of the time estimators remain above 90% or rarely fall below, but never below 80% accuracy. An empty cell means that the corresponding estimator never resulted in accuracy $\geq$90%.

As the results show, different noise levels do have an impact on the identifiability performance of Resit. In general, the linear equation models are more fragile than the non-linear ones. This is explained by the fact that the non-linear relationships tend to break the symmetry between the variables easier, see [4]. The only structural equation which always remains unidentifiable is $Y = \mathcal{N}+\mathcal{N}$, see [24].

For all other cases, all estimators reach an accuracy of over 90% for some values of i-factor. For example, all estimators perform perfectly when the noise level of the X term is comparable to the noise level of the corresponding noise term (N_y), that is $i = 1$. For other values of i, there are differences between linear and non-linear equations. Generally, the accuracy for linear cases drops if $i > 7$. However, most non-linear cases retain accuracy over 90% for much larger values of i-factor, even up to 100. Similar results are observed for the decreasing i-factors.

We can also observe differences between estimators in terms of accuracy. For example, HSIC is overall the best performing independence estimator while HSIC_IC and HSIC_IC_2 perform the worst. SH_SPACING_V is the best performing entropy estimator while SH_MAXENT1 and SH_MAXENT2 perform the worst. Some estimators show better performance for particular structural causal models, for example, SH_SPACING_V for $Y = \mathcal{U} + \mathcal{N}$; others are particularly unsuitable for some structural equations, for example, HSIC_IC and HSIC_IC2 for $Y = \mathcal{N} + \mathcal{U}$. For all non-linear equation models, SH_SPACING_V and the three Shannon kNN estimators result in accuracy close to 100% for all values of i. SH_SPACING_V also keeps its good performance in the case of linear equation models. As for independence measures, HSIC, DISTCOV, DISTCORR, and HOEFFDING perform quite similarly and are good overall. Note again, that these results are based on the assumption that in our bivariate structure only one direction of the causal relationship is present, namely $X \rightarrow Y$. Without this assumption, we cannot compare the estimates directly but rather need to compare the estimate to a derived p-value given some significance level α.

5.2   Uncertainty Scoring

Figure 2 shows the results for the Uncertainty Scoring algorithm. Recall that for these experiments we use only one estimator, the Fisher's conditional independence test. Therefore, we use different colors and styles of lines to encode structural equation models. The colours of the lines correspond to the distribution type of the noise variable N_y with the following coding: blue for $N_y \sim \mathcal{N}$, green for $N_y \sim \mathcal{U}$, and red for $N_y \sim \mathcal{L}$. The type of the lines encodes the distribution type of the cause X as follows: solid line for $X \sim \mathcal{N}$, dashed line for $X \sim \mathcal{U}$, and dotted line for $X \sim \mathcal{L}$. As in the previous experiment, the x-axis shows the values of i-factor and the y-axis shows the accuracy of causal identification. However, the results should be interpreted differently. The Uncertainty Scoring method generates a set of parents for every variable. This set can be empty or can contain cause variables. Therefore, only one structure of this result is correct and thus the y-axis of the plots in Fig. 2 shows consistent identifiability at 1, and consistent unidentifiability at 0.

We proceed to the analysis of the results. First, we can notice that the linear Gaussian model $Y = \mathcal{N} + \mathcal{N}$ is now identifiable, as it was demonstrated by the authors of this method [17]. Interestingly, for this method, the linear cases perform better than the non-linear as opposed to Resit. Only the non-linear cases where the cause X is drawn from the Uniform distribution $\mathcal{U}$ show the same performance as the linear cases. This group of models demonstrates good identifiability for $i < 1$, however the accuracy drops fast for $i > 1$. The reason for accuracy degradation lies within step 2 of the method, the conditional independence test. If noise levels are significantly different, then the independence test fails to capture the correlation between the two nodes and therefore concludes that the nodes are independent (Type II Error). However, for any given i, the ordering step always performs correctly[10].

We can also notice that models with similar structures have similar performance. For example, in Fig. 2b we can clearly identify 3 groups: 1) the group of dashed lines representing models with $X \sim \mathcal{U}$ show the best performance for $i < 1$ and the worst performance for $i > 1$; 2) the group of dotted lines corresponding to models with $X \sim \mathcal{L}$ demonstrate the worst accuracy for $i < 1$ and the best accuracy for $i > 1$; finally 3) the group of solid lines that represent the models with $X \sim \mathcal{N}$ lie in the middle. A similar observation was done for Resit as well, that is the type of the distribution of the cause variable affects the accuracy of causal discovery. If we analyze the linear cases from Fig. 2a in the same way, we can notice that here the type of the distribution of the noise variable N_y probably has more impact. Indeed, the lines overlap, but they are now grouped more by colors than by line type. Again, we can observe 3 groups: 1) the group of green lines corresponding to the models with $N_y \sim \mathcal{U}$ show worse performance for $i < 1$ and better performance for $i > 1$; 2) the group of red lines representing the models with $N_y \sim \mathcal{L}$ have better performance for $i < 1$ and worse accuracy for $i > 1$; 3) and the group of blue lines corresponding to $N_y \sim \mathcal{N}$ lies in between.

The results obtained for the Uncertainty Scoring method are summarized in Table 3. Here, each row corresponds to a combination of distribution types. The second and the third columns show the results for linear or non-linear models respectively. The values inside the table are encoded in the same way as it was done for Table 1; that is they show the ranges where the method has an accuracy around or above 90%.

---

[10] A quick test in python shell, with $i = 57$, $X \sim \mathcal{L}$ and $N_y \sim \mathcal{U}$ and 100 repetitions showed that in these runs the ordering was always correct but only in 35 runs (from the 100 repetitions) the independence tests were correct.

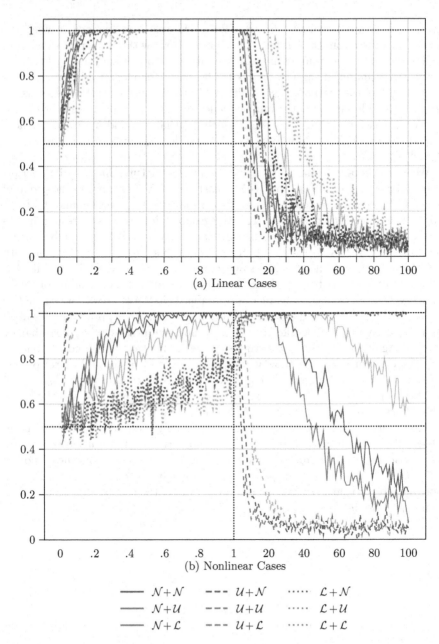

(a) Linear Cases

(b) Nonlinear Cases

$\mathcal{N}+\mathcal{N}$ $\mathcal{U}+\mathcal{N}$ $\mathcal{L}+\mathcal{N}$
$\mathcal{N}+\mathcal{U}$ $\mathcal{U}+\mathcal{U}$ $\mathcal{L}+\mathcal{U}$
$\mathcal{N}+\mathcal{L}$ $\mathcal{U}+\mathcal{L}$ $\mathcal{L}+\mathcal{L}$

Fig. 2. Results of the Uncertainty Scoring algorithm. *x-axis shows the values of i-factor and y-axis shows the accuracy of causal identification.*

Table 3. Summary for uncertainty scoring. The numbers reflect the ranges of i-factor that allow identifiability with accuracy around or above 90%.

Equation	Linear	Non-Linear
$\mathcal{N} + \mathcal{N}$	0.08–10	0.33–37
$\mathcal{N} + \mathcal{U}$	0.16–10	0.52–67
$\mathcal{N} + \mathcal{L}$	0.05–6	0.23–25
$\mathcal{U} + \mathcal{N}$	0.04–5	0.04–4
$\mathcal{U} + \mathcal{U}$	0.1–8	0.05–6
$\mathcal{U} + \mathcal{L}$	0.03–3	0.03–3
$\mathcal{L} + \mathcal{N}$	0.14–13	4–100
$\mathcal{L} + \mathcal{U}$	0.19–26	5–100
$\mathcal{L} + \mathcal{L}$	0.1–10	2–100

6   Conclusions

The results from the experiments showed that two analyzed causal discovery methods, Resit and Uncertainty Scoring, are affected by different noise scales. For significantly small noise levels in the disturbance term N_y, or significantly high noise levels, these causal discovery methods fail to capture the true causal relationship of the given structural equation model. Recall that *significantly* here depends on the model. For example, for some models, if the noise level was already twice larger then the methods failed to determine the causal direction consistently. Other models remained identifiable with 100 times higher noise levels. The range of different noise levels analyzed in this work is quite exhaustive and realistically speaking having noise levels 100 times higher than the potential cause variable is very rare. Additionally, with very high noise levels the effect of the cause variable is very likely negligible anyways. However, the discovered relationships can be useful to guide researchers in practical applications. We also observed different behavior for different distribution types (e.g., Gaussian or Uniform).

For both methods, we observed that if the variance of the noise term is smaller than that of the cause, then models remained identifiable. The opposite relationship is observed when the variance of the noise term is larger. For example, often when the standard deviation of the noise term was only half of that of the cause, the model was still identifiable. However, in several cases, if the standard deviation of the noise term was already twice larger than the standard deviation of the cause, then the model became unidentifiable. We also tested linear and non-linear models and our results show that non-linear models were still identifiable in situations where the linear models are not. For example, some non-linear models, where the noise term's variance was 100 times higher than that of the cause, were still perfectly identifiable while their linear counterparts were not.

Lastly, for Resit we used several estimators: 6 independence estimators and 6 entropy estimators. Our results show differences in terms of performance depending on which estimator is used. We observed that Hilbert-Schmidt Independence Criterion with RBF Kernel was the best independence estimator, and Shannon entropy estimator using Vasicek's spacing method was the best entropy estimator.

In our experiments, we tested only two particular methods and three different distribution types. However, similar results are expected for other methods of causal discovery with additive noise models, as their common failing point lies in the independence estimation.

Future Work. In reality, observed data does not always strictly follow a certain distribution type. As there are many different possible combinations, it would be interesting to generalize the impact of different noise levels on any distribution by using the different properties an observed distribution exhibits. Furthermore, this work does not formalize mathematically the effect of different noise levels in ANM causal discovery methods. This could be done in future work.

Acknowledgments. This work was partially supported by the European Union Horizon 2020 research programme within the project CITIES2030 "Co-creating resilient and sustainable food towards FOOD2030", grant 101000640.

Appendix

Detailed Description of Estimators

1. **HSIC**: Hilbert-Schmidt Independence Criterion with RBF Kernel[11]

$$I_{HSIC}(x, y) := ||C_{xy}||^2_{HS}$$

   where C_{xy} is the cross-covariance operator and HS the squared Hilbert-Schmidt norm.

2. **HSIC_IC**: Hilbert-Schmidt Independence Criterion using incomplete Cholesky decomposition (low rank decomposition of the Gram matrices, which permits an accurate approximation to HSIC as long as the kernel has a fast decaying spectrum) which has $\eta = 1 * 10^{-6}$ precision in the incomplete cholesky decomposition.

3. **HSIC_IC2**: Same as HSIC_IC but with $\eta = 1 * 10^{-2}$.

4. **DISTCOV**: Distance covariance estimator using pairwise distances. This is simply the L^2_w norm of the characteristic functions φ_{12} and $\varphi_1\varphi_2$ of input x, y:

$$\varphi_{12}(u^1, u^2) = \mathbb{E}[e^{i\langle u^1, x\rangle + i\langle u^2, y\rangle}],$$

$$\varphi_1(u^1) = \mathbb{E}[e^{i\langle u^1, x\rangle}],$$

$$\varphi_2(u^2) = \mathbb{E}[e^{i\langle u^2, y\rangle}].$$

With $i = \sqrt{-1}$, $\langle \cdot, \cdot \rangle$ the standard Euclidean inner product and $\mathbb{E}$ the expectation. Finally, we have:

$$I_{dCov}(x, y) = ||\varphi_{12} - \varphi_1\varphi_2||_{L^2_w}$$

---

[11] Source: https://github.com/amber0309/HSIC.

5. **DISTCORR**: Distance correlation estimator using pairwise distances. It is simply the standardized version of the distance covariance:

$$I_{dCor}(x, y) = \begin{cases} \frac{I_{dCov}(x,y)}{\sqrt{I_{dVar}(x,x)I_{dVar}(y,y)}}, & \text{if } I_{dVar}(x, x)I_{dVar}(y, y) > 0 \\ 0, & \text{otherwise,} \end{cases}$$

with

$$I_{dVar}(x, x) = ||\varphi_{11} - \varphi_1\varphi_1||_{L^2_w}, \quad I_{dVar}(y, y) = ||\varphi_{22} - \varphi_2\varphi_2||_{L^2_w}$$

(see characteristic functions under 4. DISTCOV)

6. **HOEFFDING**: Hoeffding's Phi

$$I_\Phi(x, y) = I_\Phi(C) = \left(h_2(d) \int_{[0,1]^d} [C(\boldsymbol{u}) - \Pi(\boldsymbol{u})]^2 d\boldsymbol{u} \right)^{\frac{1}{2}}$$

with C standing for the copula of the input and Π standing for the product copula.

7. **SH_KNN**: Shannon differential entropy estimator using kNNs (k-nearest neighbors)

$$H(\boldsymbol{Y}_{1:T}) = log(T - 1) - \psi(k) + log(V_d) + \frac{d}{T} \sum_{t=1}^{T} log(\rho_k(t))$$

with T standing for the number of samples, $\rho_k(t)$ - the Euclidean distance of the kth nearest neighbour of $\boldsymbol{y}_t$ in the sample $\boldsymbol{Y}_{1:T} \backslash \{\boldsymbol{y}_t\}$ and $V \subseteq \mathbb{R}^d$ a finite set.

8. **SH_KNN_2**: Same as SH_KNN but using kd-tree for quick nearest-neighbour lookup

9. **SH_KNN_3**: Same as SH_KNN but with $k = 5$

10. **SH_MAXENT1**: Maximum entropy distribution-based Shannon entropy estimator

$$H(\boldsymbol{Y}_{1:T}) = H(n) - \left[k_1 \left(\frac{1}{T} \sum_{t=1}^{T} G_1(y'_t) \right)^2 + k_2 \left(\frac{1}{T} \sum_{t=1}^{T} G_2(y'_t) - \sqrt{\frac{2}{\pi}} \right)^2 \right] + log(\hat{\sigma}),$$

with

$$\hat{\sigma} = \hat{\sigma}(\boldsymbol{Y}_{1:T}) = \sqrt{\frac{1}{T-1} \sum_{t=1}^{T} (y_t)^2},$$

$$y'_t = \frac{y_t}{\hat{\sigma}}, (t = 1, \ldots, T)$$

$$G_1(z) = ze^{\frac{-z^2}{2}},$$

$$G_2(z) = |z|,$$

$$k_1 = \frac{36}{8\sqrt{3} - 9},$$

$$k_2 = \frac{1}{2 - \frac{6}{\pi}},$$

11. **SH_MAXENT2**: Maximum entropy distribution-based Shannon entropy estimator, same as SH_MAXENT1 with the following changes:

$$G_2(z) = e^{\frac{-z^2}{2}},$$

$$k_2 = \frac{24}{16\sqrt{3} - 27},$$

12. **SH_SPACING_V**: Shannon entropy estimator using Vasicek's spacing method.

$$H(\mathbf{Y}_{1:T}) = \frac{1}{T} \sum_{t}^{T} = log\left(\frac{T}{2m}[y_{(t+m)} - y_{(t-m)}]\right)$$

with T number of samples, the convention that $y_{(t)} := y_{(1)}$ if $t - m < 1$ and $y_{(t)} := y_{(T)}$ if $t + m > T$ and $m = \lfloor\sqrt{T}\rfloor$.

References

1. Chen, W., Drton, M., Wang, Y.S.: On causal discovery with an equal-variance assumption. Biometrika **106**(4), 973–980 (2019)
2. Daniusis, P., et al.: Inferring deterministic causal relations (2012). http://arxiv.org/abs/1203.3475
3. Friedman, N., Nachman, I.: Gaussian process networks. CoRR abs/1301.3857 (2013). http://arxiv.org/abs/1301.3857
4. Hoyer, P., Janzing, D., Mooij, J.M., Peters, J., Schölkopf, B.: Nonlinear causal discovery with additive noise models. Adv. Neural. Inf. Process. Syst. **21**, 689–696 (2009)
5. Hyvärinen, A., Smith, S.M.: Pairwise likelihood ratios for estimation of non-gaussian structural equation models. J. Mach. Learn. Res. **14**, 111–152 (2013)
6. Janzing, D., Hoyer, P.O., Schoelkopf, B.: Telling cause from effect based on high-dimensional observations (2009). http://arxiv.org/abs/0909.4386
7. Janzing, D., et al.: Information-geometric approach to inferring causal directions. Artif. Intell. **182**, 1–31 (2012)
8. Judea, P.: Causality: Models, Reasoning, and Inference. Cambridge University Press (2000). ISBN 0 521(77362)
9. Kano, Y., Shimizu, S.: Causal inference using nonnormality. In: Proceedings of the International Symposium on Science of Modeling, the 30th Anniversary of the Information Criterion, pp. 261–270 (2003)
10. Kap, B.: The effect of noise level on causal identification with additive noise models (2021). https://arxiv.org/abs/2108.11320
11. Kohavi, R., Longbotham, R.: Online controlled experiments and A/B testing. Encyclopedia Mach. Learn. Data Mining **7**(8), 922–929 (2017)

12. Kpotufe, S., Sgouritsa, E., Janzing, D., Schölkopf, B.: Consistency of causal inference under the additive noise model. In: International Conference on Machine Learning, pp. 478–486. PMLR (2014)
13. Mooij, J., Janzing, D., Peters, J., Schölkopf, B.: Regression by dependence minimization and its application to causal inference in additive noise models. In: Proceedings of the 26th Annual International Conference on Machine Learning, pp. 745–752 (2009)
14. Mooij, J.M., Janzing, D., Heskes, T., Schölkopf, B.: On causal discovery with cyclic additive noise models. In: Proceedings of the 24th International Conference on Neural Information Processing Systems, pp. 639–647 (2011)
15. Mooij, J.M., Peters, J., Janzing, D., Zscheischler, J., Schölkopf, B.: Distinguishing cause from effect using observational data: methods and benchmarks. J. Mach. Learn. Res. $17(1)$, 1103–1204 (2016)
16. Nowzohour, C., Bühlmann, P.: Score-based causal learning in additive noise models. Statistics $50(3)$, 471–485 (2016)
17. Park, G.: Identifiability of additive noise models using conditional variances. J. Mach. Learn. Res. $21(75)$, 1–34 (2020)
18. Park, G., Kim, Y.: Identifiability of gaussian structural equation models with homogeneous and heterogeneous error variances (2019). http://arxiv.org/abs/1901.10134
19. Peters, J., Bühlmann, P.: Identifiability of Gaussian structural equation models with equal error variances. Biometrika $101(1)$, 219–228 (2013). https://doi.org/10.1093/biomet/ast043
20. Peters, J., Mooij, J., Janzing, D., Schölkopf, B.: Causal discovery with continuous additive noise models. J. Mach. Learn. Res. $15(1)$, 2009–2053 (2014)
21. Rebane, G., Pearl, J.: The recovery of causal poly-trees from statistical data. CoRR abs/1304.2736 (2013). http://arxiv.org/abs/1304.2736
22. Sgouritsa, E., Janzing, D., Hennig, P., Schölkopf, B.: Inference of cause and effect with unsupervised inverse regression. In: Artificial Intelligence and Statistics, pp. 847–855. PMLR (2015)
23. Shimizu, S.: LiNGAM: non-gaussian methods for estimating causal structures. Behaviormetrika $41(1)$, 65–98 (2014)
24. Shimizu, S., Hoyer, P.O., Hyvärinen, A., Kerminen, A., Jordan, M.: A linear non-gaussian acyclic model for causal discovery. J. Mach. Learn. Res. $7(10)$, 2003–2030 (2006)
25. Shimizu, S., Hyvarinen, A., Kawahara, Y.: A direct method for estimating a causal ordering in a linear non-gaussian acyclic model (2014). http://arxiv.org/abs/1408.2038
26. Silva, R., Scheines, R., Glymour, C., Spirtes, P., Chickering, D.M.: Learning the structure of linear latent variable models. J. Mach. Learn. Res. $7(2)$, 191–246 (2006)
27. Spirtes, P., Glymour, C., Scheines, R.: Causation, Prediction, and Search, vol. 81. Springer, New York (2012). https://doi.org/10.1007/978-1-4612-2748-9
28. Stegle, O., Janzing, D., Zhang, K., Mooij, J.M., Schölkopf, B.: Probabilistic latent variable models for distinguishing between cause and effect. Adv. Neural. Inf. Process. Syst. 23, 1687–1695 (2010)
29. Sun, X., Janzing, D., Schölkopf, B.: Causal inference by choosing graphs with most plausible Markov kernels. In: Ninth International Symposium on Artificial Intelligence and Mathematics (AIMath 2006), pp. 1–11 (2006)
30. Sun, X., Janzing, D., Schölkopf, B.: Causal reasoning by evaluating the complexity of conditional densities with kernel methods. Neurocomputing $71(7$–$9)$, 1248–1256 (2008)

31. Szabó, Z.: Information theoretical estimators toolbox. J. Mach. Learn. Res. **15**, 283–287 (2014)

32. Thase, M.E., Parikh, S.V., et al.: Impact of pharmacogenomics on clinical outcomes for patients taking medications with gene-drug interactions in a randomized controlled trial. J. Clin. Psychiatry **80**(6), 19m12910 (2019)

33. Wright, S.: Correlation and causation. J. Agric. Res. **20**, 557–580 (1921)

34. Young, S.W.: Improving library user experience with A/B testing: principles and process. Weave J. Libr. User Exp. **1**(1) (2014)

35. Zhang, K., Hyvarinen, A.: On the identifiability of the post-nonlinear causal model (2012). http://arxiv.org/abs/1205.2599

A Bayesian Framework for Evaluating Evolutionary Art

Augustijn de Boer$^{(\boxtimes)}$, Ron Hommelsheim , and David Leeftink

Radboud University Nijmegen, Nijmegen, The Netherlands

Abstract. Recent advances in computer-generated art (CGA) have led to a diverse state of generative art models, however, how to evaluate the works produced by these methods remains an open question, due to the subjective nature of the domain. In this work, we propose a framework for evaluating evolutionary art using a Bayesian approach.

The framework provides a method to analyse the results of a number of 'art Turing tests' (ATTs) with a Bayesian model comparison, to assess the influence the evolutionary process has on the degree to which computer-generated images are distinguishable from human generated images.

The cases where the human- and computer-generated art can and can not be distinguished are represented by the null hypothesis and the alternative hypothesis, respectively. We demonstrate the framework using Interactive Evolutionary Computation (IEC) to evolve images with a function-tree representation. These images are then used in an ATT in which $n = 11$ subjects participated. The results indicate a weak preference for the alternative hypothesis, showing that the human- and computer-generated images can not reliably be distinguished. We sketch future applications of the framework, such as evolving cellular automata or combining the framework with deep learning approaches to CGA. The framework is available as an open-source code base, and can be used by researchers and practitioners interested in evaluating their methods for generating evolutionary artworks.

Keywords: Computational creativity · Evolutionary computation · Interactive AI methods and applications · Bayesian statistics · Genetic programming

1 Introduction

Since the infancy of computers, mathematicians, programmers and eventually artists have been intrigued by the new ways in which art could be created. Cellular automata have been used to either create or modify images [11], many different types of fractals can be generated by computers easily [24], developments in deep learning in the last decade has allowed artists to create art, e.g., by using style transfer [10] and Generative Adversarial Networks [9], genetic

---

A. de Boer, R. Hommelsheim and D. Leeftink—Equal contributions.

L. A. Leiva et al. (Eds.): BNAIC/Benelearn 2021, CCIS 1530, pp. 141–152, 2022.
https://doi.org/10.1007/978-3-030-93842-0_8

algorithms can be utilized to create art by the iterative process of "survival of the fittest" [21], and the list goes on.

Here, we will focus on applying Evolutionary Algorithms for generating art. Evolutionary Algorithms are loosely inspired by the Darwinian theory of evolution by natural selection, which despite of its relative simplicity, describes all life in its enormous complexity. The fittest individuals of a population reproduce often, passing on their genes. The genes mutate and recombine, subsequently producing new individuals. This process has been abstracted and modified many times to solve problems such as parameter estimation or agent-based modeling. It has also been simulated to better understand the actual biological mechanism [18]. Furthermore, the generation of art by EAs has been explored by many artists and researchers alike in a variety of different approaches, this is commonly called Evolutionary Art (EArt) [21].

Section 2 provides a short introduction into evolutionary art, and the way it is currently evaluated. In Sect. 3, we propose a framework for evaluating EArt using a Bayesian approach. In Sect. 4 we demonstrate this framework by applying it to a specific case, in which a weak preference for the alternative hypothesis is found. We briefly discuss these results in Sect. 4.3. The results of a short questionnaire about the experience of working with the framework are discussed in Sect. 5, and we sketch future directions and applications in Sect. 7.

2 Background

Loosely inspired by Darwinian evolutionary systems, Evolutionary Algorithms (EAs) can be broken down to a few essential components [2,12]: an initialization procedure; a fitness function; a selection procedure; a crossover procedure; and a mutation procedure.

The EA cycle starts by initializing a population of individuals. These individuals are all evaluated using the fitness function, after which a number of them is selected. That selection of individuals is then crossed over and mutated to form a new population. This is repeated until some termination criterion is met.

Because the fitness function that is used is unrestricted, EAs allow human feedback as well as computer feedback to be used for evolution. When human feedback is used as a fitness function in EAs, we call this Interactive Evolutionary Computation (IEC). The dependency of the IEC framework on human evaluation as a fitness function is considered one of its core strengths. Nonetheless, the amount of control a user has over the process is still very limited; the selection, crossover, and mutation procedures are governed by pseudo-randomness.

2.1 Evaluating Computer-Generated Art

The Turing test (TT) can be used to assess whether a computer is capable of exhibiting (human) intelligent behavior [22,23]. In the TT, a subject has to distinguish a human from a computer by only communicating to them through a text channel. If the computer is indistinguishable from the human, it passes the

Turing test. Following that line of thought, to assess whether a system is creative, one could devise a Turing test specifically for art, or an 'Art Turing test' (ATT), as introduced by Boden [3]. In an ATT, a subject has to evaluate two pieces of art, one created by a computer, and one created by a human, and decide which one of them was created by a human. This way of evaluating art may seem fair at first, but Pease et al. [19] pose some objections. Mainly, their point is that the ATT does not allow the subject to interact with the art, as opposed to the classical TT, where the subject can interact with the human and the computer. Much information about the art that could influence the subject can not be taken into account this way. Similarly, the ATT does not take into account framing information. Another argument they pose is that the ATT encourages imitation, and not creativity. Lamb et al. [16] do acknowledge that the ATT is only valid in those cases where the CGA is specifically designed to imitate human art. In this paper we use an ATT to compare CGA and human art that were both made with the same method, thereby satisfying the constraints set by Lamb et al. To the best of our knowledge, we are the first to evaluate evolutionary art using the methods described here.

3   The Bayesian Framework

We propose to evaluate evolutionary art by doing a Bayesian Model Comparison (BMC) on results from an art Turing test. Here we provide an explanation of the framework and the methods used, as well as a.

3.1   Art Turing Test

We use an ATT to determine whether the evolutionary process has an influence on the degree to which the human generated images can be distinguished from computer-generated images by humans. To this end, three pools of images need to be generated by EAs.

- One pool is generated by letting a human act as a fitness function for multiple sessions of 10 generations. After the 10th generation, all images in the population are added to the pool of so-called 'human-generated' images. Note that although these images are called 'human-generated', the influence the human has on the generative process is limited. Images from this pool are indicated with h_{10}.
- One pool of computer generated images is created in the same way, but instead of using the human evaluation, we use an automatic fitness function. Images from this pool are indicated with c_{10}.
- The other pool of computer-generated images is created from purely random initial trees, i.e., they are evolved to generation 1. Images from this pool are indicated with c_1.

During the ATT, the user is to decide which of two presented images is human-generated. The pair of presented images can be one of two possible combinations, either a (h_{10}, c_{10}) pair, or a (h_{10}, c_1) pair, both being equally likely. The subject does not know which is being presented, and is not aware that this difference between the cases exists. Naturally, the images within a pair are randomly ordered when they are presented to the user.

3.2   Bayesian Model Comparison

Null Hypothesis H_0. The probability with which a participant answers correctly on the Turing test is fixed and does not depend on whether the decision was on a (h_{10}, c_1) pair or a (h_{10}, c_{10}) pair. We let z_i be 1 if the answer on the i'th Turing test was correct, and 0 if it was incorrect. We can express this in a graphical model $\mathcal{M}_0$, as shown in Fig. 1:

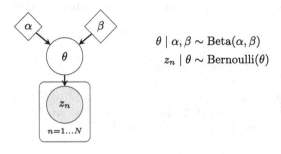

$$\theta \mid \alpha, \beta \sim \text{Beta}(\alpha, \beta)$$
$$z_n \mid \theta \sim \text{Bernoulli}(\theta)$$

Fig. 1. Graphical model $\mathcal{M}_0$ for H_0

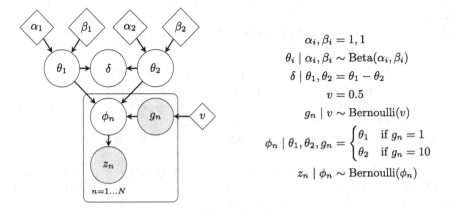

$$\alpha_i, \beta_i = 1, 1$$
$$\theta_i \mid \alpha_i, \beta_i \sim \text{Beta}(\alpha_i, \beta_i)$$
$$\delta \mid \theta_1, \theta_2 = \theta_1 - \theta_2$$
$$v = 0.5$$
$$g_n \mid v \sim \text{Bernoulli}(v)$$
$$\phi_n \mid \theta_1, \theta_2, g_n = \begin{cases} \theta_1 & \text{if } g_n = 1 \\ \theta_2 & \text{if } g_n = 10 \end{cases}$$
$$z_n \mid \phi_n \sim \text{Bernoulli}(\phi_n)$$

Fig. 2. Graphical model $\mathcal{M}_1$ for H_1

Alternative Hypothesis H_1. The probability with which a participant answers correctly on the Turing test depends on whether the decision was on a (h_{10}, c_1)

pair or (h_{10}, c_{10}) pair. The graphical model corresponding to this hypothesis can be found in Fig. 2. The variables θ_1 and θ_2 are used for each of the two possible pairs of images. In this graphical representation, if the $i'th$ decision was made on a (h_{10}, c_j) pair, we indicate that with $g_i = j$.

The Bayes Factor. The Bayes Factor (BF) was used as a measure to compare models $\mathcal{M}_0$ and $\mathcal{M}_1$. The BF is the ratio of the marginal likelihoods of the two models: $B_{10} = \frac{p(Z|\mathcal{M}_1)}{p(Z|\mathcal{M}_0)}$. To estimate the BF one can construct an hierarchical Bayesian model in which the selection for model $\mathcal{M}_0$ or $\mathcal{M}_1$ is part of the sampling process, and governed by a categorical distribution. The ratio of the frequency that each model was selected can be used as an estimate for the BF. The BF acquired this way is then interpreted according to, for example, Kass et al. [13]. Furthermore, the variable δ expresses the difference between the two cases in $\mathcal{M}_1$, in terms of how easy it was to distinguish the h_{10} images from the c_1 or c_{10} images.

4   Application

In this section we will apply our framework to a case where images are evolved by Genetic Programming. First we will provide an explanation of Genetic Programming and the type of representation that was used, then we discuss the fitness function that we propose to generate art by mimicking human evaluation. Lastly, we will analyze the results of the ATTs and briefly discuss those results.

4.1   Tree Representation

A Genetic Algorithm (GA) is a type of EA where a distinction is made between the genotype and phenotype of an individual [12]. The genotype represents the underlying structure by which a potential solution is represented. Commonly used representations for the genotype are character strings, trees, or real-valued vectors. The phenotype represents the physical traits of individuals. This distinction is central to the field of evolutionary computation, as it allows for dynamical change of the population via cross-over and mutation between genotypes of the population members. Genetic Programming (GP) [15] is a specific type of GA where the phenotype is a computer program, or—as in our demonstration—a mathematical function.

Whereas EAs such as GA and Evolution Strategies (ES) commonly use linear structures (such as bit strings and real-valued vectors) for the genotype, one can alternatively construct a non-linear genotype using a tree representation [1,12]. In this demonstration, the genotype is a tree representation (TR), and the phenotype is a mathematical function, which is applied to a grid of pixels to generate an RGB image. Here one could say that the generated image is a plot of the phenotype, or that the image is the phenotype itself. A TR is a recursive structure consisting of terminal and non-terminal nodes. Terminal nodes are either variables or constants, whereas non-terminal nodes are n-ary functions.

Crossover between two trees happens with probability p_c, by exchanging a random node in the first tree with a random node in the second tree. The children of the exchanged nodes are also moved to the other tree, so we call it a transplantation. Mutation in trees normally happens with probability p_m, by randomly changing the function of a function node, or replacing a leaf node with a new structure. We found that we already achieved pleasing results without mutation, and in literature it is stated that very low mutation rates are suitable for trees [14], so we decided to not apply mutation. In our tree evolution runs, we always set p_m to 0.

We experimented with several versions of tree representations to create RGB images. Our first representation maps every point in a 2D grid to a single numeric value, and then maps each numeric value to a RGB value using a color gradient. Our second representation creates a separate tree for each 2D color channel, and normalizes each layer separately to lay within the correct interval $[0, 255]$. These layers are then stacked to create an RGB image. Our third representation is a single tree which can map 3D coordinates to a numeric value. Like the second version, the color channels are normalized individually.

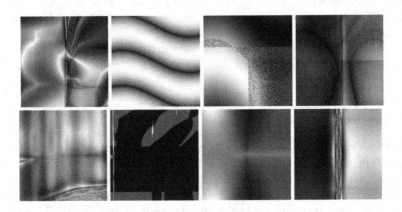

Fig. 3. Examples of tree representation-based images from c_{10}

An excellent illustrated overview of the crossover and mutation methods in these tree representations can be found on Ashley Mills' website [1].

4.2   The Mathematical Fitness Function

In this section we present ideas that went into designing the fitness function that the computer uses to evaluate the images will be presented. We hypothesise that if presented with a small population—say a population consisting of 9 individuals—a person would evaluate the individuals by the characteristics that make them stand out from the other individuals in the population. Following this line of thought, one could define a human-inspired mathematical fitness function F for an individual p, as the mean distance of individual p to each of the other individuals in the population P:

$$F_D(p) = \frac{1}{|P| - 1} \sum_{p' \in P, p' \neq p} D(p, p') \tag{1}$$

Any distance metric can be used, for example the Euclidean distance. Using the Euclidean distance does not yield very interesting images, however. Suppose in a population we have one entirely white image, and one entirely black image. The Euclidean distance if evaluated in the RGB space is maximized, since the RGB components of white are (255, 255, 255) and the RGB components of black are (0, 0, 0). As a result, these images will be assigned a high fitness, even though they are (subjectively) very uninteresting. A more interesting approach would be to use the variance of the difference of the pixel values as a distance function. Using the example of the entirely white and entirely black image again, the distance between these two images will now be 0; the difference between every pair of white and black pixels is the same. This approach yielded more interesting images, see Eq. 2.

$$D_{\text{Var}}(p, p') = \text{Var}(p - p') \tag{2}$$

The pool of c_{10} individuals used in the experiment was evolved using the function described in Eq. 1 with the distance measure from Eq. 2 as a fitness function. The pool of c_1 individuals was generated by simply randomly initializing trees. The pool of h_{10} individuals was evolved by letting a human act as the fitness function by rating the images produced by them. Starting from the root node, working downward, each node is uniformly sampled from either the binary or unary functions, or the leaf nodes. Within each category, the specific selection is again sampled uniformly from $\{+, -, \times, \div, \text{power}, \min, \max\}$, $\{\sin, \cos, \tan, \text{abs}, \sqrt{\ }\}$, and $\{x, y, z, 0.618\}$, respectively.

4.3   Results and Analysis

The h_{10} pool used here was generated by the authors, who do not have a formal art education. The experiment was done with $n = 11$ participants, each of which performed 20 ATTs, resulting in 220 binary (correct/incorrect) results. The age of the participants ranged between 20 and 27, and none of them had a formal art education. The average interaction time per participant was around 15 minutes. Of the 220 ATTs, 97 were answered correctly, about 44%. The results of the ATTs on the sub-classes are listed in Table 1.

Table 1. Results of the ATTs

	All	c_1	c_{10}
Total	220	94	126
# Correct	97	38	59
% Correct	44%	40%	47%

Table 2. Relative sampling frequencies f_s for each model

Model	rank	f_s
$\mathcal{M}_0$	1	0.468
$\mathcal{M}_1$	0	0.532

After running two Markov chains of 5000 samples for each model, our samplers over the model parameters converged nicely to some interesting distributions, which can be seen in Fig. 4. It is interesting to see that θ_1 peaks at a lower value than θ_2. This seems to imply that participants have a lower chance of answering the ATT correctly if the computer generated image is completely random, and not evolved using the automatic fitness function.

It would be premature to say that the use of the automatic fitness function actually makes the art look *less* human-like, but that is what the numbers seem to indicate. Still, the peak of θ_2 is also lower than 0.5, meaning that the human-generated images are often correctly identified.

Model $\mathcal{M}_0$ was sampled in 46.8% of the cases during the BMC. Model $\mathcal{M}_1$ was sampled in the remaining 53.2% of the cases (see Table 2), resulting in an estimated Bayes factor of 1.14. According to Kass et al. [13], this is weak support for the alternative hypothesis.

Although the BMC showed weak prefer-

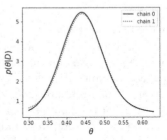

(a) θ, governing $\mathcal{M}_0$, was estimated to have a mode below 0.5.

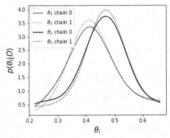

(b) θ_1 was estimated to have a lower mode than θ_2.

Fig. 4. Density estimates

ence for the alternative hypothesis, there is too little evidence to reject H_0. We can not conclude that images generated by function trees evolved using the automatic fitness function are perceived as more human-like than images generated by random function trees. However, the number of participants in our experiment was small, and with more participants it may be possible to give a more conclusive answer.

5   Questionnaire

All participants were asked to fill in a questionnaire after interacting with the evolutionary framework through the GUI. The questions and the results of that questionnaire are listed in Table 3.

The quality and responsiveness of the evolutionary process is rated positively in general, but indicate that there is still room for improvements. Question 4

Table 3. Results of the questionnaire, entries are counts

	Strongly disagree						Strongly agree
1.I enjoyed the process of making images interactively.	0	0	1	1	2	3	4
2.I have the feeling that the image is improving with increasing number of iterations.	0	0	1	3	2	1	4
3.I feel that I have control over the evolution of the images.	0	1	0	3	3	2	2
4.The generated images were surprising to me.	0	1	0	2	2	3	3
5.I find the generated images pleasant.	0	1	0	2	4	3	1
6.I want to know how the underlying mechanism works.	0	1	1	0	3	0	6

addresses the extent to which participants felt control over the evolution of the art, which resulted in a mode of 4 and 5, a median of 5 and a mean of 5. This was a positive outcome, with one outlier on the lower end. Question 5 covers the degree of surprise of the images, and was perceived positively with a mode of 6 and 7, a median of 6 and a mean of 5.36. Again, we find one low outlier with a rating of 2. Lastly, question 6 addresses the degree to which participants found the images pleasant. The results indicate a mode of 5, a median of 5 and a mean of 5.55. Again, we find one negative outlier at 2.

Based on the questionnaire results, we conclude that the IEC framework is perceived very positively. Participants generally enjoy the process of creating images and are curious about the underlying mechanisms. Furthermore, participants notice the improvement of images as a function of generations. The results also indicate room for improvement when it comes to the quality of the generated art. In particular, participants showed lower scores for control over the generated art. We hypothesize that this is related to the relative small population size (a population size of 9 is used at each iteration), which can make the process susceptible to losing the fittest individuals in the population due to the stochasticity of the crossover function. Lastly, we conclude that even though the tool is generally highly perceived, outliers exist, which indicates that there are strong differences between participants in how the application was used and perceived.

6   Code Base

A primary result of this project is an open-source code base written in Python which includes many variations of the basic components of evolutionary algorithms listed in Sect. 1, and which can be easily extended to include more. This Python code also includes a GUI that allows the user to perform the interactive evolution, and to perform the ATTs required for the proposed framework. The project can be found on GitHub [4].

7 Discussion

The demonstration of the ATT using a function-tree representation showed that participants scored worse than chance, meaning computer generated art could not reliably be distinguished from human generated art created with the IEC framework. We hypothesize that this could be caused by the lack of control of the creative process that is given to participants while using the function-tree representations. This is in line with the questionnaire results, which highlight that the evolved images using function-tree representations were generally perceived well by the participants, but the control over the evolutionary process can still be improved. We hypothesize that the choice of selection strategy can be of influence on this: by using roulette-wheel selection, individuals with high ratings are likely to stay in the population. This however also quickly filters out images with low ratings, causing the process to converge faster than desired. In contrast, different selection mechanisms such as tournament selection can cause good solutions to disappear despite high ratings, but retains solutions with low ratings better than roulette-wheel selection.

We propose several directions for future research, which may provide further improvements to the statistical framework, and the code base.

First, we believe that the use of different selection mechanisms such as steady state selection [20] and Boltzmann selection [17], or techniques like elitism [12] may improve the control of participants over the evolutionary process.

Second, the set of functions that are used to construct the function-tree can be extended. Since these directly influence the images, this can have a significant effect on their ratings. Moreover, extensions to our work could include different representations. We ourselves have experimented representing individuals as Cellular Automata (CA), such as in Conway's "Game of Life" [8]. We extended these CAs by generalizing the discrete states to intervals and the discrete time domain to acceleration, such as in Chan's "Lenia" [6,7]. Results of both representations can be seen in Fig. 5a and 5b, respectively.

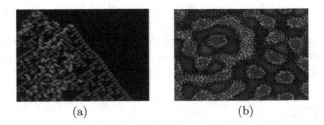

(a)   (b)

Fig. 5. (a) Cellular automaton, (b) Multi-neighborhood cellular automaton.

Third, the presented framework is readily extendable to be applied to different types of evolutionary art representations, such as representations based on deep learning. For example, Bontrager et al. (2018) [5] combine Generative

Adversarial Networks (GANs) and IEC to evolve images. Applying different representations of artworks in the presented framework is a promising direction of future research.

Fourth, the many potential uses of the framework can be exploited; for instance, one could study the influence of the evolutionary process on the perceived creativity of the process underlying the art generation with a finer granularity than was done here. In our demonstration, we generated pools of c_1 and c_{10} images, but one could easily extend that to include c_n images, and compare the influence of the generation depth on the Bayes Factor. Additionally, one could use the framework as a competition between several types of evolutionary art. Lastly, the ATT could be interpreted more freely, and instead of asking the subject which of the presented images was perceived to be more likely to be generated by a human, one could ask the subject simply which of the images he/she liked more. In a world where computer-generated art is ubiquitous, a flexible statistical framework like this may prove a valuable tool.

The questionnaire results showed that the application was found very enjoyable and quite intuitive, which is why we believe extending the framework and the code base is a venture worth pursuing.

8   Conclusion

Art is subjective. Nonetheless, complex and often interesting patterns can emerge using the techniques of algorithmic evolution. Utilizing the input of users in an Art Turing Test, we frame the task of evaluating generated art as the degree to which computer generated art can be distinguished from human generated art. Using a Bayesian model comparison, we created a framework for inferring whether the difference in degree of distinguishability is significant. The proposed automated fitness function scored worse than non-evolved function-trees in the ATT, although the results are inconclusive. We conclude that this means the method can be further improved to provide more control over the evolutionary process of generating images. We provide a framework for IEC using function-tree and CA representations, which allow the user to provide feedback on the generated individuals. The framework is open source and easily extendable to different representations, allowing for researchers and practitioners to adopt it efficiently. Results from an experiment show that the method is well-perceived in general, however improvements can still be made to the representations.

References

1. Evoart - Ashley Mills. https://www.ashleymills.com/art/evoart/
2. Back, T.: Evolutionary Algorithms in Theory and Practice: Evolution Strategies, Evolutionary Programming. Genetic Algorithms. Oxford University Press, Oxford (1996)
3. Boden, M.A.: The Turing test and artistic creativity. Kybernetes (2010)
4. de Boer, A., Leeftink, D., Hommelsheim, R.: Augub/evaluating_evolutionary_art, October 2021. https://github.com/AuguB/evaluating_evolutionary_art

5. Bontrager, P., Lin, W., Togelius, J., Risi, S.: Deep interactive evolution. In: Liapis, A., Romero Cardalda, J.J., Ekárt, A. (eds.) EvoMUSART 2018. LNCS, vol. 10783, pp. 267–282. Springer, Cham (2018). https://doi.org/10.1007/978-3-319-77583-8_18

6. Chan, B.W.C.: Lenia-biology of artificial life. arXiv preprint arXiv:1812.05433 (2018)

7. Chan, B.W.C.: Lenia and expanded universe. In: Artificial Life Conference Proceedings, pp. 221–229. MIT Press (2020)

8. Conway, J.: The game of life. Sci. Am. **223**(4), 4 (1970)

9. Elgammal, A., Liu, B., Elhoseiny, M., Mazzone, M.: CAN: creative adversarial networks, generating "art" by learning about styles and deviating from style norms. arXiv preprint arXiv:1706.07068 (2017)

10. Gatys, L.A., Ecker, A.S., Bethge, M.: Image style transfer using convolutional neural networks. In: Proceedings of the IEEE Conference on Computer Vision and Pattern Recognition, pp. 2414–2423 (2016)

11. Greenfield, G.R.: Minimalist art from cellular automata. J. Math. Arts **14**(1–2), 63–65 (2020)

12. Jong, K.D.: Evolutionary computation. Wiley Interdisciplinary Rev. Comput. Stat. **1**(1), 52–56 (2009)

13. Kass, R.E., Raftery, A.E.: Bayes factors. J. Am. Stat. Assoc. **90**(430), 773–795 (1995)

14. Koza, J.R.: Evolution of subsumption using genetic programming. In: Proceedings of the First European Conference on Artificial Life, pp. 110–119 (1992)

15. Koza, J.R.: Genetic programming: on the programming of computers by means of natural selection, vol. 1. MIT press (1992)

16. Lamb, C., Brown, D.G., Clarke, C.L.: Evaluating computational creativity: an interdisciplinary tutorial. ACM Comput. Surv. (CSUR) **51**(2), 1–34 (2018)

17. Lee, C.Y.: Entropy-Boltzmann selection in the genetic algorithms. IEEE Trans. Syst. Man Cybern. Part B (Cybern.) **33**(1), 138–149 (2003)

18. Messer, P.W.: Slim: simulating evolution with selection and linkage. Genetics **194**(4), 1037–1039 (2013)

19. Pease, A., Colton, S.: On impact and evaluation in computational creativity: a discussion of the Turing test and an alternative proposal. In: Proceedings of the AISB symposium on AI and Philosophy, vol. 39 (2011)

20. Rogers, A., Prügel-Bennett, A.: Modelling the dynamics of a steady-state genetic algorithm. Found. Genet. Algorithms **5**, 57–68 (1999)

21. Romero, J., Machado, P.: The Art of Artificial Evolution: A Handbook on Evolutionary Art and Music. Springer Science & Business Media, Heidelberg (2008). https://doi.org/10.1007/978-3-540-72877-1

22. Turing, A.M.: Computing machinery and intelligence. In: Epstein, R., Roberts, G., Beber, G. (eds.) Parsing the Turing Test. Springer, Dordrecht (2009). https://doi.org/10.1007/978-1-4020-6710-5_3

23. Turing, A.M.: Mind. Mind **59**(236), 433–460 (1950)

24. Xujian, Q.: Fractal art. J. Jilin Coll. Arts 05 (2007)

Understanding Language

Dutch SQuAD and Ensemble Learning for Question Answering from Labour Agreements

Niels J. Rouws[1,2]([✉]), Svitlana Vakulenko[1], and Sophia Katrenko[2]

[1] University of Amsterdam, 1098 XG Amsterdam, The Netherlands
[2] DEUS B.V., 1017 DL Amsterdam, The Netherlands
{niels.rouws,sophia.katrenko}@deus.ai
https://deus.ai

Abstract. The Dutch Ministry of Social Affairs and Employment has to regularly explore the content of labour agreements. Studies on topics such as diversity and work flexibility are conducted on the regular basis by means of specialised questionnaires. We show that a relatively small domain-specific dataset allows to train the state-of-the-art extractive question answering (QA) system to answer these questions automatically. This paper introduces the new dataset, Dutch SQuAD, obtained by machine translating the original SQuAD v2.0 dataset from English to Dutch (made publicly available on https://gitlab.com/niels.rouws/dutch-squad-v2.0). Our results demonstrate that it allows us to improve domain adaptation for QA models by pre-training these models first on this general domain machine-translated dataset. In our experiments, we compare fine-tuning the pre-trained Dutch versus multilingual language models: BERTje, RobBERT, and mBERT. Our results demonstrate that domain adaptation of the QA models that were first trained on a general-domain machine-translated QA dataset to the Dutch labour agreement dataset outperforms the models that were directly fine-tuned on the in-domain documents. We also compare several ensemble learning techniques and show how they allow to achieve additional performance gain on this task. A new approach of string-based voting is introduced and we showed that it performs on par with a previously proposed approach.

Keywords: Extractive question answering · Domain adaptation · Dutch

1 Introduction

The state of the art in natural language processing (NLP) field has progressed since the introduction of Transformer-based models [25]. BERT [7], one of these models, has become a baseline on numerous benchmarks due to its performance on them [22]. While language models pre-trained on English corpora are common,

© Springer Nature Switzerland AG 2022
L. A. Leiva et al. (Eds.): BNAIC/Benelearn 2021, CCIS 1530, pp. 155–169, 2022.
https://doi.org/10.1007/978-3-030-93842-0_9

other languages have fewer available resources. Devlin et al. [7] have trained a multilingual BERT model (mBERT) on 104 languages and monolingual BERT models for non-English languages are being investigated, like BERTje [5] for Dutch, for example. The main advantage of these pre-trained language models is that they can be applied to multiple downstream tasks, including question answering (QA).

The department *Cao Onderzoek en Beleidsinformatie* (COB) of the Dutch Ministry of Social Affairs and Employment regularly investigates the contents of labour agreements to evaluate existing policies or devise new ones [23]. About 30 research studies are conducted each year by the COB, and every study may include up to 80 questions to be answered for each unique labour agreement. Part of these investigations is extracting answers based on the contents of these labour agreements, which can be automated using a QA system. For this purpose, a small curated dataset composed of roughly 250 training examples is created, adopting the same format as SQuAD [20], with questions relevant to these investigations and paragraphs extracted from roughly 100 labour agreements containing the answers. The relevant paragraphs have been collected by running a baseline model, a BERT model trained on SQuAD data, on textual segments of labour agreements that have previously been identified as relevant by domain experts. The final labour agreement dataset is composed of questions regarding topics like diversity or work flexibility and relevant paragraphs from each labour agreement to make up training examples. As labour agreements are legal documents, the language used and overall document structure differ from Wikipedia texts, which are often used as corpora for pre-training language models and is also used to create the SQuAD dataset [20].

Similar datasets are created for the biomedical field, the COVID-QA dataset [17] or BioASQ [24], for example, where Jeong et al. [10] or Poerner et al. [19] apply transfer learning methods to increase performance on these datasets. Another instance where transfer learning is applied is by Hazen et al. [8] that train general domain QA models to an auto manual dataset with limited data.

This paper will compare the performance of three pre-trained language models on extractive QA for Dutch labour agreements. Three models will be considered: BERTje [5], RobBERT [6], and multilingual BERT (mBERT) [7]. These models will be trained and compared on a general domain using a SQuAD v2.0 dataset [21] which is machine translated into Dutch. The quality of the dataset will be investigated, as well as the impact of further processing on overall performance.

Fine-tuning the trained models to the domain-specific labour agreement (CAO) dataset and ensemble models will be other points of investigation. Models are expected to benefit from training on a large general domain first before being fine-tuned on the labour agreement dataset, a small domain-specific dataset. Ensembles are expected to further improve performance. Furthermore, constructing ensembles with models that excel in different types of queries will perform better than ensembles made up of identical model types [2].

The main research question addressed in this paper is:

- How do pre-trained language models perform on extractive question answering for Dutch labour agreement by using fine-tuning?

Table 1. Example question-answer pairs from SQuAD v2.0 [21] and the Dutch labour agreement dataset. Question 1 is an answerable, or positive, example, answered by the span of text in red. Question 2 on the other hand is an unanswerable, or negative, example without a valid answer present in the reference text. Question 3 originates from the labour agreement dataset, where the reference text commonly contains elements structuring documents.

Article	Normans
Reference text	The English name "Normans" comes from the French words Normans/Normanz, plural of Normant, modern French normand, which is itself borrowed from Old Low Franconian Nortmann "Northman" or directly from Old Norse Norðmaðr, Latinized variously as Nortmannus, Normannus, or Nordmannus (recorded in Medieval Latin, 9th century) to mean "Norseman, Viking"
Question 1	When was the Latin version of the word Norman first recorded?
Answer	9th century
Question 2	When was the French version of the word Norman first recorded?
Answer	*No answer*
Article	Labour agreement
Reference text	3.2 Arbeidsduur 3.2.1 Basisarbeidsduur De basisarbeidsduur is gemiddeld 36 uur per week en 1872 uur per jaar 3.2.2 Andere arbeidsduur Je kunt met je leidinggevende een andere arbeidsduur afspreken. De maximale arbeidsduur is gemiddeld 40 uur per week en 2080 uur per jaar. Je loopbaan mogelijkheden worden niet belemmerd door een kortere arbeidsduur
Question 3	Wat is de referteperiode?
Answer	per jaar

Fine-tuning the model from a machine translated general domain Dutch SQuAD v2.0 to a specific domain makes it relevant to answer the sub-questions:

- What is the influence of language filtering on a machine translated Dutch SQuAD v2.0?
- How does domain adapting QA models, trained on a general domain dataset to a specific domain, using fine-tuning compare to directly fine-tuning models on a specific domain?

Furthermore, the effectiveness of ensemble models in other applications raises the question:

- What will be the influence of ensemble models on the performance of extractive QA on Dutch labour agreements?

The contributions of this work include the evaluation of Dutch QA models trained on both a general domain and small specific domain. A fine-tuning strategy is employed which can act as an example for other Dutch QA applications with specific target domains using only a limited amount of data. Furthermore, an analysis and proposed filtering for a machine translated Dutch SQuAD v2.0 dataset is performed. The machine translated Dutch SQuAD v2.0 with additional language filtering is made publicly available[1]. This dataset can still be improved upon to reduce noisy examples due to translation in order to create better Dutch datasets for future studies on extractive QA and other downstream tasks. Finally, Dutch pre-trained language models are compared on the downstream extractive QA task on this Dutch dataset both individually and ensemble learning for small gains in exchange for more computational power.

2   Related Work

Training and evaluating Dutch QA systems with a lack of dedicated resources has been investigated by Isotalo [9]. Experiments show that machine translating datasets is a viable option to train Dutch QA systems on. Disadvantages of using machine translated data include reducing linguistic richness of translated texts, possibly resulting in easier examples. Similar works exist that study transfer learning, or domain adaption, of BERT-based models to specific domains like the COVID-QA dataset [17,19], biomedical QA [10], or QA on an automobile manual domain [8].

Möller [17] has created a QA dataset with 2k examples related to COVID-19 annotated by experts of biomedical sciences. Answers are generally longer and need to be extracted from longer reference texts compared to the general domain SQuAD dataset [20]. A RoBERTa model [13] was fine-tuned on SQuAD and evaluated on the COVID-QA dataset as baseline. EM and F1 scores were both significantly improved on by training the fine-tuned model on the COVID-QA dataset [17]. Poerner et al. [19] propose a CPU-only domain adaptation method for pre-trained language models. This approach involves learning Word2Vec [16] embeddings for text of the target domain, aligning them with the already existing embeddings of the pre-trained language model and updating the embedding layer together with a new tokenizer. A baseline BERT model trained of the SQuAD dataset [20] was adapted using this approach and performs better than prior being domain adapted.

Another example of domain adaptation of BERT models to the biomedical field is the work of Jeong et al. [10]. They apply sequential transfer learning to improve performance of models on biomedical QA. Jeong et al. [10] state that fine-tuning models on both the SQuAD dataset [20] and BioASQ [24], a biomedical QA dataset, produces better results than only training on the

---

[1] https://gitlab.com/niels.rouws/dutch-squad-v2.0.

BioASQ dataset. Furthermore, they show that fine-tuning BioBERT on natural language inference (NLI), using the MultiNLI dataset [26], followed by training on BioASQ outperforms the SQuAD approach. Additional experiments show that the order of datasets used to fine-tune matters for longer chains fine-tuning on both the MultiNLI and SQuAD datasets prior to BioASQ.

Hazen et al. [8] investigate domain adaptation to apply QA in new specific domains like an automobile manual. Their standard approach to transfer a QA model to this domain is to use general domain datasets like SQuAD [20] as starting points and training for 2 epochs to the auto manual domain. With limited data, around 200 examples were shown great performance increase on the specific domain and shows that models trained on large amounts of general data can be transfer learned with limited data of a specific domain [8].

This work will be using a machine translated Dutch SQuAD v2.0 dataset as a general domain dataset in order to adapt the domain to a legal domain using limited data extracted from labour agreements. Machine translating existing English datasets into other languages is a strategy employed by others, for instance, translating SQuAD to Spanish [4], Korean [12], or Persian [1].

3   Datasets

The models are fine-tuned and compared on two Dutch QA datasets. A large general domain machine translated Dutch SQuAD dataset and a small domain specific curated dataset composed of Dutch labour agreements.

3.1   Dutch SQuAD v2.0

Dutch SQuAD v2.0 is a machine translated, using the Google Translate API, version of the original SQuAD v2.0 [21] by Borzymowski [3][2]. Direct translations of the answers were used to find the start tokens in the translated reference text. Question-answer pairs were lost in translation if the translated answer is not present in the translated context [3]. Due to this, around 31 thousand question-answer pairs were removed in the training set of the translated version.

Despite these processing steps, noisy examples remain in the dataset containing foreign words, for example, see Table 2. Examples are either partially translated or contain large pieces of non-Dutch languages.

In order to further reduce noise in the translated dataset, language identification [15] is employed to remove noisy non-Dutch examples using Pythons langid module[3]. An example was removed if either the question or the reference text was classified as non-Dutch.

---

[2] https://github.com/borhenryk/train_custom_qa_model.

[3] https://github.com/saffsd/langid.py.

Table 2. Examples of contexts in the Dutch SQuAD v2.0 dataset removed using language identification.

Example 1:	After the Peace of Westphalia, several border territories were assigned to the United Provinces. They were federally-governed Generality Lands (*Generaliteitslanden*). They were *Staats-Brabant* (present North Brabant), *Staats-Vlaanderen* (present Zeeuws-Vlaanderen), *Staats-Limburg* (around Maastricht) and *Staats-Oppergelre* (around *Venlo*, after 1715)
Example 2:	New Delhi *is de thuisbasis van* Indira Gandhi Memorial Museum, National Gallery of Modern Art, National Museum of Natural History, National Rail Museum, National Handicrafts and Handlooms Museum, National Philatelic Museum, Nehru Planetarium, Shankar's International Dolls Museum. *en* Supreme Court of India Museum

Figure 1 shows the language distributions of both questions and answers in the Dutch SQuAD v2.0 training set. Answers are predominantly classified as English followed by Dutch and German, unlike the reference texts and questions that are predominantly Dutch. Out of 18.6k contexts, only 31 cases were classified as non-Dutch in the training set and 3 in the development set, two cases are shown in Table 2.

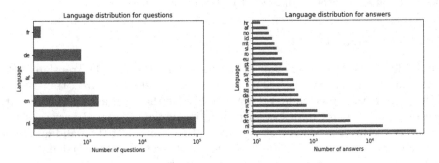

Fig. 1. Language distribution for questions and answers of the Dutch SQuAD v2.0 dataset. All languages are shown that exceed the threshold value $t = 100$.

The exact distribution of example types per dataset are shown in Table 3. Positive examples decrease each iteration, while the number of articles remains constant. The amount of negative examples only decline at the last iteration when they belong to non-Dutch questions or contexts. As a result of both translating and filtering, the proportion of positive to negative examples has shifted towards more negatives per positive example compared to the original SQuAD v2.0.

Table 3. Dataset statistics of SQuAD v2.0 [21], a Dutch SQuAD v2.0, a Dutch SQuAD v2.0 with additional language filtering (LF), and labour agreement dataset.

	English SQuAD v2.0	Dutch SQuAD v2.0	Dutch SQuAD v2.0 (LF)	Labour agreements
Train				
Total examples	130,319	99,265	95,054	241
Positive examples	86,821	55,767	53,376	165
Negative examples	43,498	43,498	41,768	76
Development				
Total examples	11,873	9,669	9,294	103
Positive examples	5,928	3,724	3,588	71
Negative examples	5,945	5,945	5,706	32

3.2 Labour Agreement Dataset

The labour agreement (CAO) dataset is a domain-specific dataset with almost 250 training examples collected from close to 100 labour agreements of Dutch businesses. Question-answer pairs were collected and curated in cooperation with experts from the Dutch Ministry of Social Affairs and Employment. Labour agreements are legally binding contracts, which is reflected in the language used in both questions and reference texts, which are relatively short compared to the SQuAD v2.0 dataset [21]. Negative examples are composed of rejected combinations of questions and reference texts. They are added to have slightly more than two positive examples per negative example, as is the case in the training set of SQuAD v2.0.

4 Approach

The different model configurations and training policies will be described that were applied to BERTje [5], RobBERT [6], and mBERT [7] in order to make meaningful comparisons.

4.1 Fine-Tuning

Initially, the three models were trained on both the unfiltered Dutch SQuAD v2.0 dataset and the language filtered Dutch SQuAD v2.0 dataset to test whether an mBERT would have an advantage due to translation errors. The fine-tuning strategy for all experiments consist of training the models for 2 epochs with a learning rate of 5e−5, batch size of 8 and AdamW [14] with $\epsilon = 1e−8$. The pre-trained models were acquired from the Hugging Face model database[4,5,6]

---

[4] https://huggingface.co/GroNLP/bert-base-dutch-cased.
[5] https://huggingface.co/pdelobelle/robbert-v2-dutch-base.
[6] https://huggingface.co/bert-base-multilingual-cased.

and used as starting points for baseline models on the CAO dataset, and the models trained on the SQuAD datasets for testing whether filtering the dataset would improve the results of the monolingual models relative to the multilingual model. The models fine-tuned on the filtered Dutch SQuAD v2.0 dataset are subsequently fine-tuned for another 2 epochs on the CAO dataset and compared to the baselines.

4.2   Voted BERT

In order to boost performance on the CAO dataset, two ensemble approaches utilizing voting mechanisms have been implemented.

The first approach votes based on the sub-strings enclosed by the output answer spans of models. Voting for the second approach, on the other hand, relies on the output scores produced by the dot product of token scores with the start and end vectors. Score voting is applied to ensemble identical models and string voting to combine mixed model types due to the different tokenizers and vocabularies of different models.

Score-Based Voting. A model fine-tuned on the filtered Dutch SQuAD v2.0 dataset is copied K times. Each model k is independently fine-tuned, following the general strategy, on the CAO dataset with a unique seed. At evaluation time, the models are combined into an ensemble that makes prediction based on the output scores of the K models. The output of a single model k is a start vector s_k and an end vector e_k of size l which is the maximum sequence length. s and e contain the logits that denote the probability of tokens in the input sequence being the start and end symbols of an answer. These probabilities are summed and normalized by K to produce the start and end vector representing the prediction of the ensemble [27]. If $\text{BERT}(x; \theta_n)$ denotes the tuple $\langle s_k, e_k \rangle$ predicted by a BERT model with parameters θ_k from the input x, this ensemble can be formulated as:

$$\text{BERT}_{VOTE}(x; \Theta) = \frac{1}{K} \sum_{k=1}^{K} \text{BERT}(x; \theta_k) \tag{1}$$

String-Based Voting. The other voted BERT approach is implemented by voting using an algorithm comparing the output strings in order to mix different BERT models. As for the score-based approach K models are fine-tuned on the CAO dataset, they are, however, different model types. One model for each type is fine-tuned and combined with the others at evaluation time. A naive variant of the algorithm votes for the most occurring exactly matching output, or defaults to the longest available prediction in the voting pool. The other version does not require the outputs of individual models to match exactly. It calculates the longest common sub-string[7] for each unique combination and votes on the longest prediction in the highest scoring combination.

---

[7] https://www.geeksforgeeks.org/longest-common-substring-dp-29/.

5   Evaluation

A description of the pre-trained language models that have been experimented on will be given in this section, in addition to the evaluation metrics used to assess and compare them.

5.1   Models

The pre-trained language models used are comparable in parameters and architecture but vary in, for example, corpora and objectives during pre-training.

BERTje. BERTje [5] is a Dutch monolingual model comparable to $BERT_{base}$ with 12 layers and cased tokenization. It has a vocabulary of 30k tokens and is pre-trained on 12 GB of corpora originating from Dutch books, TwNC, SoNaR-500, Web news, and Wikipedia. It is pre-trained on two objectives: sentence order prediction (SOP) and masked language modelling (MLM). For their MLM objective, they mask consecutive word pieces that belong to the same word instead of randomly masking single word pieces.

RobBERT. Another monolingual model is RobBERT [6], a Dutch RoBERTa based model with 12 self-attention layers, 12 heads and 117M parameters. Rob-BERT is pre-trained using the RoBERTa training regime [13] and does not include the SOP objective compared to BERTje. The OSCAR corpus was used as a dataset, which is 39 GB of Dutch text obtained from the Common Crawl corpus. It also includes their own byte pair encode (BPE) tokenizer constructed using the OSCAR corpus consisting of 40k tokens, 10k more than BERTje. The authors found that RobBERT outperforms other BERT-like models when dealing with smaller datasets.

mBERT. mBERT [7] is a multilingual model for 104 languages trained using Wikipedia texts using an MLM objective and next sentence prediction (NSP). mBERT can generalize across languages with a multilingual representation of words without an explicit training objective for this task [18].

5.2   Evaluation Metrics

We evaluated the QA models using two metrics: exact match (EM) and F1 scores. In addition to calculating EM and F1 scores on the complete datasets, scores are calculated for both the subsets of data containing only positive examples (HasAns) and negative examples (NoAns) individually to give a better insight into the performance of the models.

Moreover, we calculated the EM and F1 scores per interrogative Dutch words to gain an understanding of challenging questions. Models that excel at different question types can be combined in an ensemble to exploit strengths and compensate for weaknesses. Question types were assigned to questions by using regular expressions for Dutch interrogative words: *wie, wat, waar, waarom, wanneer, welk, welke, hoe, hoeveel*. Questions without a match for any of these words were placed in a separate category: *other*.

6   Results

This section presents the collected results to answer the research questions, starting off with the results generated from the Dutch SQuAD v2.0 dataset, followed by the results of QA systems on the labour agreement dataset.

6.1   Dutch SQuAD

Language Filtering. The effect of language filtering described in Sect. 3.1 is tested by fine-tuning BERTje [5], RobBERT [6], and mBERT [7] models on both the unfiltered and language filtered Dutch SQuAD v2.0 dataset and evaluating these models on their respective development sets. The results of this experiment are shown in Table 4 with models trained on the language filtered dataset followed by (LF). The HasAns column show the scores calculated exclusively on the subset of positive examples and NoAns scores on the subset of negative examples. mBERT achieves the highest scores on the unfiltered dataset by a large margin on all subsets of the data. While remaining the best performing model, the difference between models shrinks as RobBERT's scores improve on all fields and BERTje slightly decreases except on the NoAns section, where it becomes the best scoring model.

Table 4. Evaluation results of models, on their respective development set, fine-tuned on the unfiltered Dutch SQuAD v2.0 dataset and language filtered version. Models fine-tuned on the language filtered version are followed by (LF). The HasAns column are the evaluation scores exclusively with the subset of positive examples and NoAns scores on the subset of negative examples. **Bold** font indicates the best scores on the unfiltered dataset, and underlined font indicates the best scores on the filtered dataset.

Model	EM/F1	HasAns EM/F1	NoAns F1
BERTje	65.26/69.13	44.33/54.39	78.37
BERTje (LF)	65.05/68.72	43.62/53.89	78.53
RobBERT	63.38/67.34	43.43/53.72	75.88
RobBERT (LF)	64.64/68.55	45.43/55.54	76.73
mBERT	**67.37/71.31**	**47.80/58.03**	**79.63**
mBERT (LF)	65.69/69.35	46.40/55.89	77.81

Results per Question Type. The datasets contain a diverse mix of question types, which have been evaluated as separate subsets to identify challenging questions and compare whether the challenge exists across model types. Table 5 contains these results for all positive examples of the language filtered Dutch SQuAD v2.0 development set for the models fine-tuned on the training set.

All three models show a comparable performance distribution along the question types. *Wie*/Who and *wanneer*/when questions are among the best performing types, while *waarom*/why, *hoe*/how, and other questions score worst and have significantly large differences between EM and F1 scores. Predicting the ground truth for these question types appears to be challenging, but still parts of them are captured relatively frequently. *Wat*/What scores are surprisingly low for the high number of examples compared to other questions.

Table 5. Model scores of positive examples evaluated per question type on the filtered Dutch SQuAD v2.0 development set. Underlined scores denote the highest scores per row, and **bold** scores the highest score for a model type.

Question type	Number of examples	BERTje	mBERT	RobBERT
		HasAns EM/F1	HasAns EM/F1	HasAns EM/F1
wie/who	332	**59.34/65.41**	61.14/67.09	**61.45**/68.39
wat/what	1035	35.65/45.23	38.16/47.47	36.23/46.56
waar/where	244	35.66/49.35	35.66/52.51	38.52/51.87
waarom/why	44	20.45/41.95	22.73/35.22	11.36/33.61
wanneer/when	289	55.36/61.67	**65.74/73.51**	61.25/**69.45**
welk/which	444	50.90/57.49	52.70/59.56	53.15/59.06
welke/which	629	44.67/53.10	47.22/54.55	46.10/55.42
hoe/how	198	33.33/47.30	37.88/52.00	36.87/53.87
hoeveel/how much	324	50.00/63.49	50.62/63.66	51.85/65.45
other	103	25.24/37.51	30.10/42.58	26.21/36.15

6.2   Labour Agreement Dataset

Domain Adaptation. Table 6 shows the results of all systems trained on the labour agreement (CAO) dataset. The training strategies can be derived from the datasets following the model name. Baseline models are fine-tuned on the CAO dataset only, as opposed to domain adapted models. They are first fine-tuned on the large general domain language filtered Dutch SQuAD v2.0 (DSQuAD) followed by fine-tuning on the small domain specific CAO dataset. The results show that the baseline models are outclassed by the domain adapted version of the same model type. BERTje mainly gains performance on the negative examples and sees the least improvement on the positive examples, whereas both RobBERT and mBERT drop performance for negative examples and gain significant performance on positive examples. In addition to outperforming baseline models, domain adapted models attain higher scores on the CAO dataset than models score on the Dutch SQuAD datasets (see Table 4).

Table 6. Exact match (EM) and F1 scores of all systems evaluated on the CAO development set. **Bold** scores indicate the highest score per column, and <u>underlined</u> scores indicate the highest score per model type. Baseline models are fine-tuned on the CAO dataset (CAO) while all other systems are first fine-tuned on the filtered Dutch SQuAD v2.0 dataset followed by fine-tuning on the CAO dataset (DSQuAD + CAO). K denotes the ensemble size of score-based voted BERT systems. The final cell shows the mixed ensembles using string-based voting with LCS to indicate voting using the longest common sub-string algorithm.

System	EM/F1	HasAns EM/F1	NoAns F1
BERTje (CAO)	62.14/65.99	57.75/63.34	71.88
BERTje (DSQuAD + CAO)	66.02/71.38	59.15/66.93	**<u>81.25</u>**
BERTje (DSQuAD + CAO) (K = 3)	<u>66.99</u>/<u>73.94</u>	60.56/70.65	**<u>81.25</u>**
BERTje (DSQuAD + CAO) (K = 5)	65.05/72.78	<u>61.97</u>/<u>73.19</u>	71.88
RobBERT (CAO)	58.25/61.15	50.70/54.90	75.00
RobBERT (DSQuAD + CAO)	66.99/73.48	66.20/75.61	68.75
RobBERT (DSQuAD + CAO) (K = 3)	<u>69.90</u>/**<u>76.83</u>**	66.20/<u>76.24</u>	<u>78.13</u>
RobBERT (DSQuAD + CAO) (K = 5)	65.05/72.78	61.97/73.19	71.88
mBERT (CAO)	63.11/68.23	59.15/66.58	<u>78.13</u>
mBERT (DSQuAD + CAO)	69.90/<u>76.38</u>	67.61/**<u>77.00</u>**	75.00
mBERT (DSQuAD + CAO) (K = 3)	69.90/75.57	66.20/74.42	<u>78.13</u>
mBERT (DSQuAD + CAO) (K = 5)	**<u>70.87</u>**/75.90	**<u>69.01</u>**/76.30	75.00
BERTje + RobBERT + mBERT (DSQuAD + CAO)	**<u>70.87</u>**/76.28	67.60/75.45	<u>78.13</u>
BERTje + RobBERT + mBERT (DSQuAD + CAO) (LCS)	69.90/<u>76.47</u>	66.20/<u>75.72</u>	<u>78.13</u>

Ensemble Models. Ensemble models show in the majority of cases an increase in performance regarding single models. The score-based approach with ensemble sizes of $K = 3$ and $K = 5$ produce primarily better results than single models. Increasing the ensemble sizes also appear to benefit scores on positives examples for both BERTje and mBERT. RobBERT, on the other hand, sees a sudden decrease in performance for $K = 5$. The ensembles composed of mixed models perform generally well, achieving high overall scores. Voting using the string matching approach or largest common sub-string (LCS) approach achieve comparable results, with a trade-off between EM scores and F1 scores for positive examples.

7   Discussion

The most significant findings include the improved performance of domain adapted models compared to baseline models and slight additional gain in performance of ensemble models compared to their single model counterparts. These results were expected based on the results of similar studies of transfer learning models from general domain datasets to specific domains in the biomedical domain [10,17], for example, or on automobile manuals [8].

The ensemble models slightly improve model results as expected [27] which could be improved upon by creating ensembles of models that do not have as similar performance distributions per question type as have been found for BERTje [5], RobBERT [6], and multilingual BERT [7].

Hyperparameter optimization for BERT during fine-tuning could increase model performance. All models have been fine-tuned using a general strategy which is likely not optimal for each model type, leading to under- or overperforming models.

Improving models for the labour agreement domain could alternatively take the approach of BioBERT [11] by pre-training on data from the target domain. However, pre-training a model on corpora within a domain requires large amounts of data and computing power. Alternatively, the relatively inexpensive domain adaptation approach of Poerner et al. [19] could be explored.

7.1 Conclusion

In this paper, we examined fine-tuning pre-trained language models for a Dutch-language QA task. The models were evaluated on a general-domain machine-translated Dutch SQuAD as well as on a low-resource target domain of Dutch labour agreements. Our results show that fine-tuning the models on the language-specific QA dataset is beneficial even when such dataset is machine translated from English. This finding has important implications beyond the QA task showing that the model performance can be improved across languages by machine translating English-language resources.

We also note, however, that the domain-adapted models using fine-tuning attain higher scores on the labour agreement dataset than on the Dutch SQuAD v2.0 datasets. The cause of this is likely that a machine translated dataset contains more noise compared to a curated dataset. A limited variety of questions for the labour agreement dataset could be another reason why higher scores are attained. Our results demonstrate that the best performance can be achieved by using a mixed ensemble of mBERT, BERTje and RobBERT using string-based voting, closely followed a mBERT ensemble utilizing a score-based voting system. The best models overall reaching EM scores up to 70.87% and a F1 score of 76.28% on the target domain.

Interestingly, language filtering the machine-translated Dutch SQuAD results in decreased performance for mBERT, while RobBERT gained in performance and BERTje had only slight changes in performance. All of these results are still significantly below comparable QA models for English.

Our results provide important insights on the intricacy of domain adaptation for non-English QA models. We show that it is feasible to train QA models in a low-resource scenario which is prevalent when automating recurrent tasks in the real-world settings, such as the labour agreement investigations by the Dutch Ministry of Social Affairs and Employment.

References

1. Abadani, N., Mozafari, J., Fatemi, A., Nematbakhsh, M.A., Kazemi, A.: ParSQuAD: machine translated squad dataset for Persian question answering. In: 2021 7th International Conference on Web Research (ICWR), pp. 163–168. IEEE (2021)

2. Aniol, A., Pietron, M., Duda, J.: Ensemble approach for natural language question answering problem. In: 2019 Seventh International Symposium on Computing and Networking Workshops (CANDARW), pp. 180–183. IEEE (2019)

3. Borzymowski, H.: Henryk/BERT-base-multilingual-cased-finetuned-dutch-squad2 · Hugging Face (2020). https://huggingface.co/henryk/bert-base-multilingual-cased-finetuned-dutch-squad2

4. Carrino, C.P., Costa-jussà, M.R., Fonollosa, J.A.R.: Automatic Spanish translation of the squad dataset for multilingual question answering. arXiv preprint arXiv:1912.05200 (2019)

5. de Vries, W., van Cranenburgh, A., Bisazza, A., Caselli, T., van Noord, G., Nissim, M.: BERTje: a Dutch BERT model. CoRR abs/1912.09582 (2019). http://arxiv.org/abs/1912.09582

6. Delobelle, P., Winters, T., Berendt, B.: RobBERT: a Dutch RoBERTa-based language model (2020)

7. Devlin, J., Chang, M.-W., Lee, K., Toutanova, K.: BERT: pre-training of deep bidirectional transformers for language understanding (2019)

8. Hazen, T.J., Dhuliawala, S., Boies, D.: Towards domain adaptation from limited data for question answering using deep neural networks (2019)

9. Isotalo, L.: Generative question answering in a low-resource setting

10. Jeong, M., et al.: Transferability of natural language inference to biomedical question answering. arXiv preprint arXiv:2007.00217 (2020)

11. Lee, J., et al.: BioBERT: a pre-trained biomedical language representation model for biomedical text mining. Bioinformatics **36**(4), 1234–1240 (2020)

12. Lee, K., Yoon, K., Park, S., Hwang, S.-W.: Semi-supervised training data generation for multilingual question answering. In: Proceedings of the Eleventh International Conference on Language Resources and Evaluation (LREC 2018) (2018)

13. Liu, Y., et al.: RoBERTa: a robustly optimized BERT pretraining approach (2019)

14. Loshchilov, I., Hutter, F.: Decoupled weight decay regularization (2019)

15. Lui, M., Baldwin, T.: langid.py: an off-the-shelf language identification tool. In: Proceedings of the ACL 2012 System Demonstrations, Jeju Island, Korea. Association for Computational Linguistics, pp. 25–30, July 2012. https://www.aclweb.org/anthology/P12-3005

16. Mikolov, T., Chen, K., Corrado, G., Dean, J.: Efficient estimation of word representations in vector space (2013)

17. Möller, T., Reina, A., Jayakumar, R., Pietsch, M.: COVID-QA: a question answering dataset for COVID-19. In: Proceedings of the 1st Workshop on NLP for COVID-19 at ACL 2020 (2020)

18. Pires, T., Schlinger, E., Garrette, D.: How multilingual is multilingual BERT? (2019)

19. Poerner, N., Waltinger, U., Schütze, H.: Inexpensive domain adaptation of pretrained language models: case studies on biomedical NER and COVID-19 QA. In: Findings of the Association for Computational Linguistics: EMNLP 2020. Association for Computational Linguistics, pp. 1482–1490, November 2020. https://doi.org/10.18653/v1/2020.findings-emnlp.134, https://www.aclweb.org/anthology/2020.findings-emnlp.134

20. Rajpurkar, P., Zhang, J., Lopyrev, K., Liang, P.: SQuAD: 100,000+ questions for machine comprehension of text. arXiv preprint arXiv:1606.05250 (2016)

21. Rajpurkar, P., Jia, R., Liang, P.: Know what you don't know: unanswerable questions for SQuAD (2018)

22. Rogers, A., Kovaleva, O., Rumshisky, A.: A primer in bertology: what we know about how BERT works (2020)

23. Startup in Residence Intergov. Geautomatiseerde tekst-analyse cao's — Startup in Residence Intergov (2020). https://intergov.startupinresidence.com/nl/szw/geautomatiseerde-tekst-analyse-cao/brief
24. Tsatsaronis, G., et al.: An overview of the bioASQ large-scale biomedical semantic indexing and question answering competition. BMC Bioinform. **16**(1), 1–28 (2015)
25. Vaswani, A., et al.: Attention is all you need (2017)
26. Williams, A., Nangia, N., Bowman, S.: A broad-coverage challenge corpus for sentence understanding through inference. In: Proceedings of the 2018 Conference of the North American Chapter of the Association for Computational Linguistics: Human Language Technologies, Volume 1 (Long Papers), New Orleans, Louisiana. Association for Computational Linguistics, pp. 1112–1122, June 2018. https://doi.org/10.18653/v1/N18-1101, https://www.aclweb.org/anthology/N18-1101
27. Xu, Y., Qiu, X., Zhou, L., Huang, X.: Improving BERT fine-tuning via self-ensemble and self-distillation. arXiv preprint arXiv:2002.10345 (2020)

Verbalizing but Not Just Verbatim Translations of Ontology Axioms

Vinu Ellampallil Venugopal[1]([✉]) and P. Sreenivasa Kumar[2]

[1] University of Luxembourg, Esch-sur-Alzette, Luxembourg
vinu.venugopal@uni.lu
[2] Indian Institute of Technology, Madras, Chennai, India
psk@iitm.ac.in

Abstract. In this paper, we propose an inference-based technique to remove redundancy from natural language (NL) descriptions of Web Ontology Language (OWL) entities. The existing ontology verbalization approaches generate NL text segments that are closer to their counterpart statements in the ontology. Some of these approaches also perform grouping and aggregating of the text segments, aiming at a more fluent and comprehensive representation. However, we observed that the human-understandability of such descriptions is affected by the presence of repetitions and redundancies, and our studies show that such issues can be removed easily at the semantic level than at the NL level. We propose a novel technique called *semantic-level refinement* (or simply, *semantic-refinement*) for this purpose. Our approach aims at transforming the knowledge that is represented as a combination of less expressive (and not specific) logic-based expressions into the ones with high expressivity and specificity. This technique utilizes a predefined set of rules which are applied repeatedly on the restrictions associated with the individuals (and the concepts) to obtain a refined set of restrictions, guaranteed to be semantically equivalent to the original representation. Such refined sets of restrictions can then be verbalized to get concise descriptions of the ontology entities. Our experiments on ontologies from two different domains show that the proposed approach could significantly improve the readability of the NL texts when compared to the texts generated without a semantic-level refinement.

Keywords: Ontology verbalization · Redundancy removal · Rule-based approach

1 Introduction

Artificial Intelligence (AI) community widely uses *ontologies* for knowledge representation and reasoning. For example, the Gene Ontology[1] is now a very prominent resource in AI-powered Bioinformatics and Genomics. Another example is SNOMED CT[2], which is now fully formalized in OWL (Web Ontology Language) and widely

---

[1] http://geneontology.org/.
[2] https://www.snomed.org/snomed-ct/.

© Springer Nature Switzerland AG 2022
L. A. Leiva et al. (Eds.): BNAIC/Benelearn 2021, CCIS 1530, pp. 170–186, 2022.
https://doi.org/10.1007/978-3-030-93842-0_10

used for electronic health records related applications. It is observed recently that modeling knowledge in the form of ontologies helps to broaden the scope of cognitive AI and explainable AI (Peroni et al. (2008); Sarker et al. (2020)). However, the domain knowledge in the form of an ontology is inherently characterized by complex logical axioms, making the formalized knowledge not accessible to non-ontology communities (Dentler and Cornet (2015); Venugopal and Kumar (2020); Venugopal and Kumar (2019)). This had resulted in a large number of natural language (NL) verbalization tools for OWL ontologies such as NaturalOWL (Androutsopoulos et al. (2014)) and SWAT Tools (Third et al. (2011)). However, the existing approaches in this direction mainly strive for one-to-one translation of logical constructs into the corresponding NL fragments. Such NL translations generally contain redundancies, as a domain concept could be expressed in several different ways in an ontology using the various constructs allowed in the ontology language—and, it is not guaranteed that one would always use the best combination to formalize the knowledge. In this paper, we explore a systematic approach that removes redundancies at the logic level—preserving semantic correctness—called *semantic-refinement*. And, it is found to be complementing the ontology verbalization application by generating concise NL sentences.

Motivating Example. Consider the following axioms from People & Pets ontology[3]:

(1) `Cat_Owner ⊑ Person ⊓ Owner ⊓ ∃hasPet.Animal ⊓ ∃hasPet.Cat`
(2) `Cat_Owner(sam)`   (3) `Cat ⊑ Animal`

The controlled natural language (CNL) descriptions for the individual `sam`, generated using standard OWL verbalizers, are as follows. From now on, we refer 'description' as the NL description of an entity (*individual* or *concept*) generated from the ontology.

- *A cat-owner is a person. A cat-owner is an owner. A cat-owner has as pet an animal. A cat-owner has a cat as pet. Sam is a cat-owner. All cats are animals.*
  or (with grouping and aggregation)
- *A cat-owner is a person and an owner. A cat-owner is all of the following: something that has pet an animal, and something that has a cat as pet; Example: sam. All cats are animals.*

   As can be easily noted, these descriptions have redundant information, and attempting verbatim translation of each description logical (DL) construct has resulted in this situation. There are different types of redundancies one can observe here. The obvious type is the repetition of linguistically similar texts; e.g., "a <u>cat-owner</u> is an <u>owner</u>". The other type includes those generic restrictions which can be logically inferred from more specific restrictions; e.g., having said "A cat-owner has a cat as pet", it is not necessary to say "A cat-owner has as pet an animal." This paper deals with removing redundancies of the latter kind.

Contributions. In this paper, we propose a technique called *semantic-level refinement* (or simply *semantic-refinement*) that helps in removing the redundant (portion of the)

---

[3] http://www.cs.man.ac.uk/~horrocks/ISWC2003/Tutorial/people+pets.owl.rdf.

restrictions and forms a more comprehensive description of an ontology entity. We particularly focus on generating descriptions from $\mathcal{SHIQ}$ DL ontologies. Our proposed approach generates descriptions of individuals and concepts by first representing the associated restrictions (knowledge) using a set of DL constructs that have high expressivity and high specificity than using a set that contains less expressive and generic expressions. If we revisit our previous example, we expect our approach to generate a text similar to "sam is an owner having at least one cat as pet"; such that the redundant portion of the text "has as pet an animal" is removed (since it clearly follows from "having at least one cat as pet"). Due to page limitation, detailed proofs for the semantic correctness of the approach are made available in an extended version of the paper which we refer as *longer version*[4].

2   Related Work

Controlled Natural Languages. Over the last two decades, several CNLs such as Attempto Controlled English (ACE) by Kaljurand and Fuchs (2007), Rabbit by Hart et al. (2007), and Sydney OWL Syntax (SOS) by Cregan et al. (2007), have been specifically designed or have been adapted for ontology language OWL. All these languages are meant to make the interactions with formal ontological statements easier and faster for users who are unfamiliar with formal notations. Unlike the languages that were introduced to represent OWL in controlled English, proposed by Hewlett et al. (2005); Jarrar et al. (2006); Androutsopoulos et al. (2014), the aforementioned CNLs are designed to have formal language semantics and bidirectional mapping between NL fragments and OWL constructs. Even though these formal language semantics and bidirectional mapping enable a formal check to determine if the resulting NL expressions are unambiguous, they can result in generating a collection of unordered sentences that are difficult to comprehend. To use these CNLs as a means for ontology authoring and for knowledge validation purposes, the verbalized texts need to be properly organized. Stevens et al. (2011) have performed a detailed comparison of the systems that do such text organization. Among such systems, SWAT (Semantic Web Authoring) tools are one of the recent and prominent tools which use standard techniques from computational linguistics to make the verbalized text more readable. They have tried to give better clarity to the generated text by grouping, aggregation, and elision. Third et al. (2011) have pointed out that the NL verbalization tools such as SWAT have given much importance to the linguistic fluency of the verbalized sentences than removing redundancies from their logical forms, and hence have deficiencies in interpreting the ontology contents.

Redundancy Removal. According to Alani et al. (2006), the works related to refining ontologies have focused only on ad-hoc application settings; not focusing primarily on preserving the semantics of the axioms. A notion for removing redundancies from ontologies without affecting the overall semantics, similar to what we propose in this paper, was proposed first by Grimm and Wissmann (2011). However, they have looked at redundancy in ontologies primarily from an ontology engineering and knowledge evolution point of view and were based on the notions introduced by Liberatore (2005)

---

[4] https://orbilu.uni.lu/retrieve/83875/90647/test.pdf.

about redundant clauses in propositional logic formulas. Later, Third (2012) proposed a notion for removing redundancies in the context of ontology verbalization. In their work, the authors have established the fact that omitting "obvious axioms" while verbalization leads to a better reading experience for a human. By "obvious axioms" the author means those axioms whose semantics are in some sense obvious for an average human reader. For example, phrases such as "junior school" explicitly convey the meaning that a junior school is a school. In our work, we go further and establish that more inference-based redundancy removal could still be performed rather than just removing the morphological variants of the entity names, for greatly improving the quality and understandability of a verbalized text. Recently, Dentler and Cornet (2015) proposed four redundancy detection rules and the respective resolution methods, especially for SNOMED CT. However, there are no further efforts exist in generalizing such rules.

3 Preliminaries and Defintions

We assume that the readers are familiar with the semantics of $\mathcal{SHIQ}$ DL ontologies (Horrocks et al. (2000)). $\mathcal{SHIQ}$ DL is an extension of the well-known logic $\mathcal{ALC}$ (Schmidt-Schau and Smolka (1991)) with added support for role hierarchies, inverse roles, transitive roles, and qualifying number restrictions.

Running Example. In Fig. 1, we introduce a synthetic ontology called *academic (ACAD) ontology* which we follow throughout this paper as an example ontology.

TBox

IITStudent ≡ Student ⊓ ∀hasAdvisor.TeachingStaff ⊓
∃hasAdvisor.Professor ⊓ ∃enrolledIn.IITProgramme
IIT_MS_Student ≡ IITStudent ⊓ ≤ 1 hasAdvisor.TeachingStaff
IITPhdStudent ≡ IITStudent ⊓ ≥ 2 hasAdvisor.TeachingStaff
⊓ ≤ 1 hasAdvisor.Professor
Professor ⊑ TeachingStaff
AssistantProf ⊑ TeachingStaff
⊥ ≡ Professor ⊓ AssistantProf
⊥ ≡ IIT_MS_Student ⊓ IITPhdStudent

ABox

IITStudent(tom)
IIT_MS_Student(tom)
hasAdvisor(tom, bob)
IITPhdStudent(sam)
hasAdvisor(sam, alice)
hasAdvisor(sam, roy)
AssistantProf(alice)

Fig. 1. TBox (Terminologies) and ABox (Assersions) of ACAD ontology

Label-Set. The *label-set of an individual* is the set which contains *all* the class expressions and (existential, universal and cardinality) restrictions satisfied by that individual. A list of all label-sets from ACAD ontology is given in Table 1. The scope of the following formal definition of label-set is limited to $\mathcal{SHIQ}$ DL.

Definition 1. *Formally, the label-set of an individual* x *(represented as* $\mathcal{L}_\mathcal{O}(x)$*) is defined as:* $\mathcal{L}_\mathcal{O}(x) = \{c_i \mid \mathcal{O} \models c_i(x)\}$ *where* c_i *is of the following form:* $c_i = A \mid \exists R.C \mid \forall R.C \mid \leq nR.C \mid \geq nR.C$. *Here,* A *is an atomic concept,* C *is a class expression and* R *is a role name in ontology* $\mathcal{O}$, *and* m *and* n *are positive integers.* C *can be of the form:* $C = A \mid C_1 \sqcap C_2 \mid C_1 \sqcup C_2 \mid \exists R.C_1 \mid \forall R.C_1 \mid \leq nR.C_1 \mid \geq nR.C_1$, *where* C_1 *and* C_2 *are also class expressions.*

In the above definition, the c_is are free from disjunctions. If there exist a disjunctive clause satisfied by an individual, then the *satisfiablility* of each expression in that disjunctive clause should be checked and all such *satisfiable* expressions have to be included as conjuncts in the label-set. Clearly, then, the conjunction of all the elements in the label-set of an individual can be entailed by the ontology. That is, $\mathcal{O} \models \left(\sqcap_{i=1}^{n} c_i \right)(x)$. Here, the variable C will not be recursively expanded further to generate a large number of complex redundant expressions in the label-set. While this gives you a reasonable idea of how label-sets are generated, a more detailed account is presented in the longer version of the paper. Furthermore, the *label-set of a concept* can be defined as equivalent to the label-set of an individual that belongs to only that concept. Such a label-set could be obtained easily by introducing a synthetic individual as the member of the concept and finding its label-set.

Table 1. Label-sets from ACAD ontology (intentionally omitted ⊤ class from the label-sets)

$\mathcal{L}_{\mathcal{O}}$(tom)	= {Student, IITStudent, IIT_MS_Student, ∃enrolledIn.IITProgramme, ≤1hasAdvisor.TeachingStaff, ∀hasAdvisor.TeachingStaff, ∃hasAdvisor.Professor }
$\mathcal{L}_{\mathcal{O}}$(sam)	= {Student, IITStudent, IITPhdStudent, ∃isEnrolledIn.IITProgramme, ≥2hasAdvisor.TeachingStaff, ≤1hasAdvisor.Professor, ∀hasAdvisor.TeachingStaff, ∃hasAdvisor.Professor}
$\mathcal{L}_{\mathcal{O}}$(bob)	= {Professor, TeachingStaff}
$\mathcal{L}_{\mathcal{O}}$(alice)	= {AssistantProf, TeachingStaff}
$\mathcal{L}_{\mathcal{O}}$(roy)	= {Professor, TeachingStaff}

4   Proposed Verbalization Approach

Our verbalization process consists of three phases as shown in Fig. 2. The first phase takes an ontology as input and generates label-sets. In the second phase, we process these label-sets to a more refined form using our *semantic-refinement* technique— the main highlight of this paper. To under-

Fig. 2. Phases involved in the proposed verbalization method

stand the degree of reduction performed on a label-set, we assign a redundancy-score to the label-set while performing the reduction. Finally, we convert the restrictions in the refined label-sets into NL texts. In this section, we would first discuss the rationale for our refinement technique, and then we formally define the notion of semantic-refinement.

Consider the label-sets of the individuals from ACAD ontology given in Table 1. A label-set would give us all the restrictions (logical expressions) that are satisfied by an individual. We can effectively verbalize all or part of these restrictions to frame a meaningful definition for that individual. For example, a well formed description for the instance tom that can be generated from its label-set is of the form: *"Tom is a student who is enrolled in an IIT Programme, has one professor as advisor, and all his advisors are teaching staffs."* Here, not all labels in the label-set were considered while generating the description. Some of the generic labels (mainly role restrictions) in the label-set if verbalized directly may generate confusing descriptions, and hence they should be reduced or combined with other restrictions (if possible) to get a more specific (so-called refined) restriction. For example, if left unrefined, the restrictions ∀hasAdvisor.TeachingStaff and ∀hasAdvisor.⊤ may give rise to the description: *"all advisors are someone, and all advisors are teaching staffs"*, which may create ambiguity issues to a human reader. It is observed that to generate an unambiguous and a short description from a label-set, we have to identify redundant labels and see if they can be combined with the non-redundant labels to get a (highly expressive and more specific) refined form.

The naive method to perform the aforementioned tasks is by considering all combinations of labels and see if they can be reduced to a stricter form of logical expression. However, we could easily carryout this exhaustive process by considering labels of specific restriction types in a pre-defined order. For example, all the existential role restrictions could be considered prior to the universal role restrictions. Such a systematic process along with an ordered list of inference rules (called *refinement-rules*), that always generate stricter (more specific) forms of a given set of restriction, will ensure a fast refinement of the label-sets. Since we do this refinement of labels at the logical-level by considering their semantics, we call the refinement process as *semantic-refinement of label-sets*. The refined form of the label-set is called the *semantically-refined label-set*.

In addition to removing redundant labels in a label-set the semantic-refinement would also help in avoiding ambiguous verbalization of interim logical expressions. For example, the label: ∀hasAdvisor.Professor can appear in the label-set of an individual of IITStudent due to the axiom: IITStudent ⊑ ∀hasAdvisor.Professor. Linguistically, this label (along with the axiom) can be interpreted in two ways: either as *All advisors of IIT students are Professors* or, semantically, it can be interpreted as *Either all advisors of IIT students are Professors or* (vacuously-true case) *they do not have an advisor.* Clearly, considering the latter description, even though it is the semantically correct interpretation, may confuse a reader—especially the case when he could infer from other axioms that the vacuously-true case would not arise at all.

For identifying the cases where combinations of conditions involving qualifiers and/or number restrictions occur and to succinctly represent them, we introduce the following new constructors that have higher expressivity than the regular existential and universal restrictions.

- Non-vacuous role restriction: $\Im R.C$
  $\Im R.C^{\mathcal{I}} = \{x \in \Delta^{\mathcal{I}} | \exists y.\langle x, y \rangle \in R^{\mathcal{I}} \wedge y \in C^{\mathcal{I}} \wedge \forall z.\langle x, z \rangle \in R^{\mathcal{I}} \implies z \in C^{\mathcal{I}}\}$
- Exactly-one role restriction: $\exists_{=1} R.C$
  $\exists_{=1} R.C^{\mathcal{I}} = \{x \in \Delta^{\mathcal{I}} | (\exists y_1.\langle x, y_1 \rangle \in R^{\mathcal{I}} \wedge y_1 \in C^{\mathcal{I}} \wedge \exists y_2.\langle x, y_2 \rangle \in R^{\mathcal{I}} \wedge y_2 \in C^{\mathcal{I}}) \implies y_1 = y_2\}$
- Exactly-n role restriction: $\exists_{=n} R.C$, general case of exactly-one role restriction.

In our semantic refinement process, like any rule-based approach, the order in which the inferencing rules are applied is also important as the applicability of one rule may depend on the other. We observed that there is a notion of *strictness* associated with role restrictions which can be effectively utilized for ordering the rules, such that the redundant label selection and the application of the rules can be done simultaneously. The notion of strictness can be looked at as: if a role restriction R_1 is implied by another role restriction R_2 (i.e., $R_2 \implies R_1$), then R_1 can be said to be a stricter version of R_2. For instance, $\Im R.U$ can be said as the stricter form of $\exists R.U$ and $\forall R.U$. Similarly, $\exists_{=n} R.U$ is a stricter form of $\leq nR.U$ and $\geq nR.U$. Since we intend to find stricter forms of role-restrictions, the obvious way is to apply rules corresponding to less strict restriction types prior to those of stricter restriction types. In general, the more strict-restrictions you have in the label-set more refined your label-set is. We can easily capture this notion by finding how often we apply the rules that do this refinement. To achieve this, we associate a pre-determined weight to each rule such that on applying a rule the overall *redundancy-score* of the label-set will reduce depending on the weight of the rule. In other words, the objective of the semantic-refinement is to find the set which has the least redundancy score but yet guaranteeing the semantic-equivalence. The metric used for assigning the redundancy-score is detailed in the next section. The semantic-refinement of a label-set can be formally defined as:

Definition 2. *Given a label-set $\mathcal{L_O}$ semantically-refined label-set can be defined as the set $\mathcal{L_O}'$ such that $\forall\, x \in \mathcal{L_O}, \exists\, y \in \mathcal{L_O}' \mid y \models x$ (semantic equivalence) and in addition the set should have the least redundancy-score.*

Table 2. Details of rule sets 1–5.

Rule No.	Restriction 1	Restriction 2	Condition	Refined form
Concept Refinement rule				
1a	Concept names, whose (equality) definitions are already included in the label-set, can be removed.			
Superclass Refinement rule				
2a	U	V	$U \sqsubseteq V$	U
Existential Role Refinement rule				
3a	$\exists R.U$	$\exists S.V$	$U \sqsubseteq V$ & $R \sqsubseteq S$	$\exists R.U$
Universal Role Refinement rules				
4a	$\forall R.U$	$\forall S.V$	$U \sqsubseteq V$ & $S \sqsubseteq R$	$\forall R.U, \forall S.U$
4b	$\forall R.U$	$\forall R.V$	$V \sqsubseteq U$	$\forall R.V$
III & IV Combination rules				
5a	$\exists R.U$	$\forall R.U$		$\Im R.U$
5b	$\forall R.U$	$\exists S.V$	$U \sqsubseteq V$ & $S \sqsubseteq R$	$\Im R.U, \Im S.U$
5c	$\forall R.U$	$\exists S.V$	$V \sqsubseteq U$ & $S \sqsubseteq R$	$\Im R.U, \exists S.V$

5   Semantic-Refinement of Label-Sets

We propose seven sets of rules for refining a label-set. Each of these rule sets contain carefully chosen rules which are repeatedly applied on the selected restrictions in the label-set until no more refinement is possible. More details of the algorithm follows.

Proposed Refinement Rules. The details of the first five sets of rules are given in Table 2. Each of the rule sets are named based on the type of restriction they handle. For example, the first rule set is called *Concept Refinement rule* since it refines the atomic concepts in the label-set.

– *Concept Refinement Rule (Rule 1a).* To apply this rule, we consider all the concept names that are present in the label-sets whose definitions (i.e., the set of restrictions which defines the concept) already included in the label-set. If the set of restrictions defining a concept completely exists in the label-set, then that concept name could be treated as a redundant information and shall be removed.
– *Superclass Refinement Rule (Rule 2a).* The label-set of an individual contains all the concept names which it belongs to. Some of the concepts in these label-sets are hierarchically related (in class - super-class relationship) in the ontology, resulting in redundant labels. For example, consider the label-set $\mathcal{L}_\mathcal{O}(\text{tom})$ in Table 1, it contains the concepts IIT_MS_Student and IITStudent. Since it can be inferred from the concept IIT_MS_Student that tom is also a IITStudent, we can say that IITStudent is a redundant information (label) in the label-set. We remove such redundant labels by preserving only the most-specific concept. If the most specific concept had been already removed by Rule 1a, the next most specific concept name would be preserved in the label-set using this rule.
– *Existential Role Refinement rule (Rule 3a).* We can select two labels of the form: $\exists R.U$ and $\exists S.V$, from the label-set, as candidates for applying this rule, if $U \sqsubseteq V$ and $R \sqsubseteq S$, in the ontology. According to the existential role refinement rule, candidate labels are semantically equivalent to stating only a single restriction of the form $\exists R.U$ (which we call as the *refined form* of the labels). In general, all the rules that we cover in this paper are defined such that given a refined form and the condition which have been used for refinement, the non-refined forms of the restriction(s) could be traced back. That means, the refinement is done without affecting the semantics/meaning of the restrictions. The formal proofs of all the rules could be found at the longer version of the paper.
– *Universal Role Refinement rules (Rules 4a & 4b).* This rule set contains two rules that refine universal role restrictions.
– *III & IV Combination rules (Rules 5a, 5b & 5c).* For applying the rules in this rule set, we select combinations of existential and universal role restrictions from the label-set. The rules help in refining such combinations to a reduced form.

Table 3. Details of rule sets 6 and 7.

Rule No.	Restriction 1	Restriction 2	Condition	Refined form
Qualified Number Restriction Refinement rules				
6a	$\geq nR.U$	$\geq mS.V$	$U \sqsubseteq V$ & $R \sqsubseteq S$ & $n \geq m$	$\geq nR.U$
6b	$\exists R.U$	$\geq nS.V$	$V \sqsubseteq U$ & $S \sqsubseteq R$ & $n \geq 1$	$\geq nS.V$
6c	$\exists R.U$	$\leq nR.V$	$U \sqsubseteq V$ & $n = 1$	$\exists_{=1}R.U, \exists_{=1}R.V$
6d	$\geq nR.U$	$\leq nS.V$	$R \sqsubseteq S$ & $U \sqsubseteq V$	$\exists_{=n}R.U, \exists_{=n}S.V$
Exactly-n Role Refinement rules				
7a	$\exists R.U$	$\exists_{=1}S.V$	$U \sqsubseteq V$ & $R \sqsubseteq S$	$\exists_{=1}R.U, \exists_{=1}S.V$
7b	$\Im R.U$	$\exists_{=1}S.V$	$U \sqsubseteq V$ & $R \sqsubseteq S$	$\exists_{=1}R.U, \exists_{=1}S.V, \Im R.U$
7c	$\geq mR.V$	$\exists_{=n}R.U$	$U \sqsubseteq V$ & $m \geq n$	$\exists_{=n}R.U, \geq (m-n)R.(V \sqcap \neg U)$

The details of the next set of rule sets are given in Table 3.

– *Qualified Number Restriction Refinement rules.* In this set there are four rules. Here we mainly try to refine qualified number restriction restrictions (of the form $\leq nR.U$ or $\geq mS.V$) to stricter version of the same form or to a exactly-n restrictions.
– *Exactly-n Role Restriction rules.* In this rule set, we reduce the exactly-n role restrictions which are generated using the preceding rule-sets.

Algorithm for Semantic-Refinement. As we mentioned before, semantic-refinement helps in refining restrictions in a label-set to their stricter forms by combining them using a set of rules. The rules are applied sequentially from 1a to 7c. While applying these rules, the reduced restrictions may be removed provisionally to avoid using them in the imminent iterations. We are not removing them permanently, as we may need to use such reduced restrictions with the non-reduced ones until we are sure that none of the forthcoming rules may use such a restriction for the reduction anymore. We mark such restrictions as PRs (Provisionally Reduced ones) so that at a later stage we can remove them permanently from the label-set.

Algorithm 1 describes the steps that have to be followed for applying the rules. This algorithm works by taking pairs of restrictions from the label-set and looking for the applicability of the rules. If a rule is applicable, the restrictions will be checked for the following set of conditions to decide whether to resume the refinement or not. The below-mentioned conditions are followed to ensure a quick refinement. The rationales for considering these three conditions are detailed in the longer version of the paper.

Algorithm 1 Semantic-refinement of label-sets

```
 1: procedure SEMANTIC_REFINEMENT(L_O(x))
 2:     Mark all u ∈ L_O(x) as not PRs
 3:     Apply Concept Refinement rule and remove appropriate concept names from L_O(x)
 4:     R ← Rule-sets 2-7 ▷ list of pre-defined rules
 5:     for each rule-set rs ∈ R do
 6:         Let M, REF ← φ
 7:         for each (u, v) ∈ L_O(x)× L_O(x) AND u ≠ v do
 8:             If !MARKED_AS_PR(u) AND !MARKED_AS_PR(v)   then
 9:             for each (r ∈ rs) do
10:                 if r is applicable on (u, v) then
11:                     M ← APPLY_RULE(r, u, v)
12:                     L_O(x) ← L_O(x) ∪ M
13:                     REF ← REF ∪ {u,v}
14:                     if u ∈ M then
15:                         REF ← REF\{u}
16:                     end if
17:                     if v ∈ M then
18:                         REF ← REF\{v}
19:                     end if
20:                 end if
21:             end for
22:             end if
23:         end for
24:         MARK_AS_PR(REF)
25:         L_O(x) ←L_O(x) ∪ REF
26:         for each u ∈L_O(x) do
27:             if the restn. type of u is not used in the successive rule-sets AND MARKED_AS_PR(u) then
28:                 L_O(x) ←L_O(x)\{u}
29:             end if
30:         end for
31:     end for
32: end procedure
```

- *Condition-1:* No need to further reduce two provisionally reduced (PR) restrictions.
- *Condition-2:* If a rule combines two restrictions ($R1$ and $R2$) and generates either $R1$ or $R2$, then that $R1$ or $R2$ should not be marked as a PR.
- *Condition-3:* If the restrictions of a particular form are *not* used in successive rule-sets, the PR restrictions of such forms can be removed at an early stage.

For illustration, let us consider the label-set of the individual sam. Figure 3 shows the refinement steps and the rules in the rule sets used for the refinement. L_O(sam) is represented vertically. In the figure, the arrows represent the application of rules. The rule numbers are shown in italics. The refinement of two restrictions may sometimes result in more than one restriction. For representing such cases, the arrows are followed by brace brackets ({...}) showing the resultant restrictions.

Initially, the algorithm marks all the labels in the label-set as not PRs. Then the algorithm looks for the applicability of Rule 1a. In the figure, L_O(sam) contains the labels IITStudent and IITPhdStudent whose definitions (in the form of restrictions) are already present in the label-set. Therefore, on applying Rule 1a, they have to be removed from the label-set.

In the algorithm, lines 5–31 consider the rest of the rule-set one at a time and look for possible application of rules on pairs of restrictions in the label-set. In our example label-set, since no rules in the rule sets 2, 3, and 4 were applicable, we move to the next applicable rule set (i.e., Rule-set 5). The algorithm would then apply Rule 5c on two of the restrictions as shown in the figure and refine them to the two restrictions given in the brackets. Application of a rule will be done only if the restrictions in the pair are not marked as PR which is checked using the MARKED_AS_PR method. The *if* condition in line-8 of the algorithm will take care of this. After the application of a rule (using the method APPLY_RULE), the details of the reduced restrictions will be stored in the set variable REF. Based on Condition-2, appropriate changes are made on the contents of REF (lines 14–20). Once all the possible rules in a particular rule set are applied, the reduced restrictions will be marked as PRs (lines 24). Once the algorithm considered all pairs of labels and checked them for the applicability of all the rules in the current rule-set, Condition-3 will be checked for possible permanent removal of the PRs. The entire process will be repeated for all the succeeding rule-sets.

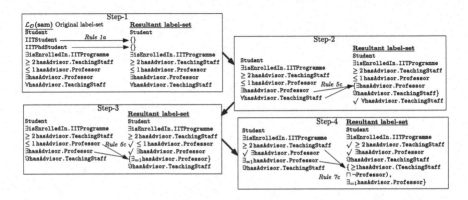

Fig. 3. Steps for the semantic-refinement of $\mathcal{L}_O(\texttt{sam})$. Arrows represent the application of rules.

Coming back to our example label-set, after the application of Rule 5c, one of the reduced restrictions is marked as PR (represented using $\sqrt{}$), while the other restriction is not marked as PR due to Condition-2. On changing the rule-set, since no other rules in Rule-set 5 were applicable, the one which is marked as PR can be permanently removed since Condition-3 is satisfied. In the forthcoming iterations of the for loop (line 5), rules in the rule-set 6 and 7 are applied in a similar fashion. In the last iteration, we will get the most refined set of labels, along with a set of restrictions that are marked as PRs. The restrictions which are marked as PRs are removed to get the refined label-set.

Redundancy Score for Label-Sets. We introduce the *redundancy-score* to quantify the degree of refinement that we perform on a label-set. Intuitively, this score is intended to capture the amount of redundancy in the NL description that is generated from a label set. This measure is defined in terms of the number of labels in the label set as it plays a role in determining the redundancy and is also based on the refinement rules that we apply while performing the reduction. Initially, the label-set will have a redundancy score of "1" where each label would equally contribute (that is, $1/n$ where

n is the number of labels in the label-set) to this score. While applying a rule, the scores (old scores) of the labels that match the antecedents of the rule are redistributed to the new labels (generated as per the consequents of the rule) after multiplying with the weight of the rule. The appropriate weight of the rule is inversely proportional to the rule number as rules are arranged in the increasing order of the amount of redundancy they remove. Therefore, the weight of the rule Rule$_j$ (denoted as w$_j$) is $1/j$. Suppose Rule$_j$ applies to the labels: $\{L_1, ..., L_r\}$, and produces labels: $\{R_1, ..., R_s\}$, then each R_i where $(1 \leq i \leq s)$ is assigned a score as follows. For example, E.g., if *oldScore* of L_1 is 1/8 and that of L_2 is 1/8, then on applying the rule: $L_1 \sqcap L_2 \rightarrow R_1 \sqcap R_2$, the new score of R_1 would be (2/8 * 1/2)*(1/2) = 1/16 and that of R_2 is again 1/16.

$$newScore(R_i) = \frac{w_j \times \sum_{k=1}^{r} oldScore(L_k)}{s} \qquad (1)$$

Those label-sets whose redundancy-score remain as "1" even after applying the semantic-refinement algorithm are treated as non-redundant label-sets. Therefore, we have to change the redundancy-score of such label-sets to "0".

Natural Language Descriptions from the Refined Label-sets. In this paper, we have considered a template similar to the following regular expression for generating descriptions of individuals and concepts, ("is") ("a") C (";" | "and")?)$^+$ (RR (";" | "and")?)$^+$

In this regex, C represents the concept name in the label-set, and RR denotes the role restriction in the label-set. The role restrictions are treated in parts. We first tokenize the role names in the constraints. Tokenizing includes word-segmentation and processing of camel-case, underscores, spaces, punctuations, etc. Then, we identify and tag the verbs and nouns in the segmented phase—as R-verb, R-noun respectively—using NLTK[5]. We then incorporate these segmented words in a *constraint-specific template*, to form a RR. For instance, the restriction ∃*hasAdvisor.Professor* is verbalized to "has at least 1 professor as advisor", using the template: <R-verb> at least <n> <C> as <R-noun> (where C corresponds to the concept present in the restriction). The constraint-specific templates corresponding to the restrictions are listed in Table 4.

6   Empirical Evaluation

We have done the empirical study to address the following two questions: **Q1:** *Does the semantic-refinement help in improving the understandability of the verbalized knowledge?* **Q2:** *Is the semantic refinement helpful in validating the correctness of ontology axioms?* For answering these questions, we present the domain experts with two representations of the same knowledge: one is from the label-sets having redundancy score "1", and the other from the refined label-sets (that is, with redundancy score < 1). We call the former as the ones from the *baseline approach* and the latter as those from the *proposed approach*. The descriptions generated using the baseline approach are similar to the texts generated using an existing ontology verbalizer. Table 5 shows the examples of the descriptions generated using both approaches.

---

[5] Python Natural Language Tool Kit: http://www.nltk.org/.

Table 4. Constraint-specific templates of the possible restrictions in a refined label-set.

Restriction	Constraint-specific template
$\exists R.C$	< R-verb > at least one < C > as < R-noun >
$\forall R.C$	< R-verb > only < C > as < R-noun >
$\geq nR.C$	< R-verb > at least < n >< C > as < R-noun >
$\leq mR.C$	< R-verb > at most < m >< C > as < R-noun >
$\Im R.C$	< R-verb > at least one < C > & only < C > as < R-noun >
$\exists_{=n} R.C$	< R-verb > exactly < n >< C > as < R-noun >

Table 5. Examples of the descriptions of individuals and concepts from PD, HarryPotter (HP) and Geographical Entity (GEO) ontologies, generated using the proposed and baseline approaches

Proposed approach	Baseline approach (with redundancy score =1)	Ontology
Bird cherry Oat Aphid: is a biotic-disorder, having at least one pest-insect and all its factors are pest-insects. (Redundancy score = 0.340)	Bird cherry Oat Aphid: is a disorder, bio-disorder, pest damage and insect damage. It is all the following: has as factor only pest-insect, has as factor only pest, has as factor only organism and has as factor something.	PD
Mite Damage: is a pest damage, having at least one mite pest and all its factors are mite pests. (Redundancy score = 0.324)	Mite Damage: is a disorder, a biotic-disorder and a pest damage. It is all the following: has as factor only organism, has as factor only pest, has as factor only mite pest, has as factor at least one thing.	PD
Hermione Granger: is a Hogwarts Student, a muggle, a gryffindor, having exactly one cat as pet. (Red. score = 0.425)	Hermione Granger: is a Hogwarts student, a student, a human, a muggle, a gryffindor. It is all the following: has a pet, has as pet a cat, has as pet only creature, has at least one creature, has at most one creature, as pet.	HP
Hogwarts Student: is a Student, is a Gryffindor or Hufflepuff or Ravenclaw or Slytherin, and having exactly one pet. (Redundancy score = 0.350)	Hogwarts Student: is a student, a human, is a Gryffindor or Hufflepuff or Ravenclaw or Slytherin. It is all the following: has a pet, has as pet only creatures, has at least one creature, has at most one creature.	HP
Aggregate of sovereign states: is not a gov. organization, is aggregate of only sovereign states and is aggregate of at least two sovereign states. (Red. score = 0.324)	Aggregate of sovereign states: is not a gov. organization and not a sovereign state. It is all the following: is aggregate of only governmental organization, is aggregate of at least two governmental organizations, is aggregate of only sovereign states and aggregate of at least two sovereign states.	GEO
Florida: is a gov. organization and a major administrative subdivision, is related to at least one nation as a part, is related to exactly one sovereign state as a member, and is a subordinate authority of at least one sovereign state. (Red. score = 0.204)	Florida: is a major administrative subdivision, an organization, a gov. organization, a subnational entity. It is all the following: is a part of at least one nation, is a subordinate authority of at least one sovereign state, is a member of at least one sovereign state and have at most one member of relationship with sovereign state.	GEO

For Q1, the domain experts were asked to rate the *degree of understanding* of the descriptions in the scale: (a) *Poor*; (b) *Medium*; (c) *Good*. And, for Q2, to measure the *usefulness* of the generated descriptions for validating the domain knowledge, the domain experts were told to choose one from the options: (a) *Valid* (b) *Invalid* (c) *Don't know* (d) *Cannot be determined*. If they cannot distinguish a given sentence to be "Valid" or "Invalid" because of their lack of knowledge, then they are instructed to choose the third option "Don't Know". Option (d) is to be selected if the expert finds it difficult to reach a conclusion on the validity of the sentence–which means, the description is either ambiguous or confusing. We have used two online available ontologies for generating descriptions: (1) *Plant Disease (PD)* ontology, and (2) *Data structures and Algorithms (DSA)* ontology. These ontologies can be downloaded from our website[6]. The PD ontology has 546 individuals, 105 concepts, and 15 object properties, and the DSA ontology has 333 individuals, 53 concepts, 19 object properties, and 11 datatype properties.

Experimental Setup. After generating descriptions from the aforementioned ontologies, since the manual evaluation of all the generated descriptions is difficult, a small number of descriptions were utilized for the study. We have selected a representative

---

[6] https://sites.google.com/site/ontoworks/ontologies (all ontologies used are available here).

set (and a heterogeneous set) of descriptions by grouping all the descriptions based on their label-sets and then randomly choosing one description from each group. From PD ontology, 31 descriptions of individuals and 10 descriptions of concepts were considered for evaluation. Similarly, from DSA ontology, 14 descriptions of individuals and 17 descriptions of concepts were chosen. Then, experts from the two domains were asked to review the verbalized descriptions. To avoid bias, the reviewers were not informed about the approach followed for generating the description, and the descriptions were randomly presented via a google form. In addition, to finding the inter-rater agreement among the experts, we have also recorded the confidence score of each reviewer for a given question such that in the case of a conflict we make a decision based on their scores. Seven experts from the PD domain and fourteen experts of DSA were involved in the study.

6.1   Results and Discussions

Figure 4, 5, 6 and 7 show the summary of the ratings given by the domain experts.

Q1: The degree of understanding of a description is identified by examining the ratings (i.e., poor, medium, or good) given by the domain experts. The domain experts were asked to choose 'poor' or 'medium' as the level of understanding if there is any ambiguity in the description. To confine the reasons for ambiguity to the fidelity to OWL constructs alone, possible (manual) grammatical error corrections have been done on the generated text—as we were not using any sophisticated NL generation techniques. Grammatical errors such as subject-verb agreement errors, verb tense errors, verb form errors, singular/plural noun ending errors, and sentence structure errors were corrected uniformly (and in an unbiased way) for both the approaches. Figure 4 and Fig. 5 show the summary of the responses (in percentage) which we received for the descriptions of PD ontology and for the descriptions of DSA ontology, respectively. In both cases, since the Fleiss' kappa scores were in the *substantial agreement* range, the overall ratings are calculated by considering the majority responses. For PD ontology, 32 out of the 41 descriptions generated using the proposed approach were rated as 'good', whereas, for those generated using the baseline approach, only 6 out of 41 texts were rated as 'good'. For DSA ontology, 23 out of 31 descriptions generated by the proposed approach were 'good', only 12 descriptions generated using the baseline approach were rated as 'good'. These results highlight the significance of the semantic-refinement process in domain knowledge understanding.

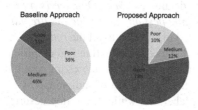

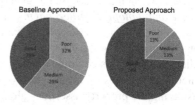

Fig. 4. Summary of the ratings obtained for the descriptions from the **PD** ontology

Fig. 5. Summary of the ratings obtained for the descriptions from the **DSA** ontology

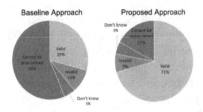

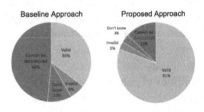

Fig. 6. Summary to determine the usefulness of the generated descriptions in validating the **PD** ontology

Fig. 7. Summary to determine the usefulness of the generated descriptions in validating the **DSA** ontology

Q2: Figure 6 and 7 show the statistics to determine the usefulness of the generated descriptions in validating the correctness of two domain ontologies. Usefulness of the generated descriptions in validating the correctness of an ontology is obtained by looking at the number of descriptions which are marked as 'Cannot be determined'. The three options: 'Valid', 'Invalid' and 'Don't know', imply that the text is useful in getting into a conclusion, whereas the option 'Cannot be determined' indicates that there is some problem in the representation. From Fig. 6 and Fig. 7, in case of the proposed approach, only 7 out of 41 descriptions from PD ontology and 4 out of 31 descriptions from DSA ontology were not useful in determining the quality of the ontology, whereas in case of the baseline approach, approximately 50% of the descriptions were not helpful. This clearly indicates that, verbalization after semantic-refinement is highly effective in applications such as ontology validation.

Discussion and Future Work. In this paper, we have formally defined the notion of redundancies in a label-set and a technique to systematically reduce the redundancies. However, the notion of redundancy is, to some extent, subjective. That is, depending on the readers' domain knowledge, the level of redundancy in the text varies. In the process of semantic-refinement, we remove the generic information from the label-set with an assumption that the human readers would be familiar with the explicit relationships between the domain entities. In that sense, a reader with poor domain knowledge may miss out on generic concept information due to the refinement process. This would be easily visible when the concept hierarchies are reduced to the specific ones alone. One possible way to overcome this problem is by including relevant (but, not all) concept names, that were previously omitted in the semantic-refinement process, in the refined label-set. E.g., in Table 5, we can further generalize the description of the concept mite damage, by including additional generic concept details, as *"Mite Damage is a pest damage and <u>a biotic-disorder</u>, having at least one mite pest and all its factors are mite pests."* Since only a generic concept name is included in addition to all the refined concepts, the meaning of the description is not affected. More investigation and empirical studies related to this could be done as a future endeavor. Another interesting method (which is not addressed in this paper) to improve the description of individuals is by considering the property assertions along with the label-sets while generating descriptions. Considering property relationships/assertions is important because validation of an ontology also involves verifying the truthfulness of the property assertions in it.

7   Conclusion

A novel approach for generating natural language descriptions of ontology entities is presented in the paper. The generated descriptions were not merely verbatim translations of logical axioms of the ontology. Instead, they were generated from a refined set of logical restrictions satisfied by individuals/concepts under consideration. We have proposed seven sets of refinement rules and an algorithm for this refinement process. We have observed that the proposed method indeed gives us short, precise, and comprehensive descriptions of individuals and concepts. Our time-budgeted empirical studies based on two ontologies have shown that the redundancy-free description of the domain knowledge is helpful in understanding the formalized knowledge more effectively and is also useful for validating them, typically for the humans who are experts of the domain under consideration.

Acknowledgements. This project is funded by Ministry of Human Resource Development, Gov. of India. We express our fullest gratitude to the participants of our evaluation process: Dr. S. Gnanasambadan (Director of Plant Protection, Quarantine & Storage), Ministry of Agriculture, Gov. of India; Mr. J. Delince and Mr. J. M. Samraj, Department of Social Sciences AC & RI, Killikulam, Tamil Nadu, India; Ms. Deepthi.S (Deputy Manager), Vegetable and Fruit Promotion Council Keralam (VFPCK), Kerala, India; Dr. K.Sreekumar (Professor) and students, College of Agriculture, Vellayani, Trivandrum, Kerala, India. We also thank all the undergraduate and post-graduate students of Indian Institute of Technology, Madras, who have participated in the empirical study.

References

Alani, H., Harris, S., O'Neil, B.: Winnowing ontologies based on application use. In: Sure, Y., Domingue, J. (eds.) ESWC 2006. LNCS, vol. 4011, pp. 185–199. Springer, Heidelberg (2006). https://doi.org/10.1007/11762256_16. ISBN 978-3-540-34545-9

Androutsopoulos, I., Lampouras, G., Galanis, D.: Generating natural language descriptions from OWL ontologies: the naturalowl system. CoRR, abs/1405.6164 (2014). http://arxiv.org/abs/1405.6164

Cregan,A., Schwitter, R., Meyer, T.: Sydney OWL syntax - towards a controlled natural language syntax for OWL 1.1. In: Golbreich, C., Kalyanpur, A., Parsia, B. (eds.) OWLED, vol. 258 (2007)

Dentler, K., Cornet, R.: Intra-axiom redundancies in SNOMED CT. Artif. Intell. Med. **65**(1), 29–34 (2015). http://dblp.uni-trier.de/db/journals/artmed/artmed65.html#DentlerC15

Venugopal, V.E., Kumar, P.S.: Difficulty-level modeling of ontology-based factual questions. Semant. Web **11**(6), 1023–1036 (2020). https://doi.org/10.3233/SW-200381

Grimm, S., Wissmann, J.: Elimination of redundancy in ontologies. In: Antoniou, G., et al. (eds.) ESWC 2011. LNCS, vol. 6643, pp. 260–274. Springer, Heidelberg (2011). https://doi.org/10.1007/978-3-642-21034-1_18 ISBN 978-3-642-21033-4

Hart, G., Dolbear, C., Goodwin, J.: Lege Feliciter: Using structured English to represent a topographic hydrology ontology. In: OWLED, volume 258 of CEUR Workshop Proceedings. CEUR-WS.org (2007)

Hewlett, D., Kalyanpur, A., Kolovski, V., Halaschek-Wiener, C.: Effective NL paraphrasing of ontologies on the semantic web. In: End User Semantic Web Interaction Workshop (ISWC 2015) (2005)

Horrocks, I., Sattler, U., Tobies, S.: Reasoning with individuals for the description logic SHIQ. CoRR, cs.LO/0005017 (2000)

Jarrar, M., Maria, C., Dongilli, K.P.: Multilingual verbalization of ORM conceptual models and axiomatized ontologies, Technical report (2006)

Kaljurand, K., Fuchs, N.E.: Verbalizing OWL in Attempto controlled English. In: OWLED, vol. 258 (2007)

Liberatore, P.: Redundancy in logic I: CNF propositional formulae. AI **163**(2), 203–232 (2005). https://doi.org/10.1016/j.artint.2004.11.002

Peroni, S., Motta, E., d'Aquin, M.: Identifying key concepts in an ontology, through the integration of cognitive principles with statistical and topological measures. In: Domingue, J., Anutariya, C. (eds.) ASWC 2008. LNCS, vol. 5367, pp. 242–256. Springer, Heidelberg (2008). https://doi.org/10.1007/978-3-540-89704-0_17

Sarker, M.K., et al.: Wikipedia knowledge graph for explainable AI. In: Villazón-Terrazas, B., Ortiz-Rodríguez, F., Tiwari, S.M., Shandilya, S.K. (eds.) KGSWC 2020. CCIS, vol. 1232, pp. 72–87. Springer, Cham (2020). https://doi.org/10.1007/978-3-030-65384-2_6

Schmidt-Schauß, M., Smolka, G.: Attributive concept descriptions with complements. Artif. Intell. **48**(1), 1–26 (1991)

Stevens, R., Malone, J., Williams, S., Power, R., Third, A.: Automating generation of textual class definitions from OWL to English. J. Biomed. Semant. **S–2**(2), S5 (2011)

Third, A.: Hidden Semantics: what can we learn from the names in an ontology? In: Proceedings of the Seventh International Natural Language Generation Conference, Stroudsburg, PA, USA, pp. 67–75. ACL (2012)

Third, A., Williams, S., Power, R.: OWL to English: a tool for generating organised easily-navigated hypertexts from ontologies. In: 10th International Semantic Web Conference (ISWC 2011), October 2011

Venugopal, V.E., Kumar, P.S.: Improving ontology verbalization using semantic-level refinement (extended abstract). In: Proceedings of the 32nd International Workshop on Description Logics, Oslo, Norway, 18–21 June 2019, volume 2373 of CEUR Workshop Proceedings. CEUR-WS.org (2019)

Transfer Learning and Curriculum Learning in Sokoban

Zhao Yang$^{(\boxtimes)}$, Mike Preuss, and Aske Plaat

LIACS, Leiden University, Leiden, The Netherlands
{z.yang,m.preuss}@liacs.leidenuniv.nl

Abstract. Transfer learning can speed up training in machine learning, and is regularly used in classification tasks. It reuses prior knowledge from other tasks to pre-train networks for new tasks. In reinforcement learning, learning actions for a behavior policy that can be applied to new environments is still a challenge, especially for tasks that involve much planning. Sokoban is a challenging puzzle game. It has been used widely as a benchmark in planning-based reinforcement learning. In this paper, we show how prior knowledge improves learning in Sokoban tasks. We find that reusing feature representations learned previously can accelerate learning new, more complex, instances. In effect, we show how curriculum learning, from simple to complex tasks, works in Sokoban. Furthermore, feature representations learned in simpler instances are more general, and thus lead to positive transfers towards more complex tasks, but not vice versa. We have also studied which part of the knowledge is most important for transfer to succeed, and identify which layers should be used for pre-training (Codes we used for this work can be found at https://github.com/yangzhao-666/TLCLS).

Keywords: Reinforcement learning · Transfer learning · Sokoban

1 Introduction

Humans are good at reusing prior knowledge when facing new problems. As a consequence, we learn new tasks quickly, a skill of great interest in machine learning. In the human brain, information received by our sensors is first transformed into different forms, and different types of transformed information are stored in different areas of our brain. When another problem arrives later on, we retrieve useful information and adjust it to better suit solving this new problem. The knowledge stored in artificial neural networks is also re-usable and transferable [31]. In supervised learning, pre-trained networks are commonly applied in computer vision [17,25] and natural language processing [3,9]. Feature representations learned from images or words overlap to some extent, which makes such feature representations reusable and transferable. In reinforcement learning (RL), transfer learning is relatively new, although with the spread of deep neural networks, reusing pre-trained models becomes possible in RL as well [1,7].

© Springer Nature Switzerland AG 2022
L. A. Leiva et al. (Eds.): BNAIC/Benelearn 2021, CCIS 1530, pp. 187–200, 2022.
https://doi.org/10.1007/978-3-030-93842-0_11

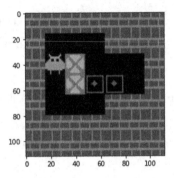

Fig. 1. An example instance of Sokoban.

Transfer learning works well in RL for recognition tasks, but tasks that rely heavily on planning are harder.

In this paper, we study transfer learning of behavior in Sokoban, a popular RL game in which planning is important [10,12]. It has already been proved that Sokoban is PSPACE-complete [8] and NP-hard problem [10]. An example instance from [22] is shown in Fig. 1. The goal of Sokoban is to control a warehouse worker that pushes all boxes onto targets. Sokoban is a challenging game where one wrong move can lead to a dead end (after a box has been pushed, it can not be pulled, and we cannot undo an inadvertent push). This non-reversibility is known to make games harder for AI agents [5]. Learning to solve Sokoban tasks is a challenge, especially in the multi-box scenario. For humans, if we have learned the basics of Sokoban (what is a box, what can an agent do), and if we are faced with a new, more complex instance, then we immediately focus on the new challenges in the instance, rather than re-learning the basics again. This building on prior knowledge saves time in the problem-solving process.

We investigate if we can achieve this kind of pretraining/fine-tuning learning in an RL agent. Our main hypothesis is that feature representations learned in Sokoban instances can be reused to improve solving other instances, and that features learned in simpler instances are more general and better transferable. We test this hypothesis by means of different experiments, in which parts of the neural network that has previously been trained on one type of instances (e.g. one box one target) are taken over (unchanged) to a new type of instances (e.g. two boxes two targets), whereas the remaining part of the network is trained on these new instances from scratch. The overall idea is that we see successful transfer if the preserved knowledge (in terms of network layers) leads to a faster learning process on the new problem type.

The main contributions of this paper are as follows: First, we show that feature representations learned in simple Sokoban instances can accelerate learning in more complex instances, indicating that curriculum learning can be used in Sokoban. Second, feature representations of simpler instances are more general and reusable than features learned in more complex instances. Third, our results confirm that in RL lower layers learn more general features. Interestingly, in some cases the best performance is achieved when more specific features are transfered, when source task and target task are similar enough to support these more specific features. Fourth, we found negative transfer from a simple supervised learning task, which tells us that choice and design of the source tasks are crucial. Fifth, we show that transferring top-fully-connected layers will not only be unhelpful but also harmful to the learning. We also used popular visualization techniques to explore potential reasons for successful transfers, which we explain in detail. Our code and test environments will be made available after blind review.

The paper is structured as follows: we first briefly review related work on transfer learning and Sokoban in the next section; then the environment and methods we are using are described in Sect. 3; Sect. 4 shows the experimental settings and results; in the last section, we conclude our work and discuss some potential future directions.

2 Related Work

De la Cruz et al. [6] studied the reuse of feature representations between two similar games: Breakout and Pong, using Deep Q Network (DQN). They used a 3-layer convolutional network. Weights learned in one game were transferred to improve learning the other game; results showed positive transfer of features between the different games. Pong and Breakout do not require planning; in our experiments, in Sokoban, we study how a curriculum of simpler instances can benefit the learning of complex instances. Spector et al. [26] used self-transfer in a DQN grid-world task to identify which parts should be transferred and which parts should be fixed, showing significant benefit of knowledge transfer.

Sokoban is a planning task that has been used as a benchmark for model-based reinforcement learning [16,22]. It has also been used in model-free RL [14,15], achieving performance competitive with model-based methods. The efficiency of AlphaZero-style curriculum learning has been shown by solving hard single Sokoban instances [11,12]. Previous works were aimed at solving single Sokoban instances; our paper focuses on the transferability of learned knowledge among *different* instances.

This transferability of learned feature representations was first studied in image classification problems [31]. It was shown that bottom layers in Convolutional Neural Networks (CNNs) extract more general features while ones extracted from back layers are more specific. In this paper, we verify this idea under RL settings.

Reinforcement learning [21,27] aims to reinforce behaviors of the learning agent by rewarding signals obtained from interactions with the environment. It has reached super-human performance in games such as Go [24], StarCraft [20,29], as well as Atari games [2] and robotic tasks. In this paper we follow the conventional MDP notation for RL [27].

Transfer learning reuses prior knowledge to improve the learning efficiency or performance in new tasks [28,30]. In reinforcement learning, higher-level knowledge such as macro actions, skills and lower-level knowledge such as reward functions, policies could be transferred. Transferring learned knowledge could take different approaches, such as reward shaping [4], learning from demonstration [19] and policy reuse [13].

3 Experimental Setup

The environment used in the paper is the Gym environment for Sokoban [23]; for the agent algorithms we follow Weber et al. [22]. Examples are shown in Fig. 2. The game is solved by controlling the agent (green sprite) to push all boxes (yellow squares) onto corresponding targets (red squares). There's no hint about which boxes should on which targets, and boxes can only be pushed; some actions are irreversible, and can leave the game in an unsolvable state. The difficulty of the game can be increased easily by putting more boxes as well as targets into generated rooms. The agent can go up, down, left, and right. The agent gets a final reward of 10 by pushing all boxes on targets. Pushing a box on a target will result a reward of 1 and a penalty of -1 for pushing a box off a target. We also give a small penalty of 0.1 for each step the agent takes.

We perform three types of experiments: (1) related tasks (source and target tasks are both RL tasks, while source tasks are to solve n-boxes Sokoban instances and target tasks are to solve m-boxes Sokoban instances, where $n \neq m$), (2) different tasks (source tasks are supervised learning (SL) tasks and target tasks are reinforcement learning (RL) tasks), and (3) different texture appearance (source and target tasks are both RL tasks, while source tasks are to solve original Sokoban instances and target tasks are to solve Sokoban instances with different texture appearance). The agent was first pre-trained on source tasks and then fine-tuned on target tasks. RL tasks are to solve 100 randomly generated n-boxes Sokoban instances. SL tasks are to recognize the location of the agent in Sokoban instances.

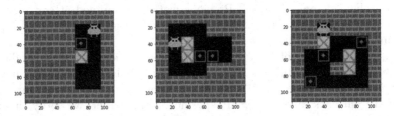

Fig. 2. Examples of Sokoban instances, increasing in difficulty from 1 box and 1 target to 3 boxes and 3 targets (Color figure online)

The overall statistics of the maps are shown in Fig. 3. As the number of objectives increases, the number of steps for the optimal solution also increases, and so does the difficulty of solving the game.

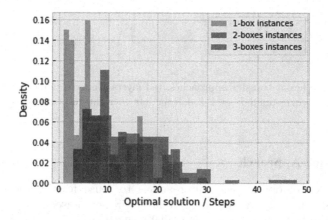

Fig. 3. Distribution of optimal solutions in different Sokoban instances.

3.1 Neural Network Architecture

The neural network we employ is taken from the DeepMind baseline [22] directly without hyper-parameter tuning. The model consists of 3 convolutional (Conv) layers with kernel size 8 × 8, 4 × 4, 3 × 3, strides of 4, 2, 1, and number of output channels 32, 64, 64. This is followed by a fully connected (FC) hidden layer with 512 units. The outputs of this FC layer will be fed into two heads: one for outputting the policy logits and one for outputting the state value. This is one of the most commonly-used architectures in RL, we selected it also in order to show what can be achieved with popular architecture. Details of architecture and hyper parameters we employ are found in Table 1.

Table 1. Hyper-parameters of the neural network and training.

Learning rate	$7 \cdot 10^{-4}$
Discount factor	0.99
Entropy coefficient	0.1
Value loss coefficient	0.5
Eps in RMSprop	10^{-5}
Alpha in RMSprop	0.99
Rollout storage size	5
No. of environments for collecting trajectories	30

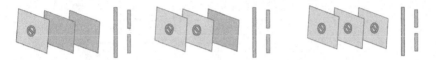

Fig. 4. Three different transfer approaches, red layers are fixed while green layers are trainable. They correspond $k = 1, 2, 3$ from left to right respectively. (Color figure online)

3.2 Transfer Approach

The main idea of our transfer approach is to reuse feature representations from source tasks learned by the Conv layers in new unseen target tasks. As detailed in the last sub-section, our model consists of 3 Conv layers and 2 FC layers. The feature representations were transferred to new tasks by copying the weights of the first k Conv layers trained in source tasks (where there are n_s boxes/targets) to initialize the new learning model in target tasks (where there are n_t boxes/targets). Then we froze these weights (they were no longer trainable) and retrained the remaining part of the model. In our experiments, $k \in \{1, 2, 3\}$, $n_s \in \{1, 2, 3\}$, $n_t \in \{1, 2, 3\}$. Please refer to Fig. 4 for an explanation of this approach. Different squares represent different layers of our neural network. The first 3 layers are Conv layers and the last two are FC layers. Reds are weights taken from pre-trained model and fixed, greens are weights reinitialized and trainable.

Solved ratios were used for evaluating agents, and evaluation executes every 1,000 environment steps. 20 randomly selected test instances were performed by the current learning agent. We say the transfer is *positive* when the performance with the transfer is better than without (training from scratch), and *negative* when the performance with the transfer is worse than without.

4   Experiments

We designed experiments with different source, target tasks and k, in order to verify the hypotheses we proposed. We experimented with Sokoban instances with 1, 2, and 3 boxes. All experiments were run for 1 million environment steps. We use abbreviations for each experiment. For instance, **s1t1k1** means source tasks are 1-box instances, target tasks are 1-box instances and we transfer and fix the 1 (first) layer. Exceptions are **sPt1k1** and **s1t1fc_game2**. **sPt1k1** stands for the source task is a supervised learning prediction task, and target task is the RL task over 1-box instances while we only keep the first layer. **s1t1fc_game2** is that the source and target tasks are both RL tasks over 1-box instances, but we transfer fully connected layers to instances with different appearance. The neural networks were trained using Advantage Actor Critic (A2C), a single threaded variant of A3C [18]. All experiments were performed 5 times with different random seeds, and figures were drawn using averaged results with 0.95

confidence interval. Heavy fluctuations were caused by irreversible actions, one irreversible action during the game could make the whole game unsolvable.

4.1   Transfer Among Related Tasks

Related tasks are tasks where the only difference between source and task is the difficulties of instances, i.e. the number of boxes and targets. (Recall that both source and task are trained on 100 different map-layouts, in all experiments.)

Figure 5 and Fig. 6 show results for training on 1-box, 2-boxes, 3-boxes instances with reusing features learned in different tasks, and we fix $k = 3$. All results showed that transferring feature representations learned in single-box instances is positive. Performance of agents (s1t1k3, s1t2k3, s1t3k3) who are using features learned from single-box instances always outperform other agents, including agents training from scratch and using features learned from other instances. The transfer, however, is not 'bi-directional', feature representations learned in multiple-box instances could not be successfully transferred to the learning in single-box instances. Their performance (s2t1k3, s3t1k3) converged to a relatively low solved ratio, which indicates that transferred features are not suitable for single-box instances. Just as humans learn more general knowledge in simpler cases, our agents also showed that the knowledge learned from single-box instances is more general and transferable than ones learned in multiple-box instances.

To further enhance performances of transferring features learned in single-box instances, we tried different k. We expected that the performance will be the best when $k = 1$ since the first layer learn the most general features. However, the results in Fig. 7 instead show that not $k = 1$ but $k = 2$ (s1t2k2, s1t3k2)

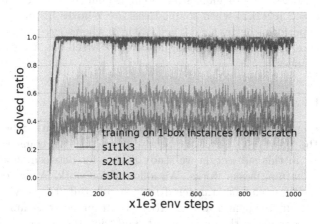

Fig. 5. Performance of transferring feature representations learned in 1-box, 2-boxes, 3-boxes instances to learning in 1-box with $k = 3$. $n_s = 1, 2, 3$, $n_t = 1$, $k = 3$. Pre-training on 1-box instances is much better than pre-training on 2 or 3 box instances when training new 1-box instances.

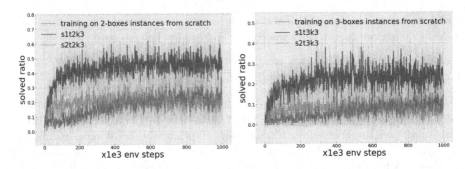

Fig. 6. Performance of transferring feature representations learned in 1-box, 2-boxes, 3-boxes instances to learning in 2-boxes (left) and 3-boxes (right) with $k = 3$. $n_s = 1, 2, 3$, $n_t = 2, 3$, $k = 3$.

perform the best. Similar to [6], features learned in the first 2 layers are still general enough for transfer; in addition, the difference between source tasks and target tasks is not as large as expected, and features learned between different instances are more overlapping than expected.

It is also interesting to see the influence of how many layers are fixed on the success of the transfer. In particular, we want to know whether a smaller k could change the negative transfer from multiple-box instances to single-box instances into positive. (We believe features from multiple and single-box instances are overlapping to some extent.) Results are shown in Fig. 8. We see that indeed the first layer (s2t1k1, s3t1k1) did learn enough general features from multiple-boxes instances to solve the single-box instances. Although agents with features only learned by the first layer could converge to decent performance in the end, the transfer is still negative. An interesting point is that $k = 3$ (s2t1k3) performs better than $k = 2$ (s2t1k2) when source tasks are 2-boxes instances. Note that $k = 2$ (s3t1k2) performs better than $k = 3$ (s3t1k3) when source tasks are 2-boxes instances. There are more overlapping features between the 2-boxes instances and single instances.

4.2 Transfer Among Different Tasks (SL/RL)

Feature representations learned from previous tasks can either be helpful or harmful. In the previous subsection we saw some positive transfer to related Sokoban tasks, in this subsection we study if transfer between supervised and reinforcement learning tasks works. We follow prior work, Anderson et al. [1] showed that features can be transferred from hand-crafted supervised learning (SL) tasks to reinforcement learning (RL). Their model was first trained to predict state dynamics of the environment, and then pre-trained hidden layers were helpful to accelerate solving RL tasks.

For transfer to different (randomly chosen) instances in Sokoban, we also formed a supervised task, which was to train a prediction model to recognize the location of the agent, shown in Fig. 9a. When humans are solving Sokoban,

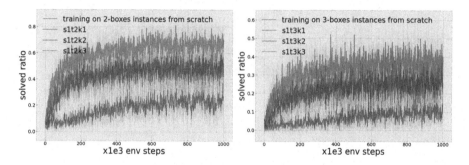

Fig. 7. Performance of transferring feature representations learned in 1-box instances to learning in 2-boxes (left) and 3-boxes (right) with different k. $n_s = 1$, $n_t = 2, 3$, $k = 1, 2, 3$.

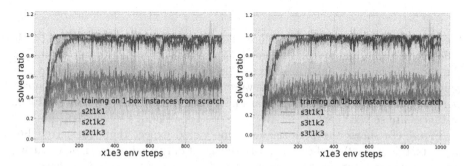

Fig. 8. Performance of transferring feature representations learned in 2-boxes (left) and 3-boxes (right) instances to learning in 1-box instances with different k. $n_s = 2, 3$, $n_t = 1$, $k = 1, 2, 3$.

we first need to know where the agent is before we draw up a plan. If we already know the location of objectives, the solving process could be faster. After the prediction model could correctly recognize where the agent is, we took feature representations of the trained model and plug them into a new agent. The first layer of learned features is fixed, and we only train the remaining part. Figure 9b shows the performance of transferring and training from scratch. We find negative transfer for (sPt1k1): the performance is much worse compare with training from scratch.

4.3 Transfer to Different Appearance

Experiments we described in previous subsections were all trying to transfer Conv layers which learned feature representations. In the next experiment, we try to make the agent utilize another part of the learned model, which are back FC layers of the whole model. The source and target tasks were both single-box instances, but the target tasks were instances with different appearances. Figure 10b is an example. The maps used for two groups of tasks were the same,

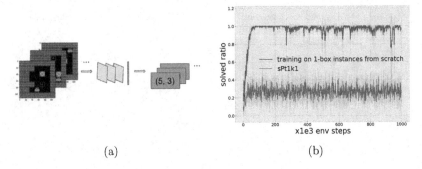

Fig. 9. (a): How SL tasks work. Input states and neural network will learn to predict locations of the agent. (b): Performance of training from scratch and training with transferred feature representations from SL tasks.

the only difference was how they look like, the appearance was changed, with different textures, and we call it Game2. Figure 10a shows the transfer approach. We took FC layers trained in source tasks and fixed them, and retrained the remaining Conv layers. Since maps were the same, solutions of the instances were the same. When Conv layers learn new feature representations successfully, instances are solved then.

Figure 11a shows the performance. One would expect that transferred FC layers (s1t1fc_game2) are faster because the agent only needs to learn new feature representations. However, the experiments did not show this result. Apparently, when the whole model is trained jointly, it has more flexibility to be trained into the final shape; when the last part of the model is fixed, the learning of the first part will be trying to cater for the last part in order to solve the problem, which made the learning slower.

4.4   Visualizing Agent Detection

In order to better understand what the network learned, we provide a visualization. We follow Yosinski et al. who showed that convolutional neural networks can detect latent objectives without explicit labels [31]. We visualized a feature map of a trained neural network on 1-box RL tasks. Figure 11b shows the latent 'agent detector' for Sokoban. The neural network automatically learned to detect the agent without giving any labels or information. Left rows are pixel inputs, right rows are outputs of one specific feature map. Yellow-green units are detected agents. We note that although the network was trained in single-box instances, it still performed quite well in multiple-box instances, which is a potential reason for the successful transfer. The agent's abilities that were learned in source tasks are useful in target tasks.

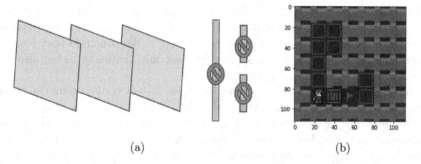

(a)   (b)

Fig. 10. (a): Transfer approach for transfer to Game2. FC layers are taken from previously training and fixed, only conv layers will be retrained. (b): An example instance in Game2. We changed appearances in Game2 with different textures of objectives.

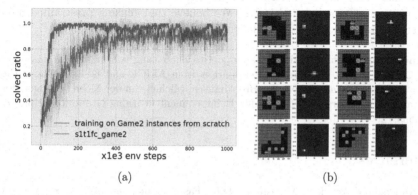

(a)   (b)

Fig. 11. (a): Training on Game2 using transferred FC layers. Its performance is worse than training from scratch. (b): The agent detector. Outputs of the twenty third feature map of the first convolutional layer, which is an agent detector learned from 1-box instances, and it's still usable in multiple-boxes scenarios. (Color figure online)

5   Conclusion and Future Work

Our experiments showed that in a reinforcement learning setting the agent in Sokoban can learn four characteristics that are similar to humans. (1) Feature representations learned previously can accelerate the new learning in other Sokoban instances. Knowledge learned in previous related tasks could be reused to accelerate new learning, transfer learning is occurring, creating an implicit learning curriculum. (2) Feature representations learned in single-box instances are more general, and are more effective for learning in multiple-boxes instances, but not vice versa. Knowledge learned in simpler tasks is more general and more effective, even in more complex tasks. Further experiments showed negative learning, that confirms these results. (3) Feature representations learned in unrelated supervised learning tasks can hurt fine-tuning performance. If the learned knowledge is required to be helpful in new coming tasks, it's better to learn from similar tasks, otherwise the choice of tasks needs to be careful. (4) Fixing the top-fully-connected layers and retraining the bottom convolutional layers slows down learning and hurts performance. We conclude that learning should have explicit order, less flexibility will not only be unhelpful but also hurt the learning process and the performance.

Our experiments showed that with a simple 5-layer convolutions/fully connected network (based on DeepMind's baseline [22]), transfer learning and curriculum learning of behavior to occur in Sokoban. This is surprising, since Sokoban is a planning-heavy problem, for which one would expect more elaborate network architectures to be necessary. Reusing pre-trained feature representations in RL fields is not well studied, and to the best of our knowledge, these are the first results show transfer learning and curriculum learning with such a simple network in such a planning-heavy behavioral task. In the future, we would like to see more utilization of pre-trained feature representations and of the entire pre-trained model in RL. We believe that reusing pre-trained model can significantly improve data-efficient reinforcement learning.

Acknowledgement. The financial support to Zhao Yang is from the China Scholarship Council (CSC). Computation support is from ALICE and DSLab. The authors thank Hui Wang, Matthias Müller-Brockhausen, Michiel van der Meer, Thomas Moerland and all members from the Leiden Reinforcement Learning Group for helpful discussions.

References

1. Anderson, C.W., Lee, M., Elliott, D.L.: Faster reinforcement learning after pretraining deep networks to predict state dynamics. In: 2015 International Joint Conference on Neural Networks (IJCNN), pp. 1–7. IEEE (2015)
2. Badia, A.P., et al.: Agent57: Outperforming the Atari human benchmark. In: International Conference on Machine Learning, pp. 507–517. PMLR (2020)
3. Brown, T.B., et al.: Language models are few-shot learners. arXiv preprint arXiv:2005.14165 (2020)
4. Brys, T., Harutyunyan, A., Taylor, M.E., Nowé, A.: Policy transfer using reward shaping. In: Proceedings of the 2015 International Conference on Autonomous Agents and Multiagent Systems, pp. 181–188 (2015)
5. Cook, M., Raad, A.: Hyperstate space graphs for automated game analysis. In: IEEE Conference on Games, CoG 2019, London, United Kingdom, 20–23 August 2019, pp. 1–8. IEEE (2019). https://doi.org/10.1109/CIG.2019.8848026
6. De la Cruz, G., Du, Y., Irwin, J., Taylor, M.: Initial progress in transfer for deep reinforcement learning algorithms. In: 25th International Joint Conference on Artificial Intelligence (IJCAI), vol. 7 (2016)
7. Cruz, G.V., Jr., Du, Y., Taylor, M.E.: Pre-training neural networks with human demonstrations for deep reinforcement learning. arXiv preprint arXiv:1709.04083 (2017)
8. Culberson, J.: Sokoban is PSPACE-complete (1997)

9. Devlin, J., Chang, M.W., Lee, K., Toutanova, K.: BERT: pre-training of deep bidirectional transformers for language understanding. arXiv preprint arXiv:1810.04805 (2018)
10. Dor, D., Zwick, U.: Sokoban and other motion planning problems. Comput. Geom. **13**(4), 215–228 (1999)
11. Feng, D., Gomes, C.P., Selman, B.: A novel automated curriculum strategy to solve hard Sokoban planning instances. Adv. Neural. Inf. Process. Syst. **33**, 3141–3152 (2020)
12. Feng, D., Gomes, C.P., Selman, B.: Solving hard AI planning instances using curriculum-driven deep reinforcement learning. CoRR abs/2006.02689 (2020). https://arxiv.org/abs/2006.02689
13. Fernández, F., García, J., Veloso, M.: Probabilistic policy reuse for inter-task transfer learning. Robot. Auton. Syst. **58**(7), 866–871 (2010)
14. Guez, A., et al.: An investigation of model-free planning. In: International Conference on Machine Learning, pp. 2464–2473. PMLR (2019)
15. Guez, A., et al.: Learning to search with MCTSnets. In: International Conference on Machine Learning, pp. 1822–1831. PMLR (2018)
16. Hamrick, J.B., et al.: On the role of planning in model-based deep reinforcement learning. In: 9th International Conference on Learning Representations, ICLR 2021, Virtual Event, Austria, 3–7 May 2021 (2021)
17. He, K., Zhang, X., Ren, S., Sun, J.: Deep residual learning for image recognition. In: Proceedings of the IEEE Conference on Computer Vision and Pattern Recognition, pp. 770–778 (2016)
18. Mnih, V., et al.: Asynchronous methods for deep reinforcement learning. In: International Conference on Machine Learning, pp. 1928–1937. PMLR (2016)
19. Nair, A., McGrew, B., Andrychowicz, M., Zaremba, W., Abbeel, P.: Overcoming exploration in reinforcement learning with demonstrations. In: 2018 IEEE International Conference on Robotics and Automation (ICRA), pp. 6292–6299. IEEE (2018)
20. Ontanón, S., Synnaeve, G., Uriarte, A., Richoux, F., Churchill, D., Preuss, M.: A survey of real-time strategy game AI research and competition in StarCraft. IEEE Trans. Comput. Intell. AI Games **5**(4), 293–311 (2013)
21. Plaat, A.: Learning to Play: Reinforcement Learning and Games. Springer, Heidelberg (2020). https://learningtoplay.net
22. Racanière, S., et al.: Imagination-augmented agents for deep reinforcement learning. In: Proceedings of the 31st International Conference on Neural Information Processing Systems, pp. 5694–5705 (2017)
23. Schrader, M.P.B.: Gym-Sokoban (2018). https://github.com/mpSchrader/gym-sokoban
24. Silver, D., et al.: Mastering the game of go without human knowledge. Nature **550**(7676), 354–359 (2017)
25. Simonyan, K., Zisserman, A.: Very deep convolutional networks for large-scale image recognition. arXiv preprint arXiv:1409.1556 (2014)
26. Spector, B., Belongie, S.: Sample-efficient reinforcement learning through transfer and architectural priors. arXiv preprint arXiv:1801.02268 (2018)
27. Sutton, R.S., Barto, A.G.: Reinforcement Learning, An Introduction, 2nd edn. MIT Press, Cambridge (2018)
28. Taylor, M.E., Stone, P.: Transfer learning for reinforcement learning domains: a survey. J. Mach. Learn. Res. **10**, 1633–1685 (2009)
29. Vinyals, O., et al.: Grandmaster level in StarCraft II using multi-agent reinforcement learning. Nature **575**(7782), 350–354 (2019)

30. Xu, W., He, J., Shu, Y.: Transfer learning and deep domain adaptation. In: Advances in Deep Learning. IntechOpen (2020)
31. Yosinski, J., Clune, J., Bengio, Y., Lipson, H.: How transferable are features in deep neural networks? Advances in Neural Information Processing Systems, pp. 3320–3328 (2014)

Reinforcing Decisions

Proximal Policy Optimisation for a Private Equity Recommitment System

Emmanuel Kieffer[1]([📧]), Frédéric Pinel[1], Thomas Meyer[3],
Georges Gloukoviezoff[2], Hakan Lucius[2], and Pascal Bouvry[1]

[1] University of Luxembourg, Esch-sur-Alzette, Luxembourg
{emmanuel.kieffer,frederic.pinel,pascal.bouvry}@uni.lu
[2] European Investment Bank, Luxembourg, Kirchberg, Luxembourg
{g.gloukoviezoff,h.lucius}@eib.org
[3] SimCorp Luxembourg SA, Luxembourg City, Luxembourg
thomas.meyer@simcorp.com

Abstract. Recommitments are essential for limited partner investors to maintain a target exposure to private equity. However, recommitting to new funds is irrevocable and expose investors to cashflow uncertainty and illiquidity. Maintaining a specific target allocation is therefore a tedious and critical task. Unfortunately, recommitment strategies are still manually designed and few works in the literature have endeavored to develop a recommitment system balancing opportunity cost and risk of default. Due to its strong similarities to a control system, we propose to "learn how to recommit" with Reinforcement Learning (RL) and, more specifically, using Proximal Policy Optimisation (PPO). To the best of our knowledge, this is the first attempt a RL algorithm is applied to private equity with the aim to solve the recommitment problematic. After training the RL model on simulated portfolios, the resulting recommitment policy is compared to state-of-the-art strategies. Numerical results suggest that the trained policy can achieve high target allocation while bounding the risk of being overinvested.

Keywords: Reinforcement learning · Private equity · Control system

1 Introduction

Private equity is an alternative asset class which refers to direct investments in non-listed companies made at different stages of their development to create added value. These companies are then sold few years later with the expectation to obtain a significant capital gain. Early investments in strong performing companies help them to develop their business and make them more profitable. Contrary to the public equity market, private equity investments are not easily accessed as stocks and bonds. Recently, private equity has been included in the portfolios of institutional investors such as pension funds, sovereign wealth funds, etc. These institutional investors have been building sizable allocation by investing "indirectly"

© Springer Nature Switzerland AG 2022
L. A. Leiva et al. (Eds.): BNAIC/Benelearn 2021, CCIS 1530, pp. 203–217, 2022.
https://doi.org/10.1007/978-3-030-93842-0_12

to private companies through private equity funds. Indeed, managing such a less traditional asset class requires a high level of expertise to properly enter and exit direct investments. This explains their preferred modus operandi to invest indirectly as so-called limited partners (LP) through limited partnership funds in which they commit a certain amount of capital for a given period of time. Commitments are irrevocable and called at the discretion of the fund's management, i.e., the general partner (GP), to decide how investments should be realised. The committed capital is gradually draw down during the so-called investment period which last several years. To complicate matters, stakes in these funds are illiquid [7] which enforce LP investors to be extremely cautious when it comes to recommit into new funds to limit the risk of default. Generally, the committed capital is an upper-bound of the total capital finally called by a fund. A significant part ($\approx 10\%$) of the initial capital is generally never invested as described in [18]. Furthermore, committed capital waiting to be called is generally pictured as dry powder. Prequin[1] reported in November 2020 that North American private equity firms are sitting on almost \$980bn in reserves. This uncalled capital dramatically impacts investors' exposure (see [12]). In practice, LP investors therefore run so-called overcommitment strategies, i.e., committing more capital in aggregate than actually available as dedicated resources, with the gap expected to be filled by future distributions from investments made in other existing funds. These strategies thus increase the liquidity risk when the fund is only few years old when the likelihood to be called is the highest. LP investors need to setup a commitment-pacing strategy, i.e., on how to size and time their commitments, in order to achieve and maintain a target allocation while complying with the liquidity constraints imposed by the uncalled capital. As reported in [3] and [9], few investigations have been engaged to evaluate the cost of maintaining uncalled capital. This is the reason why the current existing models still remain rudimentary and depend on spreadsheet-based and "trial-and-error" approaches. These manually-designed strategies are often error-prone and naive although the opportunity cost, i.e., the cost of being underinvested, and the risk of default in case of overinvestment can be very damaging for LP investors.

In this work, we propose to investigate an approach relying on Reinforcement Learning to learn how to size and time dynamic recommitments. The latter can be formulated as a RL problem to discover reliable recommitment policies using a Proximal Policy Optimisation algorithm. Recommitment policies can be assimilated as control policies which should maintain a target allocation minimizing the opportunity cost while preserving investors from the risk of default.

The remainder of this paper is organized as follows. The next section provides a state of the art on existing recommitment strategies. Section 3 introduces formally the Private Equity Recommitment Problem (PERP). Section 4 described the Proximal Policy Optimisation algorithm applied on the RL version of the PERP introduced in Sect. 5. Experiment setups and results are discussed in

---

[1] https://www.preqin.com/insights/research/blogs/what-private-equitys-record-dry-powder-haul-means-for-the-industry.

Sect. 6 and 7. Finally, the last section provides our conclusions and proposes some possible perspectives.

2   Related Works

Recommitment strategies are essential to keep investors constantly invested at some target allocation. To the best of our knowledge, few studies have tried to model this as an optimisation problem. They generally rely on some rules of thumb lacking robustness and flexibility. In [4], authors considered that the entire private equity allocation should be recommitted to new funds every year without taking into account past portfolios evolution. Nevin et al. in [11] based their recommitment strategy on average rates of distributions and commitments. New commitments should be made if the committed capital does not reach a target threshold to compensate the difference. This strategy assumes constants rates which seems very illusory over time. In [18], de Zwart et al. proposed recommitment strategies for funds aiming to maintain stable the exposure to PE. The strategy's key feature is the level of new commitments in a given period which depends on the current portfolio's characteristics. Importantly, de Zwart's strategies does not require to forecast funds'cashflows. Although they consider 100% PE portfolios, their last suggested strategy is a first attempt to design dynamic recommitment strategies relying on past portfolio development. Finally, Oberli et al. in [12] extended de Zwart's work to multi-asset class portfolios including stocks and bonds. These two last contributions solely rely on handcrafted recommitment strategies to control the investment degree (ID), i.e., PE exposure. While they are innovative and improving attempts without the need to forecast future cashflows, they have been built on specific and limited datasets with given market conditions. Building recommitment strategies in various market conditions is a challenging task. In this work, we investigate Reinforcement Learning to discover promising recommitment policies using the policy-based PPO algorithm. Policy-based algorithms [13,15] have been motivated by the fact that solving a RL problem is all about finding a sequences of actions even for value-based algorithms [6,10]. Discovering and predicting the best actions avoid the computational burden to compute all state values. Besides, when the action space is continuous or very large, policy-based approaches are more attractive than values as we do not need to solve an optimisation problem to select the best action.

3   Problem Description

This section describes the Private Equity Recommitment (PERP) by considering a single LP investor owning a 100% private equity portfolio. To minimize the opportunity cost, the investor's primary target is to remain fully invested while avoiding cash shortage. Let us define $\mathcal{P}(t) = \{f\}_{i=1}^{M}$ the set of active funds in the portfolio at time t. In order to measure its degree of investment, the fraction of total allocated capital that is actually invested can be computed as follows:

$$ID(\mathcal{P},t) = \frac{\sum\limits_{f \in \mathcal{P}(t)} NAV(f,t)}{\sum\limits_{f \in \mathcal{P}(t)} NAV(f,t) + Cash(\mathcal{P},t)} \tag{1}$$

where $\sum\limits_{f \in \mathcal{P}(t)} NAV(f,t)$ represents the sum of all Net Asset Value (NAV) for the underlying funds in the portfolio at period t. $Cash(\mathcal{P},t)$ accounts for the global uninvested cash in the portfolio, i.e., uncalled capital and possible distributions. Ideally, the investment degree ID should be as close as possible to 1. A trivial but not viable solution would be to bring $Cash(\mathcal{P},t)$ to 0 but this is without counting on future and inopportune capital calls exceeding the investor resources capacities. Becoming a defaulting investor once capital has been committed is subject to strong financial and reputational penalties. The PERP is therefore a challenging problematic for LP investors as they constantly need to stay close to the boundary without over-crossing it. In [18], authors modelled the problem as a sequence of single-period portfolio optimisation problems maximizing subsequent investment degrees using the following formulation:

$$\min_{C(\mathcal{P},t)} E_t \left[(1 - ID(\mathcal{P},t+1))^2 \right] \tag{2}$$

where the $C(\mathcal{P},t)$ represents the optimal amount of capital to be recommitted at t. Note that this model only determines the optimal recommitment level with regards to the next period. This is debatable as the committed capital is called progressively over the investment period, i.e., roughly during the first 6 years. With respect to formulation Eq. (2), the optimal level of commitment at period t is therefore:

$$C(\mathcal{P},t) = E_t \left(\frac{Cash(\mathcal{P},t) + D(\mathcal{P},t+1) - \sum_{i=1}^{\tau} \gamma_{t+1,i+1} C(\mathcal{P},t-i)}{\gamma_{t+1,1}} \right) \tag{3}$$

with E_t the conditional expectation, $Cash(\mathcal{P},t)$ the uninvested cash in the portfolio, $D(\mathcal{P},t)$ representing distributions for the next period, $C(\mathcal{P},t-i)$ the capital committed i period ago and $\gamma_{t+1,i+1}$ is the fraction of the capital committed i periods ago. $\gamma_{t+1,i+1}$ enables to compute the total capital called at the end of quarter $t+1$, i.e.,

$$CC(\mathcal{P},t-i) = \sum_{i=0}^{\tau} \gamma_{t+1,i+1} C(\mathcal{P},t-i) \text{ with } \tau \text{ representing the maximum fund}$$

age at which capital can still be called. Interested readers can refer to [18] for more details about the proof.

One can observe that the analytical solution requires to forecast distributions (see [8,16]) at $t+1$ and the fraction of the capital committed in the past that will be called. Although prediction models can be developed to approximate future distributions, it is very unlikely to *guess* future capital calls as direct investments in private companies are made at the discretion of the fund's management.

Some works [12,18] in the literature have tried to cope with this issue by engineering strategies using only available and past quantities. These strategies can be likened "heuristics" to approximate the optimal amount to be recommitted at each period and are defined as follows:

- $DZ^1(\mathcal{P}, t) = D(\mathcal{P}, t)$;
- $DZ^2(\mathcal{P}, t) = D(\mathcal{P}, t) + UC(\mathcal{P}, t - 24)$;
- $DZ^3(\mathcal{P}, t) = \frac{1}{ID(\mathcal{P}, t)} \times (D(\mathcal{P}, t) + UC(\mathcal{P}, t - 24))$

Strategy $DZ^1(\mathcal{P}, t)$ recommits only current distributions at t while the strategy $DZ^2(\mathcal{P}, t)$ incorporates the uncalled capital made 24 quarters ago, i.e., $UC(\mathcal{P}, t - 24)$. The inclusion of this quantity is based on the observation that unallocated but committed capital for older funds that already passed their maximal NAV's peak is unlikely to be called. These funds are typically in the divestment period. The last strategy $DZ^3(\mathcal{P}, t)$ scales recommitments obtained from $DZ^2(\mathcal{P}, t)$ with the inverse of the current investment degree. If the investment degree is high, the recommitted capital will be decreased. Conversely, a low investment degree will amplify the recommitted capital. This allows to perform some kind of active control to adjust the level of recommitment to reach and remain stable at a target allocation.

In this paper, we propose to learn an active control system to recommit at each period. Instead of relying on cashflow predictions and strategies' engineering which require strong expert knowledge, we posit that recommitment policies could be learnt using a policy-based algorithm introduced in the next section.

4   Proximal Policy Optimisation

As aforementioned in Sect. 2, the number of approaches relying on policy learning has flourished since recent years. They all try to find a trade-off between fast training and stability. Making large steps in the policy update can be disastrous, especially for on-policy algorithms which could never recover from subsequent updates. Among all existing alternatives in the literature, we considered the Proximal Policy Optimisation (PPO) algorithm [15] due to its simplicity. Although the PPO algorithm was released long after the Trust Region Policy Optimisation (TRPO) [13] which was the first of its kind, the PPO policy update is simpler but empirically seems to perform at least as well as TRPO relying on a second-order approach. But before diving into the stability improvement proposed in the PPO algorithm, let us recall the foundations, i.e., the vanilla policy gradient. Let π_θ represents a policy as a function of the parameter θ, the current state s_t, the taken action a_t and the received reward r_t at time t. A trajectory τ is a sequence of states and actions representing the path taken by an agent. In Reinforcement Learning, the goal is to discover the trajectory maximizing the expected return $J(\theta) = \mathbf{E}_{\pi_\theta}[R(\tau)]$ by updating sequentially the weights θ as follows: $\theta_{k+1} = \theta_k + \alpha * \nabla_\theta J(\theta_k)$ where $\nabla_\theta J(\theta_k)$ represents the policy gradient and is expressed as $\nabla_\theta J(\theta) = \mathbf{E}[R(\tau)\nabla_\theta \log \pi_\theta(a_t|s_t)]$. $R(\tau)$ can take different forms as suggested in [14]:

- The total reward trajectory: $\sum\limits_{t=0}^{\infty} r_t$

- The future reward from action a_t or rewards-to-go: $\sum\limits_{t=t'}^{\infty} r'_t$

- Future reward with baseline: $\sum\limits_{t=t'}^{\infty} r'_t - b(s_t)$
- State-action value function: $Q^{\pi_\theta}(s_t, a_t)$
- Advantage function: $A^{\pi_\theta}(s_t, a_t) = Q^{\pi_\theta}(s_t, a_t) - V^\pi(s_t)$

All the previous choices lead to the same expected value but have different variance. The formulation using the advantage function is extremely common as it uses the state-action value function and the estimation value of the state as baseline to reduce the variance of the gradient. The PPO algorithm relies on an estimation of the advantage function and tries to avoid parameter updates that change the policy too much at one step. In the same way as TRPO, the loss function is built to measure of how policy π_θ performs relatively to an old policy $\pi_{\theta_{old}}$:

$$\mathcal{L}(\theta, \theta_{old}) = \mathbf{E}\left[A^{\pi_\theta}(s_t, a_t)\frac{\pi_\theta(a_t|s_t)}{\pi_{\theta_{old}}(a_t|s_t)}\right] \tag{4}$$

While the TRPO algorithm uses the hard constraint $D_{KL}(\theta||\theta_{old}) < \lambda$ to limit the KL-divergence between both policies, the PPO algorithm relaxes the hard constraints and:

- either penalizes the KL-divergence directly in the loss function. This is the PPO-penalty version which we did not consider in this work.
- or clips the ratio $\frac{\pi_\theta(a_t|s_t)}{\pi_{\theta_{old}}(a_t|s_t)}$ in the loss function to remove incentives for the new policy to get far from the old policy. Note that the KL-divergence is not used anymore as constraints nor as a penalty.

The PPO-clip algorithm considered in this work is depicted in Algorithm 1. Contrary to the penalty version in which penalty coefficients are adjusted automatically during training, PPO-clip requires a static hyper-parameter ϵ use to clip the ratio between the policies. Due to space restriction, we will not go further into details but more explanations can be obtained from the original paper [15].

5   Private Equity Recommitment as RL Problem

As described in Sect. 3, the PERP can be solved using two main methodologies. While the first one relies on cashflow forecasting, the second one engineers recommitment functions only using past and current quantities from portfolios. Instead of building explicitly these functions, one could consider a Markov Decision Processes (MDP) to model a recommitment system and searches for the best policy in order to maintain a target investment degree while minimizing the risk of default.

Algorithm 1. PPO-clip version

1: Initialize policy parameters θ_1 and value function parameters ϕ_1
2: **for** $k \in \{1, ..., M\}$ **do**
3:     Sample a set of trajectories $\{\tau_i\}_{i=1}^{M}$ using the policy π_{θ_k}
4:     Create a batch $\mathcal{B}$ of transitions (s_t^i, a_t^i, r_t^i) $\forall t \in \{1, ..., |\tau_i|\}$ $\forall i \in \{1, ..., M\}$
5:     Compute rewards-to-go $\hat{\mathcal{R}}_t^i$, i.e. rewards from action a_t^i, $\forall t \in \{1, ..., |\tau_i|\}$ $\forall i \in \{1, ..., M\}$
6:     Estimate the advantages $A^{\pi_{\theta_k}}(s_t^i, a_t^i)$ using the value function V_{ϕ_k}
7:     Perform policy update:

$$\theta_{k+1} = \arg\max_{\theta} \frac{1}{M} \sum_{i=1}^{M} \frac{1}{|\tau_i|} \sum_{t=1}^{T_i} \left[\min\left(A^{\pi_\theta}(s_t^i, a_t^i) \frac{\pi_\theta(a_t^i|s_t^i)}{\pi_{\theta_{old}}(a_t^i|s_t^i)}, g\left(\epsilon, A^{\pi_\theta}(s_t^i, a_t^i)\right) \right) \right]$$

with $g\left(\epsilon, A^{\pi_\theta}(s_t^i, a_t^i)\right) = \text{clip}\left(\frac{\pi_\theta(a_t^i|s_t^i)}{\pi_{\theta_{old}}(a_t^i|s_t^i)}, 1-\epsilon, 1+\epsilon \right)$

8:     Perform value function update by minimizing mean-squared error:

$$\phi_{k+1} = \arg\min_{\phi} \frac{1}{M} \sum_{i=1}^{M} \frac{1}{|\tau_i|} \sum_{t=1}^{T_i} \left[V_\phi(s_t^i) - \hat{\mathcal{R}}_t^i \right]^2$$

9: **end for**

5.1   Modelling

Figure 1 illustrates how the PERP can be turned into a Reinforcement Learning problem. Each state s_t represents the portfolio position at time t and contains the following information:

- $ID(\mathcal{P}, t)$: Investment degree at time t
- $D(\mathcal{P}, t)$: Distributions obtained from divestments at time t
- $CC(\mathcal{P}, t)$: Capital called at time t
- $UC(\mathcal{P}, t - 24)$: Uncalled capital from commitment made 24 quarters ago
- $Cash(\mathcal{P}, t)$: Portfolio cash at time t
- $NAV(\mathcal{P}, t)$: Net Asset Value at time t

The state s_t gives us the opportunity to control the amount of recommitted capital at time t, i.e., the continuous action a_t depicted in Fig. 1. So far, the RL model is trivial to obtain. However, we need to be extremely cautious regarding the reward provided to the agent. Although we could define the reward by minimizing the deviation to the ideal investment degree as done in Eq. (2), there is no control on the risk of default. Two alternatives open to us: (1) either we train on multiple portfolios per episode and adjust the objective using the standard deviation or (2) we constrain the agent to remain below the fateful boundary, i.e., $ID(\mathcal{P}, t) = 1.0$. Needless to say, alternative (2) is more challenging for the agent but we argue that it will be more generalizable than alternative (1). For this purpose, we define a local reward r_t^{valid} and a global reward r_τ^{ID}. While the former is applied after each action (recommitment), the second one only occurs at the end of a valid episode. We recall that a valid episode ends when the maximum number of steps has been reached. The agent is rewarded after each action depending on whether the future state of the portfolio is valid:

$$r_t^{valid} = \begin{cases} 0 \text{ if } ID(\mathcal{P}, t+1) > 1 \\ 1 \text{ if } else \end{cases}$$

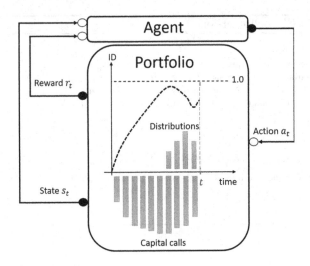

Fig. 1. Reinforcement learning of private equity policies

If a situation of default happens, the episode is stopped and does not reach the maximum number of steps allowed. The accumulated reward obtained during the episode would finally correspond to the number of periods in which the portfolio remained valid. This reward function strictly increases monotonically to drive the agent to simply learn to provide valid episodes. Once the agent has learnt to recommit, i.e., it reaches the maximum number of steps per episode, it receives an additional and final global reward $r_\tau^{ID} = \sum_{t=1}^{T} ID(\mathcal{P}, t)$ where T is the maximal number of steps per episode. Note that the sum could be replaced by the min to maximize the worst investment degree obtained during an episode. Finally, the total reward of a valid episode is the accumulated local reward added to the shifted global reward:

$$r_\tau = r_\tau^{ID} \times 10^{(digits(T)+1)} + \sum_{t=1}^{T} r_t^{valid} \tag{5}$$

where $digits(T)$ is the number of digit of T. For an episode lasting 100 steps, $\#digit(100) = 2$. This shifting mechanism is a constraint handling approach to make sure that non-valid episodes are guaranteed to receive a total reward lower than valid ones.

5.2 Synthetic Cashflows

Private equity data is a sensitive topic. Private equity players generally protect their rich cashflow histories. Although some financial data providers propose commercial libraries for very specific periods and economies, their data are generally incomplete. Historical cashflows's data capture the fund's dynamics which is an essential information for training. Multiple works including [18] and [12] relied on commercial libraries to draw conclusions or train their own model. In this work, we adopt another strategy to simulate portfolio evolution over time. Since 1973, the Yale University's endowment has been investing in private equity using a methodology for modelling illiquid assets proposed by Takahashi and Alexander (see [16]). Referred to as the *mother of all cashflows's models*, this Yale-model can be applied to private equity and real asset funds (e.g. natural resources and infrastructures). Although, according to Takahasi and Alexander, the generated projections fit historical data, the cashflows are modelled as deterministic which limit their applicability.

Instead of depending on a commercial solution to acquire historical cashflows which are often expensive and incomplete, synthetic fund cashflows have been preferred in this work as they represent a more practical solution. This is the reason why we decide to rely on an alteration of the Yale-model to make it probabilistic. These synthetic cashflows are created by funnelling data generated by the robust and tried-and-tested, albeit over-simplistic, Yale-model through a noise-adding algorithm to construct a new dataset. The resulting dataset shows the statistical features and the useful patterns needed for capturing the liquidity risks associated with portfolio of funds. The synthetic cashflows considered in this work have been provided by T.Meyer, an expert in private equity and co-author of this paper.

6   Experimental Setups

In order to fairly evaluate the resulting recommitment policies with the state of the art, simulations have been performed according to the parameters described in [18]. Due to the lack of secondary market, a portfolio cannot be bought instantaneously. We empirically created initial but mature portfolios over a year by committing equal capital to 16 randomly selected private equity funds. We also apply 30% initial overcommitment in setting up all portfolios to be in line with the experiments performed in [18].

A portfolio simulation consists in recommitting some capital to new selected fund every quarter. The amount of capital is determined by the current policy sampled from the critic network (see Algorithm 1). Table 1a details the simulation parameters while Table 1b described the PPO-clip parameters. A single portfolio simulation last 104 quarters, i.e., 26 years. Capital is recommitted uniformly into 4 randomly selected funds. The number of portfolio simulations is therefore equal to the number of episodes:

$$\#episodes = \frac{steps\_per\_epoch \times epochs}{104} = 125000 \qquad (6)$$

Strategies $DZ^i(\mathcal{P}, t)$ for $i \in \{1, 2, 3\}$ proposed in [18] have been evaluated with the same parameters and over the same period. All experiments presented in this paper were carried out using the HPC facility of the University of Luxembourg [17]. The python library SpinningUp [1] has been considered for the PPO-clip implementation. A distributed implementation using OpenMPI [5] has been considered to work with multiple environment in parallel. The discount parameter γ has been set to 1.0 since an episode's length is finite and last 26 years. The clip ratio ϵ has been set to 0.2 and represents how far can the new policy go from the old policy while still improving the objective. PPO-clip 's networks, i.e., actor and critic have both two hidden layers of 64 nodes. The ReLU function [2] has been chosen as activation function.

Table 1. Parameters

Parameters	Training	Validation
Cashflows frequency	quarterly	quarterly
Investment period	26 years	26 years
Funds per recommitment	4	4
Fund selection	random	random
Number of simulated portfolios	#episodes	1000

(a) Simulation parameters

Parameters	Value
Steps_per_epoch	26000
Gamma	1
Epochs	500
# episodes	125000
Clip_ratio ϵ	0.2
Pi_lr / vf_lr	$3e^{-4}$ / $1e^{-4}$
Hidden layers	[64, 64]

(b) PPO-clip parameters

7   Experimental Results

With regards to the experimental setups described in the previous section, Fig. 2 illustrates the average rewards recorded during policy optimisation/training. One can easily observe that the PPO-clip algorithm required few epochs to generate valid policies. The average rewards curve then steadily increases to reach what we can consider as a plateau in terms of improvements. Indeed, we can note periodic falls indicating that the algorithm have strong difficulties to improve more significantly the investment degree without breaking the cash constraint. When arrived at the rupture point, a policy yielding non-valid episodes is more likely to be generated leading to a steep fall in terms of overall rewards. When a fall occurs, the algorithm tries to recover until the next rupture. This pattern can be easily observed in Fig. 2. Due to the shifting constraint handling approach implemented in this work, non-valid and valid episodes do not have the same reward scale which explains these deep reward falls every time the algorithm encounters a non-valid episode.

The best policy obtained after training is depicted in Fig. 2. In order to validate results, the obtained policy has been applied on a test set of 1000 portfolios. After recording the investment degree evolution and the validity of each portfolio, the average investment degree as well as the surrounding 95% confidence interval have been computed and are depicted in Fig. 3. We first observe that the percentage of overinvested portfolios remains extremely low, i.e. $\approx 0.7\%$.

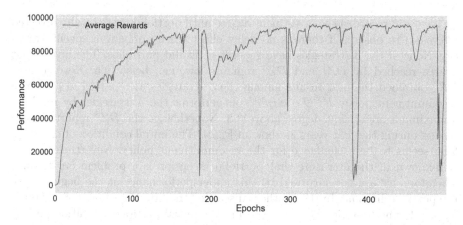

Fig. 2. Evolution of the average rewards per epoch

The investment degree varies strongly during the first 6 years going from 0.4 to almost 1.0. After the first 6 years, the average investment degree slightly increases to remain stable around 0.9.

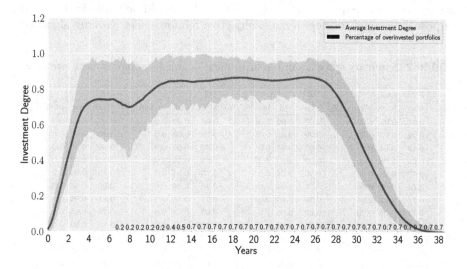

Fig. 3. Best policy obtained with the PPO-clip algorithm

We now compare the investment degree obtained with state-of-the-art strategies engineered in [18], namely DZ^i for all $i \in \{1, 2, 3\}$. Each DZ^i have been applied on the same test set. Table 2 reports the average investment degree, the standard deviation of the investment degree and the fraction of overinvested portfolios obtained for each strategy including the best policy recommitment $PPO - clip^{best}$. Although the active recommitment period only lasts 26 years, we have still recorded the investment degree until portfolios were totally divested (38 years) to observe if there is no delay effect when applying a specific strategy. None of the 3 strategies have generated invalid portfolios. The investment degree reached by DZ^1 and DZ^2 remains low, i.e., below 0.6. Nevertheless, DZ^3 obtained the best results among the 3 strategies as reported in [18]. The recommitment policy $PPO - clip^{best}$ outperforms the 3 strategies by reaching a maximum investment degree above 0.8. Nonetheless, the DZ^3 reports better results during the first years as show in Fig. 4. The initial condition of the portfolio seems to be a challenge for the recommitment policy. Nevertheless, it is well-known in the literature that portfolio inception is a problem on its own. Therefore, we are not surprised by this under-performance at the beginning of the portfolio lifetime. In [18], authors discarded the first three years of the portfolio's lifetime to avoid the influence from the initial portfolio formation period.

Regarding the percentage of overinvested portfolios, it comes as no surprise to encounter some invalid portfolios when getting closer to $ID(\mathcal{P}, t) = 1.0$. This is due to cashflow variability which is very difficult to predict. An alternative would be to replace the strong cash constraint by a soft one taking the form of an additional objective. Most of the LP investors generally own multi-class asset portfolios. If liquidity is missing due to an unexpected capital calls, more liquid assets could be sold. Of course, such a situation should be tempered and the injected cash required to satisfy capital calls should be minimized. For this purpose, one could consider a multi-objective reinforcement learning algorithm.

Table 2. Summary statistics of the investment degree in recommitment strategies

Years	$PPO - clip^{best}$			DZ^1			DZ^2			DZ^3		
	Mean	Std	Invalid (%)	Mean	Std	Invalid (%)	Mean	Std	Invalid (%)	Mean	Std	Invalid (%)
0	0.07	0.02	0.00	0.07	0.02	0.0	0.07	0.02	0.0	0.07	0.02	0.0
1	0.29	0.03	0.00	0.29	0.03	0.0	0.29	0.03	0.0	0.30	0.03	0.0
2	0.52	0.04	0.00	0.52	0.04	0.0	0.52	0.04	0.0	0.55	0.03	0.0
3	0.68	0.06	0.00	0.69	0.04	0.0	0.69	0.04	0.0	0.75	0.03	0.0
4	0.73	0.06	0.00	0.75	0.04	0.0	0.75	0.04	0.0	0.83	0.03	0.0
5	0.74	0.07	0.00	0.76	0.04	0.0	0.76	0.04	0.0	0.85	0.04	0.0
6	0.74	0.07	0.08	0.71	0.05	0.0	0.71	0.05	0.0	0.81	0.05	0.0
7	0.71	0.08	0.20	0.63	0.05	0.0	0.63	0.05	0.0	0.74	0.05	0.0
8	0.71	0.07	0.20	0.56	0.04	0.0	0.57	0.05	0.0	0.70	0.04	0.0
9	0.75	0.05	0.20	0.54	0.03	0.0	0.56	0.03	0.0	0.72	0.04	0.0
10	0.80	0.05	0.20	0.56	0.03	0.0	0.58	0.03	0.0	0.76	0.03	0.0
11	0.84	0.05	0.23	0.58	0.02	0.0	0.60	0.02	0.0	0.79	0.03	0.0
12	0.85	0.05	0.40	0.59	0.02	0.0	0.62	0.02	0.0	0.81	0.03	0.0
13	0.85	0.05	0.58	0.59	0.02	0.0	0.62	0.02	0.0	0.81	0.03	0.0
14	0.84	0.06	0.70	0.58	0.02	0.0	0.60	0.02	0.0	0.79	0.03	0.0
15	0.85	0.06	0.70	0.56	0.02	0.0	0.58	0.02	0.0	0.77	0.03	0.0
16	0.85	0.06	0.70	0.55	0.02	0.0	0.57	0.02	0.0	0.76	0.03	0.0
17	0.86	0.06	0.70	0.54	0.02	0.0	0.57	0.02	0.0	0.76	0.03	0.0
18	0.86	0.07	0.70	0.55	0.02	0.0	0.58	0.02	0.0	0.77	0.02	0.0
19	0.86	0.07	0.70	0.55	0.02	0.0	0.58	0.02	0.0	0.78	0.02	0.0
20	0.85	0.07	0.70	0.55	0.02	0.0	0.58	0.02	0.0	0.79	0.02	0.0

(continued)

Table 2. (*continued*)

Years	$PPO-clip^{best}$			DZ^1			DZ^2			DZ^3		
	Mean	Std	Invalid (%)	Mean	Std	Invalid (%)	Mean	Std	Invalid (%)	Mean	Std	Invalid (%)
21	0.85	0.08	0.70	0.55	0.02	0.0	0.58	0.02	0.0	0.78	0.02	0.0
22	0.85	0.08	0.70	0.54	0.02	0.0	0.58	0.02	0.0	0.78	0.02	0.0
23	0.85	0.08	0.70	0.54	0.02	0.0	0.57	0.02	0.0	0.77	0.02	0.0
24	0.86	0.08	0.70	0.54	0.02	0.0	0.57	0.02	0.0	0.77	0.02	0.0
25	0.86	0.08	0.70	0.54	0.02	0.0	0.57	0.02	0.0	0.77	0.02	0.0
26	0.85	0.08	0.70	0.54	0.02	0.0	0.57	0.02	0.0	0.78	0.02	0.0
27	0.81	0.09	0.70	0.53	0.02	0.0	0.56	0.02	0.0	0.76	0.02	0.0
28	0.73	0.08	0.70	0.49	0.02	0.0	0.52	0.02	0.0	0.71	0.03	0.0
29	0.62	0.08	0.70	0.44	0.02	0.0	0.46	0.02	0.0	0.62	0.03	0.0
30	0.50	0.07	0.70	0.37	0.02	0.0	0.39	0.02	0.0	0.51	0.03	0.0
31	0.38	0.06	0.70	0.29	0.02	0.0	0.31	0.02	0.0	0.40	0.03	0.0
32	0.27	0.05	0.70	0.21	0.02	0.0	0.22	0.02	0.0	0.29	0.03	0.0
33	0.17	0.04	0.70	0.14	0.02	0.0	0.14	0.02	0.0	0.19	0.03	0.0
34	0.09	0.02	0.70	0.07	0.01	0.0	0.08	0.01	0.0	0.10	0.02	0.0
35	0.04	0.01	0.70	0.03	0.01	0.0	0.03	0.01	0.0	0.05	0.01	0.0
36	0.01	0.01	0.70	0.01	0.01	0.0	0.01	0.01	0.0	0.02	0.01	0.0
37	0.00	0.00	0.70	0.00	0.00	0.0	0.00	0.00	0.0	0.00	0.00	0.0
38	0.00	0.00	0.70	0.00	0.00	0.0	0.00	0.00	0.0	0.00	0.00	0.0

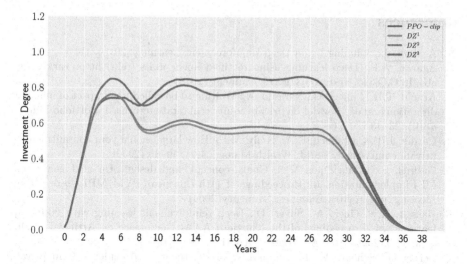

Fig. 4. Comparison between de Zwart's strategies [18] and the policy obtained with the PPO-clip algorithm

8   Conclusion

Recommitting into new PE funds is crucial for LP investors to maintain high allocation to private equity. Current methodologies rely on cashflow forecasting and over-simplistic approaches which are lacking of flexibility. Although this problem is a key of major importance, few works have attempted to develop a robust and flexible recommitment system. Perhaps, this is due to the lack of data. This is the reason why we adopted a different strategy consisting in learning recommitment policies through Reinforcement Learning. Using synthetic cash-flows build from the traditional but proven Yale-model, we applied Proximal Policy Optimisation to the Private Equity Recommitment Problem to maximise the investment degree while avoiding cash shortage situations by constraining the agent. Results obtained after training confirm that the recommitment policy outperform the strategies engineered in [18] while limiting the fractions of invalid portfolios. This work was a first proof of concept and subsequent experiments will be performed using different RL algorithms. Future works will investigate a strategy to handle the cash constraint more efficiently. Another avenue for research would be to model the cash constraint as a soft constraint, typically by considering it as a second objective. Both opportunity cost and cash shortage are two conflicting objectives. Finally, this work could be extended to take into account multi-class asset portfolios.

Acknowledgment. E. Kieffer acknowledges the support of the European Investment Bank through its STAREBEI programme.

References

1. Achiam, J.: Spinning Up in Deep Reinforcement Learning (2018)
2. Agarap, A.F.: Deep learning using rectified linear units (relu) http://arxiv.org/abs/1803.08375, arxiv:1803.08375Comment (2018)
3. Arnold, T.R., Ling, D.C., Naranjo, A.: Waiting to be called: the impact of manager discretion and dry powder on private equity real estate returns. J. Portfolio Manag. **43**(6), 23–43 (2017)
4. Cardie, J.H., Cattanach, K.A., Kelly, M.F.: How large should your commitment to private equity really be? J. Wealth Manag. **3**(2), 39–45 (2000)
5. Gabriel, E., et al.: Open MPI: Goals, concept, and design of a next generation MPI implementation. In: Proceedings of 11th European PVM/MPI Users' Group Meeting, pp. 97–104. Budapest, Hungary(2004)
6. Hasselt, H.v., Guez, A., Silver, D.: Deep reinforcement learning with double q-learning. In: Proceedings of the Thirtieth AAAI Conference on Artificial Intelligence, pp. 2094–2100. AAAI 2016, AAAI Press (2016)
7. Lerner, J., Schoar, A.: The illiquidity puzzle: theory and evidence from private equity. J. Financ. Econ. **72**(1), 3–40 (2004)
8. de Malherbe, E.: Modeling private equity funds and private equity collateralised fund obligations. Int. J. Theor. Appl. Financ. **07**, 193–230 (2004)
9. Meyer, T.: Hidden in plain sight-the impact of undrawn commitments. J. Altern. Investments **23**(2), 94–110 (2020)
10. Mnih, V., et al.: Playing atari with deep reinforcement learning http://arxiv.org/abs/1312.5602, arxiv:1312.5602Comment (2013)
11. Nevins, D., Conner, A., McIntire, G.: A portfolio management approach to determining private equity commitments. J. Altern. Investments **6**(4), 32–46 (2004)
12. Oberli, A.: Private equity asset allocation: how to recommit? J. Private Equity **18**(2), 9–22 (2015)

13. Schulman, J., Levine, S., Abbeel, P., Jordan, M.I., Moritz, P.: Trust region policy optimization. In: Bach, F.R., Blei, D.M. (eds.) ICML. JMLR Workshop and Conference Proceedings, vol. 37, pp. 1889–1897. JMLR.org (2015). http://dblp.uni-trier.de/db/conf/icml/icml2015.html#SchulmanLAJM15

14. Schulman, J., Moritz, P., Levine, S., Jordan, M., Abbeel, P.: High-dimensional continuous control using generalized advantage estimation. In: Proceedings of the International Conference on Learning Representations (ICLR) (2016)

15. Schulman, J., Wolski, F., Dhariwal, P., Radford, A., Klimov, O.: Proximal policy optimization algorithms. CoRR abs/1707.06347 (2017). http://dblp.uni-trier.de/db/journals/corr/corr1707.html#SchulmanWDRK17

16. Takahashi, D., Alexander, S.: Illiquid alternative asset fund modeling. J. Portfolio Manag. 28(2), 90–100 (2002)

17. Varrette, S., Bouvry, P., Cartiaux, H., Georgatos, F.: Management of an academic HPC cluster: the UL experience. In: Proceedings of the 2014 International Conference on High Performance Computing and Simulation (HPCS 2014), pp. 959–967. IEEE, Bologna, Italy (2014)

18. de Zwart, G., Frieser, B., van Dijk, D.: Private equity recommitment strategies for institutional investors. Financ. Anal. J. 68(3), 81–99 (2012)

Regular Decision Processes for Grid Worlds

Nicky Lenaers[1] and Martijn van Otterlo[1,2(✉)]

[1] Open University, Heerlen, The Netherlands
martijn.vanotterlo@ou.nl
[2] Radboud University, Nijmegen, The Netherlands

Abstract. Markov decision processes are typically used for sequential decision making under uncertainty. For many aspects however, ranging from *constrained* or *safe* specifications to various kinds of temporal (*non-Markovian*) dependencies in task and reward structures, extensions are needed. To that end, in recent years interest has grown into combinations of reinforcement learning and temporal logic, that is, combinations of flexible behavior learning methods with robust verification and guarantees. In this paper we describe an experimental investigation of the recently introduced *regular decision processes* that support both non-Markovian reward functions as well as transition functions. In particular, we provide a tool chain for regular decision processes, algorithmic extensions relating to online, incremental learning, an empirical evaluation of model-free and model-based solution algorithms, and applications in regular, but non-Markovian, grid worlds.

Keywords: Sequential decisions · Safe reinforcement learning · Non-Markovian dynamics · Regular decision process · Linear temporal logic

1 Introduction

Sequential decision making under uncertainty, often simply denoted by its core algorithmic subfield *reinforcement learning* (RL) [34, 36, 39], has been showing a huge amount of progress the last decades. Among the recent breakthroughs is the progression of DeepMind's RL methods solving the board game Go [32], chess, Atari computer games, the real-time strategy game StarCraft II, and lately chip design [26]. The algorithms employ combinations of (Monte Carlo) planning and value function approximation using deep neural networks.

Underlying typical RL systems is the *Markov decision process* (MDP) [30] in which *states* carry all necessary information to choose (optimal) *actions*. The *Markov property* dictates that given the present, the future is *independent* of the past. To scale to more complex problems, one can exploit *structure* in the space of state(-action) spaces, or policies or value functions, to utilize abstractions and approximations, for example as *value function approximation*, state space

L. A. Leiva et al. (Eds.): BNAIC/Benelearn 2021, CCIS 1530, pp. 218–238, 2022.
https://doi.org/10.1007/978-3-030-93842-0_13

abstractions [37], and hierarchical decompositions, cf. [36]. Many current *deep* RL algorithms too assume the environment behaves as an MDP [38].

To scale to larger problems, the Markov property is no longer adequate, and one may require dependence on a *history* of events and observations. For example, consider a robotic waiter working in a restaurant. It needs to deliver food and beverages to tables, but only *after* it has been requested by guests, and at the end the guests need to pay the price of the items delivered earlier. However, keeping a history of every possible event that ever occurred soon becomes practically infeasible. One well-known class of non-Markov MDP extensions is the *partially observable* MDP [33] in which the current state can be represented as a *probability distribution* over (latent) state features, denoted a *belief state*. Despite the existence of effective POMDP algorithms, many in robotics domains, the general class of POMDPs is computationally much more complex than MDPs, it is not easy to decide what the belief state should include exactly, and how much history should be included, and updating and interpreting the belief states is non-trivial.

A prominent RL direction [23] is to model dependence on the arbitrary past *explicitly* resulting in non-Markovian variants of MDPs. Inspired by seminal work [3] the idea is to utilize modern logical languages such as *linear temporal logic* [29] to represent goals and reward functions over past traces, and to employ formal computer science techniques (e.g. *automata*, *verification* and *model-checking*) in decision making. A core idea here is to *compile* a temporal specification of a reward function into an automaton that *monitors* the fulfillment of the temporal formula. Monitors allow for *compiling* the original non-Markov problem back into the MDP framework such that all existing algorithms, including deep RL, can be employed. This fruitful marriage of RL and formal verification combines flexible behavior learning algorithms with formal performance guarantees.

One motivation for employing temporal logic in RL comes from the ability to elegantly specify complex reward structures as in the waiter example, where earnings depend on an ordered series of events in the history. Another, more general, motivation is the need to *constrain* RL behaviors using (declarative) knowledge about which behaviors are desired or considered *safe* [15], for example to teach an autonomous car how to drive while still obeying traffic rules. Transparent safety of learned behaviors is often part of a general desire for AI systems to behave *responsibly* and *explainable* [19,24,28].

In this paper we empirically investigate algorithmic variations in one of the most recently introduced models, *regular decision processes* (RDP) [6], in which reward functions *and* transition functions can be specified using temporal logic. We employ RDPs specifically for *grid worlds*, which are archetypical problem scenarios in RL and allow for focused experimentation with new representations and algorithms. More specifically, our contributions are i) a novel *tool chain* implementing RDPs, utilizing existing algorithms and tools for RL and model checking, ii) an empirical investigation of the recently introduced RDPs in grid worlds, iii) algorithmic RL extensions to learn RDP behaviors based on Monte Carlo value estimation and incremental (online) compilation of RDPs, and iv) initial steps towards an (empirical) investigation of the trade-offs between temporal logical specifications and the complexity of learning. The paper is organized as follows: we first provide all necessary background in the next section, after which we discuss our approach in Sect. 3, then we continue with an extensive experimental evaluation in Sect. 4 and we conclude in Sect. 5.

2 Background

Here we will formalize MDPs and basic solution algorithms, after which we introduce non-Markov reward functions and their corresponding temporal logic formalizations. Furthermore we introduce the general compilation of logical specifications into automata functioning as monitors that can be combined with the original MDP into *extended* MDPs, which can be solved using off-the-shelf solution methods. In addition, we describe automata-based *shaping* techniques to deal with the resulting sparse MDPs. Last we introduce RDPs, which support non-Markovian aspects in both reward and transition functions.

2.1 Markov Decision Processes

An MDP M is a tuple $M = \langle S, A, T, R \rangle$, where S is the set of states, A the set of actions, $T : S \times A \times S \rightarrow [0, 1]$ the *transition function* yielding a transition probability and $R : S \times A \times S \rightarrow \mathbb{R}$ the real-valued *reward function*. Actions only applicable in state s are denoted $a \in A(S)$. A *policy* maps to each state $s \in S$ an action $a \in A$ and is denoted π. Additionally, a *discount factor* $\gamma \in [0, 1]$ is used to discount rewards obtained in the future.

As said, MDPs adhere to the *Markov Property*: given the present (s_t), the future (s_{t+1}) is independent on the past (s_{t-1}). In other words, everything that is needed to learn from the past is *embedded* in the present state s_t. The Markov Property holds for all states $s \in S$ and is formally expressed as:

$$p(s_{t+1}|s_t) = p(s_{t+1}|s_1, s_2, \ldots, s_t)$$

A labelling function $\mathcal{L} : S \rightarrow 2^P$, where P is a finite set of atomic propositions and S the set of states enables a state representation using *features*.

Solving an MDP comprises computing an optimal policy. A policy is optimal iff it maximizes the expected discounted sum of rewards for every state $s \in S$. Methods for solving decision making problems are generally divided into *model-based* and *model-free* methods [34]. Model-based methods, generally called *dynamic programming* (DP), can employ the full model (T and R) to *plan* optimal sequences of actions. Model-free methods, generally called *reinforcement learning* (RL), do not have knowledge of the model and require sampling, i.e. trial-and-error learning and use that experience to find optimal policies.

Dynamic Programming (DP) methods such as *value and policy iteration* find optimal policies typically by employing a *value function* that expresses for each state *how good* is it for the agent to be in that particular state, and it represents the (expected) discounted future reward that can be obtained from that state, by employing a particular policy. The equation used to calculate a state value is known as the *Bellman Equation*, which formalizes how a state's value, denoted

$v(s)$, is evaluated in terms of expected returns, expressing a relationship between the value of a state and the values of its successor states. DP algorithms use it *iteratively* to update the value of all states until convergence to the *optimal value function* $v^*(s)$ using the following *Bellman Optimality Equation*:

$$v^*(s) = \max_{a \in A} \sum_{s' \in S} T(s'|s, a) \left[R(s, a, s') + \gamma \, v^*(s') \right]$$

An optimal action a for s is computed using $v^*(s)$, T and R.

Where DP methods are concerned with *computing* a value function, RL tries to *learn* value functions using returns obtained from *interaction* with the MDP. In order to find a policy in absence of a model, one needs the *state-action value* for each action $a \in A$ in state $s \in S$, denoted $q(s, a)$, in order to determine the best policy. A straightforward extension of the previous update rule results in $q^*(s, a) = \sum_{s' \in S} T(s'|s, a) \left[R(s, a, s') + \gamma \max_{a' \in A} q^*(s', a') \right]$. *One-step* RL algorithms employ it to *update* action-values after each step in the environment and select their actions based on $\pi^*(s) = \arg\max_a q(s, a)$.

In addition to *bootstrapping* methods above, where values of states (and actions) are computed using other values, one can employ more unbiased estimation methods for model-free RL such as *Monte Carlo estimation* (MC) in which a value is estimated based on the average return of full sample traces in the MDP, cf. [34]. In Sect. 3 we employ MC as our model-free RL algorithm for RDPs.

2.2 Non-Markovian Decision Processes

If rewards depend on more than just the current state, we end up with Non-Markovian Reward Decision Processes (NMRDPs) [3], a subset of Non-Markovian Decision Processes (NMDPs). Temporal logic can be used to specify the conditions under which reward is obtained. As with MDPs, the states of an NMRDP can be enhanced by labelling function $\mathcal{L} : S \to 2^P$ and propositions P, where each state $s \in S$ is a valuation over P, thus $s \in 2^P$.

Formally, an NMRDP is denoted as the tuple $M = \langle S, A, T, \bar{R} \rangle$, where S, A and T are as in an MDP, and $\bar{R}$ is defined as $\bar{R} : (S \times A)^* \to \mathbb{R}$. In words, the reward is specified as a real-valued function over finite state-action sequences, or *traces*, where a trace captures the history of states and is denoted $h = \langle s_0, \ldots, s_k \rangle$. Because the reward is now dependent on the full history, it no longer fits to define state or state-action values as before. Instead, a temporally extended reward function for a given trace h and reward formulae φ is [4]:

$$\bar{R}(h) = \sum_{1 \leq i \leq n : h \models \varphi_i} r_i \tag{1}$$

where the set of pairs $\{(\varphi_i, r_i)_{i=1}^n\}$ is assumed to be specified for $\bar{R}$. That is, an agent receives reward r_i at state $s \in S$ of trace h that satisfies temporal formula φ_i. The value of a trace h is in turn defined as the accumulation of rewards obtained during trace traversal, possibly discounted by discount factor γ [4]. The value of such a trace can now formally be defined as follows:

$$v(h) = \sum_{k=1}^{|h|} \gamma^{k-1} \, \bar{R}(\langle h(1), h(2), \ldots, h(k)\rangle)$$

where discount factor $\gamma \in [0, 1]$ as usual and $h(k)$ denotes the pair (s_{k-1}, a_k). Because NMRDPs define the value of traces instead of individual states, a policy no longer maps states to actions as before. Instead, a policy for an NMRDP is a mapping from histories to actions. The value of a policy in terms of expected return thus becomes the expected discounted sum of rewards over a possibly infinite amount of traces. The distribution over traces is defined by the initial state s_0, the transition function T and policy π. The expected value of infinite traces can formally be defined as $v_\pi(s) = E_{h \sim M, \pi, s_0} v(h)$.

2.3   Temporal Logic, Automata and Product MDPs

Temporal logic to express non-Markovian aspects has a history [3, 29] containing, e.g., Linear Temporal Logic [29] (LTL). It uses the standard Boolean connectives of propositional logic, i.e. $\wedge$, $\vee$ and $\neg$, with the addition of temporal connectives G (*always*), F (*eventually*), X (*next*) and U (*until*). More recent variations restrict to finite traces: *Linear Temporal Logic over Finite Traces*, denoted LTL$_f$, and *Linear Dynamic Logic over Finite Traces* which allows for regular expressivity [12]. Using LDL$_f$, goals can be as expressive as regular expressions while at the same time providing a more attractive specification syntax. Formally, LDL$_f$ formulae ϕ can be built using an atomic property tt for the logical *true*, a propositional formula φ and a path expression ρ, which is a regular expression over propositional formulae ϕ. In addition to regular expression constructs, ρ uses a test construct $\varphi?$, indicating to only continue evaluation when φ evaluates to *true*. The LDL$_f$ formalism, as presented by [12], is expressed in Eqs. (2) and (3).

$$\varphi ::= tt \mid \neg\varphi \mid \varphi_1 \wedge \varphi_2 \mid \langle \varrho \rangle \varphi \tag{2}$$

$$\varrho ::= \phi \mid \varphi? \mid \varrho_1 + \varrho_2 \mid \varrho_1; \varrho_2 \mid \varrho^* \tag{3}$$

Intuitively, one may interpret LDL$_f$ formula $\langle \varrho \rangle \varphi$ as stating that, from the current step in the trace, there exists *at least one* (cf. $\exists$) execution path that satisfies regular expression ϱ such that the last step in the trace satisfies φ. Conversely, $[\varrho]\varphi$ states that, from the current step in the trace, *all* (cf. $\forall$) execution paths satisfying regular expression ϱ are such that the last step in that execution path satisfies φ. For example, to formalize the property of a robotic waiter to always serve guests after they have placed an order, the formula $[true*](order \rightarrow \langle true^*; served \rangle) end$ can be used.

Temporal formulae specified using LDL$_f$ can be compiled into Deterministic Finite Automata (DFA) [4]. Formally, a DFA for formula φ is denoted $A_\varphi = \langle 2^P, Q, \delta, F, q_0 \rangle$, where 2^P is the input alphabet containing all truth assignments to propositions in P, Q is the state space, δ the transition function, F the set of accepting states and q_0 the initial state.

Core properties that can be expressed in LDL$_f$ are *safety* and *liveness* [12]. A safety property is used to indicate that *something bad should never happen*,

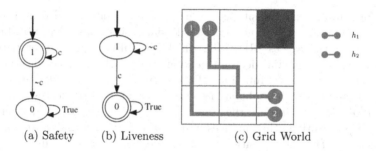

Fig. 1. (left) Automata for LDL$_f$ formulae: a) $[true^*]\langle c^*\rangle end$, b) $\langle true^*; c; true^*\rangle end$ (right) A grid world modeled as an RDP

or *something good always holds*, and can be expressed as $[true^*]\langle c^*\rangle end$, where c indicates the good condition and the asterisk ($*$) indicates c holds at every step up until and including the last step of the trace. That is, *until the end of the trace*, c holds. Conversely, a liveness property indicates that some condition should be met *before the end of the trace* and can be expressed as $\langle true^*; c; true^*\rangle end$, where c is the condition to be met. In words, *eventually before the end of the trace*, c holds. Figures 1a and 1b visualize this.

Solving an NMRDP $M = \langle S, A, T, \{(\varphi_i, r_i)_{i=1}^m\}\rangle$, with temporal formulae φ_i and r_i the corresponding rewards, is tackled by formulating the *extended* MDP M' as $M' = \langle S', A, T', R'\rangle$ that is *equivalent* to M in the sense that states can be mapped in such a way that the mapping yields identical transition probabilities for T and T'. Each formula φ_i is compiled into an equivalent automaton, as in Fig. 1a and 1b, and the *cross-product* between the original NMRDP M and these automata is computed, resulting in the extended MDP M'. Some straightforward choices should still be made about discounting to prevent infinite reward exploitation and whether rewards belonging to a formula φ can be obtained only once or multiple times. We omit formal details of this standard construction (but cf. [4,21]) and refer here to an example later in this paper: Fig. 5 shows a grid world MDP where a red square needs to be avoided, something which is specified using the LDL$_f$ formula $\varphi \equiv [true^*]\langle(\neg x_{is1} \wedge \neg y_{is2})^*\rangle end$, and where the extended MDP depicted in Fig. 9 is the result of the cross product between the automaton representing φ, the grid world MDP, and the automaton representing an additional formula expressing a reward of $+50$ when reaching the top right corner. Note that the extended model is again an MDP where typical RL and DP algorithms can be employed.

2.4   Regular Decision Processes: Non-Markovian Dynamics

The concept of an NMRDP can be extended to a decision process in which not only the reward function, but the transition function too can depend on the arbitrary past, and where both are represented using a logic like LDL$_f$ As described in Sect. 2.3, these, in turn, can be compiled into automata, which allows for rewards and transitions to be *monitored*, and compiled into product models yielding an MDP. Such non-Markovian transitions were introduced in regular decision processes (RDP) [6], which is a fully observable, probabilistic, non-Markovian, sequential decision making model, where successor states and rewards can be stochastic functions of the entire history. Just like before, RDP states are endowed with a labeling function over a set of predicates.

An RDP M is defined as the tuple $M = \langle P, S, A, Tr_L, R_L, s_0 \rangle$, where P is the set of propositions that induces state-space S with initial state s_0, A the set of actions, Tr_L the transition function and R_L the reward function, where both Tr_L and R_L are now non-Markovian. Transition function Tr_L is defined by a finite set T of quadruples of the form $(\varphi, a, P', \pi(P'))$, where φ is an LDL$_f$ formula over P, $a \in A$ an action, $P' \subseteq P$ the set of propositions $p \in P$ that are affected by a when φ holds and $\pi(P')$ the distribution over proposition in P' that describe the post-action distribution. The reward function R_L is specified using a finite set R of pairs (φ, r), where φ is an LDL$_f$ formula over propositions in P and $r \in \mathbb{R}$ a real-valued reward. It is assumed that for the quadruples in T, the value of variables not in P' are not affected by action a [6]. If the set $\{(\varphi_i, a, P'_i, \pi_i(P')) \mid i \in I_a\}$ defines all quadruples for a, then all formulae φ_i must be *mutually exclusive* such that $\varphi_i \wedge \varphi_j$ is inconsistent for $i \neq j$. In other words, no two formulae φ_i and φ_j can hold at once if both apply to action a and φ_i and φ_j are not identical. In addition, let $s'|_{P'}$ denote the restriction of s' to properties in P'. Then, Tr_L is defined as $Tr_L((s_0, \ldots, s_k), a, s') = \pi(s'|_{P'})$ if quadruple $(\varphi, a, P', \pi(P'))$ exists such that $s_0, \ldots, s_k \models \varphi$ and s_k and s' agree on all variables in $P \backslash P'$. That is, given trace $s_0, \ldots, s_k$, action a and quadruple $(\varphi, a, P', \pi(P'))$ with formula φ that is satisfied by $s_0, \ldots, s_k$, s' is a possible next state if it assigns the same value to all propositions not in P'. If this is the case, then the transition probability equals the probability π assigns to $s'|_{P'}$. In all other cases, $Tr_L((s_0, \ldots, s_k), a, s') = 0$.

As an illustration, consider Fig. 1c, outlining a 3×3 grid world with the upper-left state s_{11} being the initial state and the upper-right state s_{31} being a terminal state. Let us define a transition that intuitively states that, when an agent goes east in the bottom-left state s_{13} and ends up in the bottom-center state s_{23}, immediately followed by going east *again* in s_{23}, the probability of ending up in the bottom-right state s_{33} is set to 0.1, denoted $\pi(s_{33}|\{x_{is2}, x_{is3}\}) = 0.1$. Otherwise, $Tr(s_{23}, e, s_{33}) = 1$. In other words, the transition from s_{23} to s_{33} depends on the transition from s_{13} to s_{23}. In addition, the propositions affected by this transition are defined by P' such that $P' \subseteq P = \{x_{is2}, x_{is3}\}$. All other propositions are not affected by said transition. Both transitions can be captured by LDL$_f$ formula φ_1 and φ_2 as $\varphi_1 = \langle true^*; \neg x_{is1} \vee \neg y_{is3}; x_{is2} \wedge y_{is3} \rangle end$ and $\varphi_2 = \langle true^*; x_{is1} \wedge y_{is3}; x_{is2} \wedge y_{is3} \rangle end$. Given φ_1 and φ_2, we can define a quadruple for e that uses φ_1 or φ_2 respectively as $(\varphi_1, \{x_{is3} \wedge y_{is3}\}, 1)$ and $(\varphi_2, e, \{x_{is3} \wedge y_{is3}\}, 0.1)$. For brevity, we assume these are the only quadruples for e, conforming to exhaustiveness and mutual exclusion [6]. Then, let us define two traces h_1 and h_2 that each reach s_{33} differently as $h_1 = \langle s_{11}, s_{12}, s_{13}, s_{23}, s_{33} \rangle$ and $h_2 = \langle s_{11}, s_{12}, s_{22}, s_{23}, s_{33} \rangle$. Then, using the aforementioned quadruple for e, the affected propositions P' and the definition of Tr_L, i.e. $Tr_L((s_0, \ldots, s_k), a, s') = \pi(s'|_{P'})$, the transition functions on h_1 and h_2 from s_{23} to s_{33} can be calculated as $Tr_L(h_1, e, s_{33}) = \pi(s_{33}|\{x_{is2}, x_{is3}\}) = 1$ and $Tr_L(h_2, e, s_{33}) = \pi(s_{33}|\{x_{is2}, x_{is3}\}) = 0.1$.

Solving an RDP involves the well known construction of an *extended* MDP as a product of all automata monitoring the satisfaction of (transition and reward) LDL$_f$ formulae combined with the initial RDP state space [4,12], resulting in an MDP that can again be solved by off-the-shelf algorithms. Note that, because of the combinatorial nature of this construction, the extended MDP does not necessarily scale well. The equivalence between the RDP and the constructed MDP entails that optimal policies found in the constructed MDP can be mapped back to the RDP, thus yielding optimal policies for the initial RDP.

The product models employed in non-Markovian decision process solutions grow quickly with the number of formulas, see the example in Sect. 2.3. The result of non-Markovian dependencies is that paths to receiving rewards can become long, and complicate typical bootstrapping RL methods and exploration. One general solution for MDPs is *reward shaping* [27] (RS): giving intermediate rewards to speed up learning, with the restriction that the extra rewards do not alter the optimal policy. So-called *potential-based* RS replaces the original reward function $R : S \times A \times S \to \mathbb{R}$ by an alternative reward function $R'(s, a, s') + F(s, a, s') \to \mathbb{R}$, where $F(s, a, s')$ is a *shaping reward function*. In turn, this function can be applied to *potential-based* RS of the form $F(s, a, s') \to \gamma\Phi(s') - \Phi(s)$ for some $\Phi : S \to \mathbb{R}$. The way in which RS is applied inherently depends on the representation of the reward function. For NMRDPs an opportunity arises to utilize the structure of the DFA representing a reward function [10]. Every step in the extended MDP can be given a reward proportional to the *distance* in that DFA to an accepting state (i.e. when the original reward would be given).

2.5   Related Work

The typical MDP context is well studied and there is an abundance of algorithms and representations [30,34,36,39]. Endowing MDPs with non-Markovian goal and reward functions has a history with seminal work on model-based settings [3,35] and more recently several subclasses are considered (e.g. probabilistic vs. deterministic) [4,5]. The most recent addition to the field are the general *regular decision processes* [6] we employ here. One aim of all these methods is to scale MDPs to more complex problems. However, another main reason to utilize temporal logics for reward specifications is that it opens up many new possibilities for *reward function engineering*, resulting in more intuitive and technically useful ways to specify tasks and goals. A more general view, based on automata as *transducers* [9] improves on the technical part by merging the non-Markovian parts into a single structure.

The use of temporal logics [12,29] in model-free RL settings is a recent trend [23], and comes with additional requirements since the model of the environment is unknown. Many ideas here come from *constrained* or *safe* [15] forms of RL, where the policy space is restricted either before learning, or during action selection, based on a notion what are (un)desired actions. Safety issues have obvious connections with *model checking* [16] and some recent RL approaches instantiate that connection for safe RL [2,13]. Very recently, several approaches have appeared combining formal temporal logic with RL [4,7,9–11,22]. Some focus more on the representational devices such as *reward machines* [7], some study additional mechanisms such as *shaping* to aid in the more complex learning process [27], and others introduce variants such as *geometric* LTL to capture a different semantics of goals [25]. Overall, variations exist in different logics, different underlying automata (e.g. DFA vs Mealy) and inference algorithms, and different RL algorithms to solve the resulting extended MDPs.

The meaning of "model-free" has variations here, since one can assume that nothing is known, or that at least the reward formula is (which is quite believable when we want an agent to adhere to certain rules or restrictions). In the latter case one can use the monitor automata states as extra state information and apply any form of deep function approximation [18]. In general, reward and transition functions may need to be learned from traces for fully general RL systems. In the temporal logic settings we describe, this typically amounts to *automaton induction* algorithms that can work on examples of traces (positive or negative) in deterministic or even probabilistic settings, which contains notoriously hard settings, but some promising work is emerging [8,14,20]. In the context of RDPs, initial work with a Mealy machine representation shows promise [1]. In addition, temporal logic allows for declarative and intuitive models, hence in terms of explainability in RL many possibilities are left, and only some work is just emerging [19].

3   Approach and Software Design

In this paper we develop a new *tool chain* for the recently introduced RDPs and experiment with algorithmic variations, specifically applied to grid worlds (cf. [21]). Figure 2 graphically shows a simplified high-level overview of how decision processes, temporal logic and model checking intertwine. Currently no software tool can conveniently model, visualize and solve all RDPs, which motivates our particular approach. Secondly, RDPs are introduced very recently and not much empirical evidence has been gathered so far [1,10]. Also the familiar grid worlds in general are underrepresented in the temporal logical RL community despite their abundance in basic RL research, and despite their ability to quickly show insight into models. In general we follow the main paths through Fig. 2, where rectangles, diamonds and circles represent formalisms (or models), processes and artifacts, respectively. On the left we see temporal logics such as LTL_f/LDL_f used to define non-Markov decision models, as we have seen in the previous sections, where we also described how these can be compiled into (extended) MDPs, which can then be solved by traditional MDP algorithms. Note that NMDPs are not solely dependent on temporal logic, but require other input such as a state space definition. In the lower-most flow, temporal formulae can be used to define

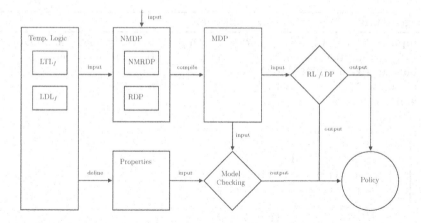

Fig. 2. Conceptual/tool chains

system properties that can be verified using *model checking*[1]. Finally, experimental learning algorithms can be combined with formal verification methods to produce a policy.

Our prototype integrates existing software tools. First, an integration is made with FLLOAT [6], a tool that allows to construct automata from LTL_f and LDL_f formulae. Because the prototype is a TypeScript (TS) web application, and FLLOAT is built with Python, a small web server is put in place to communicate with FLLOAT. Communication then occurs by making HTTP requests from the prototype through a *Browser HTTP Layer* to the FLLOAT application through a *Server API Layer*. In addition, an integration with a browser-based Graphviz extension called Viz.js[2] was made. It allows for *visualization* of automata within the prototype. Input to the software prototype is defined in terms of TS variables, stored in a single TS file an presented during execution at runtime.

3.1 Compilation: From RDP to MDP

A core component in our approach is the conversion of NMDPs to MDPs for both *off-line*, i.e. before learning, and *on-line*, i.e. during learning, use cases. Intuitively, one can think of the off-line case as a model-based control problem, where the reward function and transition function are fully known to the agent. However, in contrast to other work, we compute the extended MDP *incrementally*. On the other hand, the on-line case can be thought of as a model-free control problem where the agent has to interact with the environment to learn an optimal behavior. Also here the algorithm constructs the extended MDP incrementally, but now only in the areas of the state-action space that are actually experienced by the agent in

---

[1] In the current paper there is no room to highlight it, but model-checkers such as Storm (https://www.stormchecker.org/) can be employed for shaping and shielding purposes (and more) in this tool chain, cf. [21]).

[2] https://github.com/mdaines/viz.js.

Algorithm 1: NMDP to MDP (off-line)

input : NMDP $M = \langle S, A, T, R \rangle$ with LDL$_f$ reward automata Q_i^R and LDL$_f$
transition automata Q_j^T, with $Q_k \leftarrow Q_i^R \cup Q_j^T$ for convenience
output: Extended MDP $M' = \langle S', A', T', R' \rangle$

1 $t \leftarrow 0$; $s_t' \leftarrow s_0' \leftarrow (q_{1,0}, q_{2,0}, \dots, q_{k,0}, s_0)$; $A' \leftarrow A$; $S, T, R \leftarrow \emptyset$
2 **while** $s_t' \notin S'$ **do**
3       $s_t \leftarrow \tau(s_t')$
4   **for** $a \in A(s_t)$ **do**
5           $s_{t+1} \leftarrow T(\mathcal{L}(s_t), a)$
6   **for** $q_{k,t} \in Q_{k,t}$ **do**
7               $q_{k,t+1}' \leftarrow \texttt{transition}(q_{k,t}, \mathcal{L}(s_{t+1}))$
8           $s_{t+1}' \leftarrow (q_{1,t+1}, q_{2,t+1}, \dots, q_{k,t+1}, s_{t+1})$
9           $S' \leftarrow S' \cup \{s_{t+1}'\}$
10          $T'(s_t', a, s_{t+1}') \leftarrow T(\mathcal{L}(s_t), a, \mathcal{L}(s_{t+1}))$
11          $R'(s_t', a, s_{t+1}') \leftarrow \texttt{sum\_accept}(Q_{i,t+1}^R)$
12          $s_t' \leftarrow s_{t+1}'$
13 **return** M'

---

the interaction with the environment. In addition, in this model-free setting it is assumed that the agent has access to only the states of the automata tracking the formulae, just like in other works (e.g. [18]). Throughout the algorithms, automata for rewards are indicated by Q_i^R and automata for transitions are indicated by Q_j^T and their union is denoted Q_k.

The compilation of an NMDP can exploit knowledge of the known dynamics/reward model. Algorithm 1 outlines our algorithm, generalized to NMDPs. It incrementally builds an extended MDP *off-line* by incorporating all LDL$_f$ automáta such that only reachable states are generated. Here, off-line means the compilation is done before solving the final MDP. The transition function in Algorithm 1 on Line 10 abstracts away the different transition dynamics between NMRDPs and RDPs by using labelling function $\mathcal{L}$, making it applicable to both models. Furthermore, the state space generated by Algorithm 1 is *minimal* because it only generates states that are reachable, and thus solution algorithms do not waste time on irrelevant states. The resulting MDP can be solved using e.g. *value iteration*, cf. [21].

Because in the model-free setting the reward function and transition dynamics are not known a priori, compilation cannot occur in a similar fashion as in Algorithm 1. We employ a different, *online, incremental* approach in Algorithm 2. Similar to the off-line algorithm it *incrementally* builds the extended MDP, only here the automata Q_i^R for rewards and automata Q_j^T for transitions are *not* known to the agent. Hence, Q_k is not defined as input like it is for Algorithm 1. Furthermore, the extended MDP is not fully defined in terms of dynamics of transitions and rewards. This, in turn, requires an environment capable of handling LDL$_f$ automata for rewards and transitions. In addition to Algorithm 2, a step function first gets the current state s_t from the environment using $s_t \leftarrow \texttt{env.snapshot}()$. In addition, all automata are retrieved through $Q_{k,t} \leftarrow \texttt{env.get\_automata\_states}()$.

Algorithm 2: NMDP to MDP (on-line)

---

    input : Environment `env` with n-step limit per episode, exploration factor ϵ, discount factor γ and `max_episodes`

    output: Policy π

1 $s_t \leftarrow s_0 \leftarrow$ `env.reset()`; $Q(s,a) \leftarrow$ `arbitrary()` for all $s \in S, a \in A(s)$; $\pi \leftarrow$ `arbitrary()`

2 **repeat**

3   ep $=$ `generate_episode`$(n, A(s_t), \pi, \epsilon)$

4      $T \leftarrow |\text{ep}|$

5      $G \leftarrow 0$

6   **foreach** *step of* ep, $t = T - 1, T - 2, \ldots, 0$ **do**

7         $G \leftarrow \gamma G + r_{t+1}$

8         $Q(s_t, a_t) \leftarrow G$

9         $\pi(s_t) \leftarrow \arg \max_a (Q(s_t, a))$

10 **until** `max_episodes`;

11 **return** π

Then, for each $q_{k,t} \in Q_{k,t}$, both the original state and all automata states transition to their subsequent states through $s_{t+1} \leftarrow$ `env.transition`(s_t, a) and $q_{k,t+1} \leftarrow$ `transition`$(q_{i,t}, \mathcal{L}(s_{t+1}))$ respectively. Automata are then updated through `env.set_automaton_state`$(Q_k, q_{k,t+1})$ the reflect the state transition. Finally, when $Q_{k,t}$ has been iterated over, i.e. all automata have transitioned, a next state is generated by $s'_{t+1} \leftarrow (q_{1,t+1}, q_{2,t+1}, \ldots, q_{k,t+1}, s_{t+1})$, i.e. the MDP state is extended with each *monitor* state. In addition, the rewards for all automata currently in an accepting state are summed by $r \leftarrow$ `sum_accept`$(Q_{k,t+1} \backslash Q_{i,t+1}^T)$. Indeed, the better part of Algorithm 2 aligns with first-visit MC [34], except that the underlying problem definition is assumed to be non-Markovian and hence compiled *on-line* from NMDP to MDP.

Similar to Algorithm 1, Algorithm 2 generate only reachable states and is therefore *minimal*. This is due to the transition function of automata being defined as $q_{k,t+1} \leftarrow$ `transition`$(q_{i,t}, \mathcal{L}(s_{t+1}))$, where a transition cannot occur if the target state is unreachable. Due to the nature of RL, the implicitly extended MDP contains only states actually encountered by an agent through interaction with the environment. Note that, as opposed to Algorithm 1, Algorithm 2 does *not* contain all information on the history of states per se. Due to the trial-and-error nature of MC, some states might remain unobserved after Algorithm 2 has completed. Therefore, an optimal policy π^* is only guaranteed in the limit.

4   Experiments

Our experimental evaluation focuses on RDPs for grid worlds, utilizing a model-free online MC algorithm. Our experimental evaluation focuses on RDPs for grid worlds, utilizing a model-free online MC algorithm. Overall, the goal is to empirically assess various aspects of RL for RDPs, with a focus on the relation

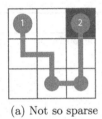 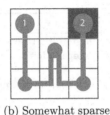 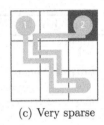

(a) Not so sparse   (b) Somewhat sparse   (c) Very sparse

Fig. 3. Experiment 1 - Goals for on-line compilation with RL

between RDP elements and final learning performance in the resulting extended MDP. For more experiments, (also model-based, value iteration), cf. [21]. In this section we target four different empirical questions: **R1**: *How does learning performance relate to goal sparsity/complexity?*, **R2**: *How can shaping help for complex goals?*, **R3**: *What are the implications of safety properties on learning performance?*, and **R4**: *What is the relation between learning performance and non-Markovian dynamics?*

4.1   Experiment 1: Goal Sparsity

This experiment aims at relating *goal sparsity* to the performance fist-visit MC. Here, goal sparsity describes the accumulated minimum length of traces h_i accepted by LDL$_f$ formulae φ_i. The idea is to increase the grid world size, while keeping reward formulae constant, such that the traces increase in length due to an increase in the size of the state space. To illustrate this, temporal formulae encoding liveness properties are used such that the number of steps to satisfy a formula increases with the grid world size. The minimum length of a trace h_i is measured in terms of the minimum number of states contained in h_i for it to be accepted. The quantitative measurement is defined by the relative frequency of values within 10% of the maximum value. This range is deemed acceptable for a solution as it follows from the value used for ϵ, being $\epsilon = 0.1$, that generates exploration noise. Data is gathered over 50 runs, where each run consists of 1000 episodes with a maximum of 50 steps per episode. Furthermore, $\gamma = 1$. In order to consistently increase the goal sparsity when the grid world size is increased, the agent always starts in state s_{11} and an episode is terminated when the agent reaches s_{13}, after which a new episode is initiated until the maximum number of episodes is reached. Figure 3 outlines three goals, each rewarded $+1000$, with Fig. 3a being the least sparse where goal state are adjacent, Fig. 3b being somewhat sparse where goal states require the agent to travel through the center of the grid and Fig. 3c being the most sparse where the agent is required to go reach the far-right state and then go back to its initial state again. The goals encoded in LDL$_f$ as $\langle true^*; x_{is2} \wedge y_{is3}; true^*; x_{is3} \wedge y_{is3}; true^* \rangle end$, $\langle true^*; x_{is1} \wedge y_{is3}; true^*; x_{is2} \wedge y_{is2}; true^*; x_{is3} \wedge y_{is3}; true^* \rangle end$ and $\langle true^*; x_{is3} \wedge y_{is3}; true^*; x_{is1} \wedge y_{is1}; true^* \rangle end$ respectively.

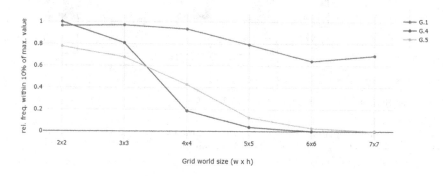

Fig. 4. Rel. freq. within 10% of max. value

Figure 4 outlines the results for this experiment. It shows that the latter two goals quickly become harder to solve in this setting, as there is a steep decline in optimal behaviour between grid world sizes 3×3 and 4×4. In addition, the graph shows that for the more sparse goals the chance of finding optimal behaviour under the conditions outlined for this setting for a grid world of 7×7 becomes nil. Thus, the observed data indicates there is a relation between goal sparsity and the performance of first-visit MC.

4.2 Experiment 2: Reward Shaping

Recall that for Experiment 1, sparser goals quickly become harder to solve. Therefore, this experiment aims to apply RS to an RDP construction from Sect. 3 so as to identify whether the performance of MC can be improved when using a potential function from Sect. 2.4. In addition, Algorithm 2 will be used for on-line compilation in a model-free setting. A preliminary experiment showed that for a 5×5 grid world, in which $\langle true^*; x_{is1} \wedge y_{is5}; true^*; x_{is3} \wedge y_{is3}; true^*; x_{is5} \wedge y_{is5}; true^* \rangle end$ is used, an optimal policy is rarely found [21]. Therefore, this experiment outlines the effect of applying a potential function for RS. For this experiment, a 5×5 grid world is used, transitions are deterministic and MC is applied as the RL learning algorithm. The reward for the goal is set to $+1000$. Figure 5a outlines a possible optimal trace for the given goal. The quantitative measurements are defined by the averaged returns per episode and the size of the extended MDP. A total of 50 runs with each 1000 episodes and a maximum of 50 steps per episode is used. Parameters are defined as $\gamma = 1$ and $\epsilon = 0.1$. The agent always starts an episode in state s_{11} and an episode is terminated when the agent reaches s_{51}, after which a new episode is initiated until the maximum number of episodes is reaches.

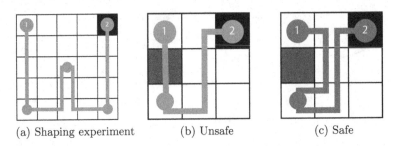

(a) Shaping experiment   (b) Unsafe   (c) Safe

Fig. 5. (a) Possible optimal trace for reward shaping experiment, (b)–(c) Possible optimal traces for safety experiment (Color figure online)

Figure 6 plots the results for this experiment. From Fig. 6a it can be observed that a shaped reward takes somewhat longer to learn, but the averaged return is significantly higher for the 5×5 grid world. More specifically, the averaged return for unshaped rewards shows that unshaped rewards are, on average, not received, as the trend remains just below zero. Finally, Fig. 6b outlines that shaped rewards reach far more states when compared to unshaped rewards. Given the observation that unshaped rewards are, on average, not received, all states reachable only after a goal is satisfied are very rarely explored for unshaped rewards. Hence, the size of the extended MDP is significantly smaller.

As an intuitive evaluation of the observed results, recall the 5×5 grid world as outlined in Fig. 5a. Finding a trace that follows the critical path for the given goal without a potential function is then inherently hard. Consider, for example, the trace outlined by Fig. 5a. This trace contains 16 consecutive steps, where the agent may stray from the path at each one of these steps with a probability ϵ. Even if the agent reaches the end of the trace in the case of unshaped rewards, the back-propagation of the reward value may be insignificant when it updates the state-action value of state s_{11}, as the agent only gets rewarded for the trace when it finally reaches terminal state s_{51}. In turn, on average, the agent might only obtain the unshaped reward relatively rarely, leaving most of the states that account for the latter part of the trace uncharted. Note that, as discussed, this result is accounted for in Fig. 6b. Conversely, a shaped reward encourages the agent to better follow the critical path, in turn increasing the probability of satisfying the reward formula by its trace and thus increasing the number of explored states in the extended MDP generated by Algorithm 2. In general, it can be observed that shaped rewards make learning perform better, while at the same time increasing the size of the (encountered) state space and the number of steps required in optimal traces.

When reward shaping is applied, a significant increase in MC performance can be observed from Fig. 7 for a 5×5 grid world. Where the unshaped reward decreases rapidly between 3×3 and 4×4 grid world, the shaped reward decreases significantly less over the course of the increasing grid world sizes.

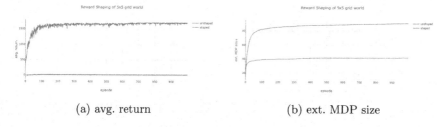

(a) avg. return   (b) ext. MDP size

Fig. 6. MC performance for unshaped vs. shaped rewards.

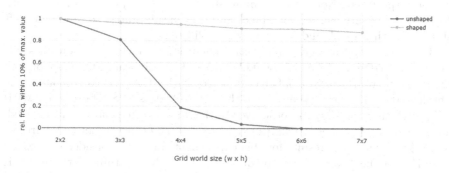

Fig. 7. Rel. freq. within 10% of max. value for unshaped and shaped rewards

4.3   Experiment 3: Safety

The goal of this experiment is to empirically measure the effects of safety properties on the performance of learning. Here, a preemptive shield [2] is applied such that the agent is provided a list of safe actions upon action selection. Moreover, on-line compilation as outlined in Algorithm 2 is applied. Next, a 3×3 grid world is used and modeled as an RDP in which first-visit MC is applied as an RL learning algorithm. Transitions are deterministic to reduce experiment complexity. The quantitative measurement is defined by the performance of the learning algorithm. A total of 50 runs is performed, each of which consists of 1000 episodes and a maximum of 50 steps per episode. Furthermore, $\gamma = 1$ and $\epsilon = 0.1$. The agent always starts in state s_{11} and an episode always terminates when the agent reaches state s_{31}. Goal $\langle true^*; x_{is1} \wedge y_{is3}; true^* \rangle end$ is specified for which the agent is rewarded $+50$ for reaching state s_{13}, i.e. the bottom-left state. A step cost of -1 is rewarded with each step the agent takes in the environment. An additional safety property $[true^*] \langle (\neg x_{is1} \wedge \neg y_{is2})^* \rangle end$ is specified in LDL_f where the agent should never visit unsafe state s_{21}. Figure 5 outlines possible optimal traces for unsafe and safe situations in Fig. 5b and

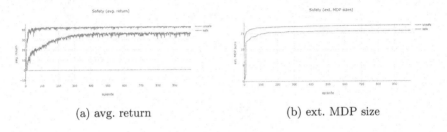

(a) avg. return   (b) ext. MDP size

Fig. 8. MC performance for safety

Fig. 5c respectively. Note that terminal states, i.e. the top-right states in both Figs. 5b and 5c, are marked solid black and that unsafe states, i.e. the center-left states in both Figs. 5b and 5c are marked solid red.

First, in order to verify no unsafe condition is met, Fig. 9 outlines the extended MDP for this experiment. Because of a technical index mapping, an unsafe state would have a label that starts with $(1, 2, \ldots)$, corresponding to unsafe state s_{12}. As can be observed, there is no state $s' \in S'$ of extended MDP M' for which $\tau(s') \to s_{21}$. In other words, the unsafe state is never encountered. Therefore, safety property $[true^*]\langle(\neg x_{is1} \land \neg y_{is2})^*\rangle end$ is never violated. Furthermore, Fig. 8 plots the results for this experiment. Let us reconsider the results from Fig. 8a and Fig. 8b. It can be observed that, when learning performance is decreased, the size of the state space has become smaller. However, the intuition is that, when less states are to be explored, performance is generally increased. It appears, then, that RL performance is not necessarily dictated by the size of the state space. To account for what does impact the decreased learning performance, let us reconsider the experiment setup. Where state s_{13} in Fig. 5b can be reached from two states, i.e. s_{12} and s_{23}, the same state can only be reached from a single state s_{23} in Fig. 5c. This observation leads to the conjecture that RL performance is related to the *accessibility* of states required to satisfy goal formulae. That is, when states have less paths by which they can be reached, RL performance decreases.

4.4 Experiment 4: Non-Markovian Transitions

This experiment focuses on non-Markovian transition models. Here, on-line compilation using Algorithm 2 will be used in a model-free setting, with first-visit MC. The quantitative measurements are defined by the averaged returns per episode, the averaged number of steps per episode and the size of the extended MDP. The experiment consists of 50 runs, each 1000 episodes with a maximum of 50 steps per episode. Furthermore, $\gamma = 1$ and $\epsilon = 0.1$. The grid world is defined by a 5×2 rectangle. The agent always starts an episode in state s_{11} and state s_{51} is defined as a terminal state. There is a single goal $\langle true^*; x_{is3} \land y_{is1}; true^*\rangle end$ rewarded when reaching s_{41} of $+10$, with the addition of a step cost encoded in LDL_f valued as -1.

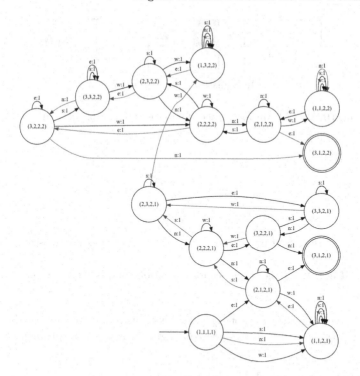

Fig. 9. Product MDP for safety experiment

The first set of 50 runs uses non-deterministic transitions. That is, in every state of the grid world the agent has a 0.8 probability of ending up in the next state and a 0.2 probability of remaining in its current state. For example, when in s_{21} and taking action s, there is a 0.8 probability that we end up in s_{22} and a 0.2 probability to remain in s_{21}. The transition from s_{31} for action e is defined by $\langle true^*; x_{is3} \wedge y_{is1} \rangle end$ and will be different for the regular transition defined below. A possible optimal trace is visually displayed in Fig. 10a.

The second set of 50 runs uses regular transitions. Now, when the agent reaches s_{31}, a transition $\langle true^*; x_{is2} \wedge y_{is1}; x_{is3} \wedge y_{is1} \rangle end$ is defined that depends on whether the agent came from state $_{21}$ or not. In case the previous state was s_{21}, the transition of action e in s_{31} is defined as a 0.1 probability of ending up in s_{41} and a 0.9 probability of remaining in s_{31}. Otherwise, the same transition probabilities used for the non-deterministic transitions apply, i.e. a 0.8 probability of ending up in s_{41} and a 0.2 probability of remaining in s_{31}. Here, the transition in s_{31} is regularly defined and depends on a history of states. A possible optimal trace for regular transitions is given in Fig. 10b.

From Fig. 11, we observe that regular non-deterministic transitions, when compared to non-regular ones, induce a harder problem for a model-free setting, while the size of the state space is only increased by one additional state that

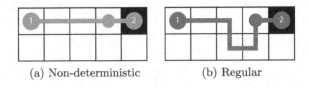

(a) Non-deterministic   (b) Regular

Fig. 10. Possible optimal traces for transition complexity variations

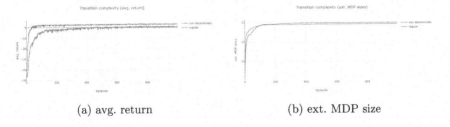

(a) avg. return   (b) ext. MDP size

Fig. 11. MC performance for transition complexity variations

keeps track of whether or not s_{21} has been visited. In other words, a small increase in size can evidently generate a significantly harder problem.

5   Conclusions and Future Work

We have introduced a new tool chain to compute with regular decision processes, and experimented with novel algorithmic variations with the aim to gain insight in how complexity of temporal logic formulas relates to the complexity of learning algorithms such as MC RL for the resulting extended MDPs. We have shown that by increasing the world size for similar built formulas problems get harder (**R1**), but also that reward shaping on the automata representing those formulas can really help learning, *and* exploration (**R2**). The safety experiments (**R3**) have shown less states do not necessarily result in easier learning tasks, and the non-Markov transitions experiments (**R4**) showed that these only caused a small increase in state space size, but did complicate learning a lot more.

Our overall conclusions of the experiments point to our main future work direction. It seems that there are complex relations between i) the complexity and properties of the temporal formulae defining the non-Markovian aspects, ii) the resulting size and connection structure of the extended MDP, and iii) the learning performance of online RL algorithms for the extended MDP. Much more work is needed to evaluate a temporal specification for a particular problem, and assess its influence on the complexity of learning the original task in the presence of the new rule. For MDPs there is much work on measures relating to e.g. homomorphism and abstraction [36,37] and work is starting to emerge to gain more insight in the logical side [31] but their interaction needs study.

Other future work should focus on *representations* and *applications*. For the first, there is much to be gained by utilizing existing formal methods, for example the use of transducers and Mealy machines [9] trading off the size of the state space with compositional modeling. Equally important is to focus more on utilizing model checking tools [2,16]. Application-wise, there are plenty of opportunities to utilize the methods in this paper, for example to constrain RL dialogue agents, in medical domains with logically represented medical guidance and regulations, or to implement coaching strategies in RL coaching agents [17].

References

1. Abadi, E., Brafman, R.I.: Learning and solving regular decision processes. In: IJCAI (2020)
2. Alshiekh, M., Bloem, R., Ehlers, R., Könighofer, B., Niekum, S., Topcu, U.: Safe reinforcement learning via shielding. In: AAAI (2018)
3. Bacchus, F., Boutilier, C., Grove, A.: Rewarding behaviors. In: AAAI (1996)
4. Brafman, R., Giacomo, G.D., Patrizi, F.: LTLf/LDLf non-Markovian rewards (2018)
5. Brafman, R.I., De Giacomo, G.: Planning for LTLf/LDLf goals in non-Markovian fully observable nondeterministic domains. In: IJCAI (2019)
6. Brafman, R.I., De Giacomo, G.: Regular decision processes: a model for non-Markovian domains. In: IJCAI (2019)
7. Camacho, A., Icarte, R.T., Klassen, T.Q., Valenzano, R.A., McIlraith, S.A.: LTL and beyond: formal languages for reward function specification in reinforcement learning. In: IJCAI (2019)
8. Camacho, A., McIlraith, S.A.: Learning interpretable models expressed in linear temporal logic. In: ICAPS (2019)
9. De Giacomo, G., Favorito, M., Iocchi, L., Patrizi, F., Ronca, A.: Temporal logic monitoring rewards via transducers. In: KR (2020)
10. De Giacomo, G., Iocchi, L., Favorito, M., Patrizi, F.: Reinforcement learning for LTLf/LDLf goals. arXiv preprint arXiv:1807.06333 (2018)
11. De Giacomo, G., Iocchi, L., Favorito, M., Patrizi, F.: Foundations for restraining bolts: reinforcement learning with LTLf/LDLf restraining specifications. In: ICAPS (2019)
12. De Giacomo, G., Vardi, M.Y.: Linear temporal logic and linear dynamic logic on finite traces. In: AAAI (2013)
13. Fulton, N., Platzer, A.: Safe reinforcement learning via formal methods: toward safe control through proof and learning. In: AAAI (2018)
14. Furelos-Blanco, D., Law, M., Jonsson, A., Broda, K., Russo, A.: Induction and exploitation of subgoal automata for reinforcement learning. J. Artif. Intell. Res. **70**, 1031–1116 (2021)
15. Garcia, J., Fernández, F.: A comprehensive survey on safe reinforcement learning. J. Mach. Learn. Res. **16**(1), 1437–1480 (2015)
16. Giaquinta, R., Hoffmann, R., Ireland, M., Miller, A., Norman, G.: Strategy synthesis for autonomous agents using PRISM. In: Dutle, A., Muñoz, C., Narkawicz, A. (eds.) NFM 2018. LNCS, vol. 10811, pp. 220–236. Springer, Cham (2018). https://doi.org/10.1007/978-3-319-77935-5_16

17. Hassouni, A., Hoogendoorn, M., van Otterlo, M., Barbaro, E.: Personalization of health interventions using cluster-based reinforcement learning. In: Miller, T., Oren, N., Sakurai, Y., Noda, I., Savarimuthu, B.T.R., Cao Son, T. (eds.) PRIMA 2018. LNCS (LNAI), vol. 11224, pp. 467–475. Springer, Cham (2018). https://doi.org/10.1007/978-3-030-03098-8_31

18. Jothimurugan, K., Alur, R., Bastani, O.: A composable specification language for reinforcement learning tasks. In: NeurIPS (2019)

19. Kasenberg, D., Thielstrom, R., Scheutz, M.: Generating explanations for temporal logic planner decisions. In: ICAPS (2020)

20. Kim, J., Muise, C., Shah, A., Agarwal, S., Shah, J.: Bayesian inference of linear temporal logic specifications for contrastive explanations. In: IJCAI (2019)

21. Lenaers, N.: An empirical study on regular decision processes for grid worlds. Master's thesis, Department of Computer Science, Faculty of Science, Open University (2021)

22. Li, X., Vasile, C.I., Belta, C.: Reinforcement learning with temporal logic rewards. In: IROS (2017)

23. Liao, H.C.: A survey of reinforcement learning with temporal logic rewards (2020)

24. Liao, S.M.: Ethics of Artificial Intelligence. Oxford University Press, Oxford (2020)

25. Littman, M.L., Topcu, U., Fu, J., Isbell, C., Wen, M., MacGlashan, J.: Environment-independent task specifications via GLTL. arXiv preprint arXiv:1704.04341 (2017)

26. Mirhoseini, A., et al.: A graph placement methodology for fast chip design. Nature **594**(7862), 207–212 (2021)

27. Ng, A.Y., Harada, D., Russell, S.J.: Policy invariance under reward transformations: theory and application to reward shaping. In: ICML (1999)

28. van Otterlo, M.: Ethics and the value (s) of artificial intelligence. Nieuw Archief voor Wiskunde **5**(19), 3 (2018)

29. Pnueli, A.: The temporal logic of programs. In: Proceedings of the 18th Annual Symposium on Foundations of Computer Science (1977)

30. Puterman, M.L.: Markov Decision Processes: Discrete Stochastic Dynamic Programming. Wiley, Hoboken (1994)

31. Romeo, Í.Í., Lohstroh, M., Iannopollo, A., Lee, E.A., Sangiovanni-Vincentelli, A.: A metric for linear temporal logic. arXiv preprint arXiv:1812.03923 (2018)

32. Silver, D., et al.: Mastering the game of go with deep neural networks and tree search. Nature **529**(7587), 484–489 (2016)

33. Spaan, M.T.J.: Partially observable Markov decision processes. In: Wiering, M.A., van Otterlo, M. (eds.) Reinforcement Learning. ALO, vol. 12, pp. 387–414. Springer, Heidelberg (2012). https://doi.org/10.1007/978-3-642-27645-3_12

34. Sutton, R.S., Barto, A.G.: Reinforcement Learning: An Introduction. The MIT Press, Cambridge (2018)

35. Thiébaux, S., Gretton, C., Slaney, J., Price, D., Kabanza, F.: Decision-theoretic planning with non-Markovian rewards. JAIR **25**, 17–74 (2006)

36. Van Otterlo, M.: The Logic of Adaptive Behavior, Frontiers in Artificial Intelligence and Applications, vol. 192. IOS Press, Amsterdam (2009)

37. Wang, H., Dong, S., Shao, L.: Measuring structural similarities in finite MDPs. In: IJCAI (2019)

38. Wang, H., et al.: Deep reinforcement learning: a survey. Front. Inf. Technol. Electron. Eng. **21**, 1726–1744 (2020). https://doi.org/10.1631/FITEE.1900533

39. Wiering, M.A., Van Otterlo, M.: Reinforcement Learning. Adaptation, Learning, and Optimization, vol. 12. Springer, Heidelberg (2012). https://doi.org/10.1007/978-3-642-27645-3

MoveRL: To a Safer Robotic Reinforcement Learning Environment

Gaoyuan Liu$^{(\boxtimes)}$, Joris De Winter, Bram Vanderborght, Ann Nowé, and Denis Steckelmacher

Vrije Universiteit Brussel, Brussel, Belgium
`gaoyuan.liu@vub.be`

Abstract. The deployment of Reinforcement Learning (RL) on physical robots still stumbles on several challenges, such as sample-efficiency, safety, reproducibility, cost, and software platforms. In this paper, we introduce MoveRL, an environment that exposes a standard OpenAI Gym interface, and allows any off-the-shelf RL agent to control a robot built on ROS, the Robot OS. ROS is the standard abstraction layer used by roboticists, and allows to observe and control both simulated and physical robots. By providing a bridge between the Gym and ROS, our environment allows an easy evaluation of RL algorithms in highly-accurate simulators, or real-world robots, without any change of software. In addition to a Gym-ROS bridge, our environment also leverages MoveIt, a state-of-the-art collision-aware robot motion planner, to prevent the RL agent from executing actions that would lead to a collision. Our experimental results show that a standard PPO agent is able to control a simulated commercial robot arm in an environment with moving obstacles, while almost perfectly avoiding collisions even in the early stages of learning. We also show that the use of MoveIt slightly increases the sample-efficiency of the RL agent. Combined, these results show that RL on robots is possible in a safe way, and that it is possible to leverage state-of-the-art robotic techniques to improve how an RL agent learns. We hope that our environment will allow more (future) RL algorithms to be evaluated on commercial robotic tasks.

Github repository: https://github.com/Gaoyuan-Liu/MoveRL

1 Introduction

Reinforcement Learning is a Machine Learning approach that allows an agent to learn what action to execute in which situation, to maximize a scalar reward [14]. On robots, Reinforcement Learning has the potential of allowing to learn near-optimal controllers on challenging tasks, on which classical methods such as planning are not applicable, for instance due to the unavailability of a good model, or high stochasticity or unexpected events around the robot. However, in practice, Reinforcement Learning is not often used on robots.

Several challenges currently prevent the use of Reinforcement Learning on robots, such as safety, sample-efficiency, the ease of implementation of RL on

© Springer Nature Switzerland AG 2022
L. A. Leiva et al. (Eds.): BNAIC/Benelearn 2021, CCIS 1530, pp. 239–253, 2022.
https://doi.org/10.1007/978-3-030-93842-0_14

robots from a software perspective, and the trust designers must have in RL to use it. In this paper, we propose a new OpenAI Gym [3] environment that allows real-world robotic experiments to be performed, addressing these two challenges:

Software Compatibility with Robots. Existing Reinforcement Learning environments that have robots in mind, such as the Gym Mujoco environments [3], the DeepMind control suite [25], or PyBullet environments [28], implement environment-specific robotic arms or bodies (not industry-standard robots), using embedded simulators (not a connection to an industry-standard simulator). As such, these environments can be used to show that RL works on robots in theory, but do not help implementing RL on a real-world robot. Our main contribution, MoveRL, interfaces an RL agent with the Gym API to ROS, the Robot OS, used by industry-standard simulators (such as Gazebo) and robots. This allows direct learning on the robot, or easy transfer of an agent learned in simulation to a physical robot (without having to re-implement anything).

Safety. The Robot OS comes with many packages that allow to build complete robotic systems, with planning, collision avoidance, simultaneous localization and mapping, ... In this paper, we use MoveIt [4] to transform an action selected by an RL agent into a motion plan for a robot, while avoiding collisions with obstacles. MoveIt gets its knowledge about obstacles from the ROS network, which means that it is inherently compatible with simulators (that know where obstacles are) and depth cameras, that produce the same information on real robots [11].

Our empirical results in the Gazebo simulator, using a simulated real-world robot (the Franka Emika Panda manipulator), show that combining an unmodified implementation of PPO [23] from the stable-baselines3 [21] with a ROS environment is possible, and that leveraging MoveIt for action execution allows to prevent almost every collision, even in the early stages of learning.

2   Notations

The Reinforcement Learning literature considers an agent that executes actions in a Markov Decision Process, defined by a tuple $\langle S, A, R, T, \mu_0, \gamma \rangle$. S is the state space, that can be either discrete or continuous. In this paper, we consider continuous state-spaces, in which each state is a vector of several real values. A is the action space. In this paper, we consider a continuous action space, in which each action is a vector of real values. $R(s, a, s')$ is the reward function, that produces a single real value after a transition from state s to s', caused by the execution of action a. $T(s, a)$ is the transition function, that maps a state and an action to a new state. μ_0 is the initial state distribution, that defines in which state the agent may start an episode, and $\gamma < 1$ is a real value, the discount factor.

Most Reinforcement Learning literature follows the notation described above. However, roboticians use other notations, that appear in the literature related to

ROS and MoveIt, and that we sometimes use in this paper when interfacing with these components. We provide a brief summary of the differences of notation in the table below:

RL	Meaning	Motion planning
s	State (observation)	q (if joint angles) p (if end-effector position)
a	Action	q_i (target joint angles)
r	Reward	r or c (cost $c = -r$)

3   Related Work

Our main contribution allows a Reinforcement Learning agent to interface with the Robot OS, for easy control of simulated or physical robots, with the use of a motion planner to ensure safety. We now provide a related work review of other approaches at robotic environments for Reinforcement Learning, techniques that allow to make a Reinforcement Learning agent safer, and motion planning libraries.

3.1   RL Robotic Environment

To tackle various challenges in robot RL [14], numerous robotic RL environments are developed with different platforms. A brief survey of robotic RL environment frameworks can be found in [13] and [9]. Each work emphasises specific merits with regards to particular issues. In this paper, we only review frameworks which are wildly accepted as benchmark, and particularly, we discuss how they consider safety when learning.

Mujoco. To improve the reproducibility in RL robotics research, SURREAL [8] is built on the MuJoCo simulation environment and physics engine [26]. Mujoco is widely used for RL environments, and frameworks with the same physics engine can be found in [1,20,29]. Such projects usually focus on theoretical RL research, and lack compatibility with robotic software such as the Robot OS. Moreover, the use of Mujoco requires a license id (free for academic purposes, paid otherwise).

PyBullet. PyBullet is an open-source physics engine, used by [28] to implement several Reinforcement Learning environments in simulated 3D spaces. These environments allow the agent to control every joint of the robots, but do not provide any safety mechanism or collision avoidance. An RL environment for a quadcopter is developed with PyBullet by [18], but collision avoidance is not considered, even though it appears crucial for a quadcopter.

Gazebo. Gazebo is an open-source simulator with a graphical interface, and an interface to the Robot OS ROS [6]. A Gym environment for interacting with Gazebo is proposed in [15], but collisions are allowed to happen in the simulator, which makes replacing the simulator with a real-world robot impractical. However, because Gazebo and ROS have large communities that developed many industry-proven tools, we base our main contribution on these two pieces of software, and add MoveIt for collision avoidance.

3.2 Safe Reinforcement Learning

RL safety is normally defined as a mechanism which can ensure reasonable system performance and/or respect safety constraints during the training or validation processes.

Definition and Survey. RL safety approaches can be categorized in two classes: tuning the optimization criterion of the algorithm to encourage safe behavior, and directly intervening on the exploration of the agent to prevent unsafe actions from being executed.

With the optimization approach, maximizing the long-term reward can generate statistically safer policy, but does not necessarily avoid the rare occurrences of damage, neither ensures safety during training. The exploration approach provides a *shielding* mechanism that modifies or prevents unsafe actions [10]. Several approaches to Safe RL, belonging to the two classes described above, are reviewed in [27].

Safe Exploration. In this paper, we focus our attention onto Safe RL approaches that consider physical issues, and in particular prevent physical damage. In a danger-sensitive learning environment, such as robotics, the importance of damage avoidance is higher than obtaining high rewards. Therefore, a shielding layer maintaining zero-constraint-violations throughout whole learning process is necessary.

[22] introduce *safe exploration*, more specifically Constrained Reinforcement Learning, and address two challenges: 1) the difficulty of designing reward functions that nicely balance punishing unsafe actions, and encouraging the agent to learn the desired skill; 2) the fact that eventually learning the optimal safe policy does not guarantee that no unsafe action has been performed while learning.

[5] consider that some states can be identified as unsafe, and propose a method to avoid these states. In [19], a safety layer is applied in a real-robot system, the safety layer modifies possibly risky actions to the closest valid alternatives which satisfy safety constrains, but such constraints are difficult to define especially when the environment is noisy or uncertain. Similar structured safety guarantee is also utilized in [2].

When positioning this paper in relation to existing work, it is important to note that existing work focuses on preventing the execution of specific unsafe actions, and let the designer define what an unsafe action is. In this paper, we use MoveIt to automatically detect what would be unsafe actions, freeing the designer from this task. Moreover, existing work considers that moving from a safe state to a safe state is safe. This is not the case in practice, as we explain in Sect. 4.7: the path between two safe states may go through a wall, and therefore be unsafe. Our contribution detects these unsafe actions.

3.3   Path Planning

Path planning is one of the most fundamental problems in autonomous robotics, particularly, in the scenarios where robots have to execute tasks in an environment with obstacles. Sampling-based methods offer a solution to overcome the complexity of deterministic robot planning algorithms for a robots with many degrees of freedom (many joints). A comprehensive survey can be found in [7]. An open-source library for sampling-based motion planning OMPL (Open Motion Planning Library) is proposed by [24], and is integrated in an open-source framework, MoveIt!, that offers an state of the art path planning based on several well-known libraries. MoveIt also integrates implementations of useful robotics functions, such 3D perception, kinematics calculation and control[1].

4   Contribution

Our main contribution is a Gym environment, that allows to interface unmodified Reinforcement Learning agents written in Python with a simulated or physical robot exposed on ROS-Noetic, the Robot OS, a collection of libraries and network protocols that allow components of robotic systems (hardware, software, planners, ...) to communicate in an industry-standard way. We also leverage MoveIt, a state-of-the-art motion planner, for efficient action execution and collision avoidance.

The general architecture of our main contribution, MoveRL, is depicted in Fig. 1. Every time-step, the agent receives an observation and reward from the environment, and selects a *raw action*, a desired position of the robot, not yet guaranteed safe. The raw action passes through a collision monitor, based on MoveIt, that observes the current position of obstacles and verifies the action. Verifying the action relies on the possibility to simulate its outcome, which is possible on physical robots by using *co-simulation* (a simulated version of the robot runs in parallel with the physical robot, an approach very common in industrial robotics and transparently supported by ROS). In this paper, we only use pure simulation, and leave co-simulation with a physical robot to future work.

If the raw action will cause a collision, it is discarded, leading to no movement of the robot for this time-step, and a punishment given to the Reinforcement Learning agent. If the raw action is safe, the planner computes a collision-free path to guarantee the safety during execution. Our action shielding mechanism ensures that no collision happens when the agent moves.

---

[1] https://MoveIt.ros.org/.

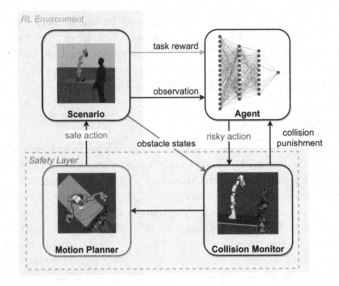

Fig. 1. Our MoveRL framework. Our safety layer leveraging the MoveIt motion planner contains 2 modules: 1) a collision monitor, that detects actions that lead to collisions, and 2) a motion planner, that plans a collision-free path to reach the target locations encoded in (previously-identified) safe actions.

We now detail all the software components of our proposed MoveRL. Our implementation is available at https://github.com/Gaoyuan-Liu/MoveRL.

4.1   The Gym Environment

To be compatible with standard RL algorithm implementations, such as in Stable Baseline 3 [21], our contribution needs to be implemented as an OpenAI Gym [3] environment. A Gym environment is a Python class that contains attributes that describe its state and action spaces (both Box in our case), and methods that allow actions to be executed in the environment. The *reset* method resets the environment to an initial state, and returns the first observation of the episode. The *step* method takes an *action* as input, passes to ROS and MoveIt for safe execution, and produces a new state (*observation*) and *reward*. We describe all these steps in more detail later. A *done* signal is also returned by *step*, and allows the environment to choose when an episode should terminate.

4.2   Observation Space

Since we consider kinematics observation, we make an assumption that the position of obstacles can be detected by sensors, or is available in simulation. The observation space contains two parts: the state of the robot, and the state of the obstacles. For the robot state, we developed two environments with two different kinds of observation: joint angles $\mathbf{q} = [q_1, q_2, ..., q_n]$

for an n degrees-of-freedom robot, and end-effector <u>position</u> and orientation $\mathbf{p} = [p_x^{ee}, p_y^{ee}, p_z^{ee}, o_x^{ee}, o_y^{ee}, o_z^{ee}, o_w^{ee}]$, for tasks in which the robot has an end-effector such as a gripper. For obstacle state, the agent can observe the position and orientation of the obstacles: $[p_x^{obs}, p_y^{obs}, p_z^{obs}, o_x^{obs}, o_y^{obs}, o_z^{obs}, o_w^{obs}]$. Our environment class can adjust the size of state space according to the number of obstacles in the simulation.

Note that the agent observes the position and orientation of the obstacles (cylinders, spheres, rods, cubes), but not their shape or dimensions. This is not a problem, as an RL agent is perfectly able to learn what positions in relation to the center and orientation of an obstacle will translate to negative rewards. So, the agent sorts of learns the shape of the obstacles by feel, and does not need to be provided that information.

4.3   Action Space

Our environment exposes a continuous action space, for which actions are vectors of real values. More precisely, we consider that the action produced by the agent is a target configuration of the robot, so a list of real values that define the angle at which every joint of the robot must be set. Robotics libraries call this set of angles q_i, and the Reinforcement Learning literature calls this a. The action space is constrained by the physical abilities of the robot, with joint position limits $q_{i,\text{limit}}$ and joint velocity limits $\dot{q}_{i,\text{limit}}$.

The physical constraint on the speed of a joint requires careful engineering of how the agent produces an action. Given a time-step duration Δt, we must ensure that the action $q_{i,\text{cmd}}$ produced by the agent, and sent to the environment, differs (in absolute value) from the previous action by at most $\Delta t \cdot \dot{q}_{i,\text{limit}}$, for every element of $q_{i,\text{cmd}}$. We must also ensure that the action $q_{i,\text{cmd}}$ is part of the allowed range of joint angles $[q_{i,\text{min}}, q_{i,\text{max}}]$.

We implement these constraints as follows: the policy of the agent produces the change in joint positions $\Delta q_{i,\text{cmd}}$, instead of the absolute value of the joint positions $q_{i,\text{cmd}}$. Then, we clip $\Delta q_{i,\text{cmd}}$ to $[-\Delta t \dot{q}_{i,\text{limit}}, \Delta t \dot{q}_{i,\text{limit}}]$, produce $q_{i,\text{cmd}} = q_{i,\text{prev timestep}} + \Delta q_{i,\text{cmd}}$, and clip $q_{i,\text{cmd}}$ to the range $[q_{i,\text{min}}, q_{i,\text{max}}]$. This clipped value is sent to the environment, that uses MoveIt to detect and avoid collisions.

4.4   Why Do We Need Sequences of Actions?

Most tasks on which we evaluate our framework consist of moving the end effector of a robot to a specific target location. Given the action set described above, it may seem logical that only one action is necessary for that: putting the robot in the pose that puts the end effector at the target location. However, in practice, a sequence of actions is needed for the following reasons:

- The time-step has a fixed duration and the robot cannot move infinitely quickly, so the actions have to progressively bring the robot close to the target location;

- Even if state of the art, MoveIt has difficulties planning motions on long distances, especially when there are concave obstacles in the scene. Reinforcement Learning is particularly useful in this case, as its optimization of the discounted sum of rewards allows the agent to take actions that move away from the goal in the short term, but allow to reach it in the long term.

4.5 Reward Function

The reward function is customized for each specific task, but always consists of the sum of two terms: a task-specific reward and a task-agnostic safety term, $r = r_{\text{task}} + r_{\text{safety}}$.

We describe r_{task} in the next sections. r_{safety} is 0 when an action would cause no collision, and some negative constant when an action is detected as being unsafe (and cancelled). The choice of the constant is described in our experiments, and needs to be large enough that the agent learns to avoid states that can potentially lead to collisions (especially when there are moving obstacles), but not too much, so that the agent does not become too conservative (and learns a policy that remains immobile, for instance).

4.6 Initial States and Termination

Every episode, we initialize the simulated robot to a random pose, to ensure good exploration. The episode terminates when the end effector of the robot reaches a pre-defined goal position, or after 100 time-steps.

4.7 Safety Guarantee

After having described the different components of our environment (state space, action space, ...), we now discuss the different types of collisions that can be detected by MoveIt, and provide details on how we query MoveIt from a Gym environment. A full description with code would go beyond the page limit of this paper, but the complete source code that we use in our experiments is available on Github (link in the abstract).

Collision Types. To comprehensively consider the potential risk during training, we categorize collisions into three types:

(a) self collision: two parts of robot itself collide with each other; (b) pose collision: the commanded configuration $q_{i,\text{cmd}}$ collides with objects in the environment; (c) path collision: the direct path between two configurations contains collisions with objects in the environment. Figure 2 shows examples of these three types of collisions.

Avoiding self-collision and pose collision during learning can be achieved by constrained inverse kinematics and state-validation checking at each time-step. However, the avoiding path collisions is more challenging, and tends to be neglected in the Safe RL literature since it is difficult to do state validation

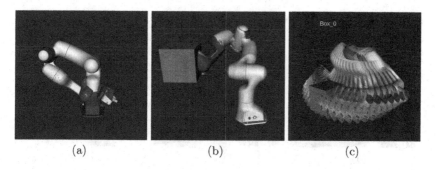

Fig. 2. (a) Self collision (b) Pose collision (c) Path collision

checking continuously. Therefore, even when the state for two adjacent steps are safe, the direct path (without planning) can still collide with obstacles. We give an unified solution to avoid the aforementioned three types of collision, which is integrating MoveIt as an safety layer in the RL environment.

Collision Detection. The MoveIt provide package `Planning Scene` allows to manage an abstract representation of the environment surrounding a simulated or physical robot. This environment can contain obstacles of two possible types: scene object and octomap [12].

Scene objects have an explicit shape, such as a 3D mesh or a primitive shape (cylinder, box, sphere). It is used when a coarse obstacle is enough, for instance a big cylinder around a human, to encoder a general area that has to be avoided. An Octomap is built from a depth camera (or produced by a simulator), and allows to precisely measure the presence of an obstacle around the robot, without having to model it. The trade-off between precision and efficiency can be adjusted with the resolution parameter of the octomap.

Once the Planning Scene has been defined (and kept updated by the simulator or sensors, using ROS network messages that the Gym environment does not even need to bother with), MoveIt is able to detect collisions using libraries such as the FCL (Flexible Collision Library) [17].

We stress that the use of ROS allows to transparently interface our Gym environment with many well-regarded robotic packages, Planning Scene being only one. Other packages allow to stream updates to the position of the obstacles from a variety of sensors (and are usually shipped with the sensors), or to visualize various aspects of the scene (for instance, visualizing how a physical robot senses its surrounding). Figure 3 shows that it is possible to visualize a textured 3D render of a scene, along with information about the obstacles in it, and what motion planning has to be performed.

Path Planner. It's worth noting that the direct path between two valid poses can still contain collisions, which we term as path collision. To avoid path collisions, a local planner is necessary, and will run every time-step, to produce a

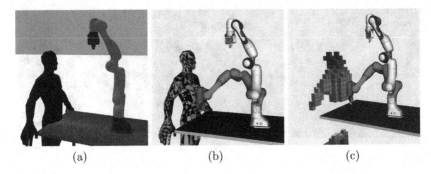

(a)   (b)   (c)

Fig. 3. The collision detection methods in MoveIt. (a) Gazebo simulation (b) Collision detection with scene object (c) Collision detection with octomap. The white arm indicates current pose, the orange arm indicate the commanded pose, and the red parts indicate the collision links.

full motion from the pose of the robot on one time-step, to its pose at the next time-step.

For each time-step, given a valid action command, a planner plans a collision-free local path based on the present knowledge of the position of obstacles. In order to reduce the time consumption of training and minimize the planning delay, our primary consideration for choosing the most appropriate planner is efficiency and completeness. Therefore, we evaluated planners available in MoveIt by their solving time and path length, which can reflect the planners' efficiency in either planning and execution phases [16].

The planners' time consumption and planned path length on a benchmark task (putting a robotic arm into a desired pose) are shown in Fig. 4. We note that our objective is not to identify the absolute best planner, but to provide an informed choice of planner for our Reinforcement Learning experiments. RRT and its derivative show merits in both planning time and path length. Therefore, we choose the RRT planner in our experiments.

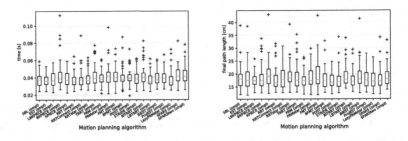

Fig. 4. *Left:* Planner planning-time comparison, *right:* Planner final path length comparison.

Goal-Reaching Task. We now define a goal-reaching task, and detail how it is implemented with MoveIt. To achieve the goal-reaching task, we define a dense reward (non-zero whenever there is movement during a time-step), that is proportional to the change in distance between the end-effector's current position and the goal position. The task reward can be formalized as:

$$r_{\text{task}}(s) = \begin{cases} \kappa \Delta d(s) + r_{\text{goal}} & \text{if } s \text{ is close to } s_{\text{goal}} \\ \kappa \Delta d(s) & \text{otherwise} \end{cases}$$

where $r_{\text{task}}(s)$ is the task reward given to the agent when reaching state s, $\Delta d(s)$ is the distance between the end-effector in state s and the target end-effector location, r_{goal} is a fixed positive reward given when the target location is reached, and κ is a weighting constant, allowing to balance r_{task} and r_{safety}. The actual values of r_{goal} and κ are given in the next section.

5   Experiment

While our main contribution is a Gym environment that allows to learn tasks in ROS-based robotic environments with standard Reinforcement Learning algorithms, we also provide experimental results, that show that:

- Our framework, that we call MoveRL, works and actually allows an un-modified PPO agent to learn a task;
- Collisions can indeed be avoided, thanks to MoveIt, which allows simulated robots to be replaced with physical robots if need be.

5.1   Learning Scenarios

In our experiments, the robot learns to fetch the goal point with its end-effector by adjusting 7 joint angles. We consider 3 scenarios around this task, that differ in what kinds of obstacles are around the robot:

1. **Table:** The table holding the robot is the only exterior obstacle, thus self-collisions are considered as the major risks in this scenario.
2. **Human:** The robot and a human worker share a single workspace. The goal point is located between the human and the robot. Self-collisions and pose collisions would be the major risks. The human is modelled with basic shapes such as cylinders.
3. **Case:** The robot has to reach a goal location inside a box/case (walls with an opening on top). Finding how to enter the case is challenging in this task and benefits from the use of Reinforcement Learning. The thin walls of the case lead to possible path collisions (in addition to self-collisions and pose collisions).

The 3 training scenarios are illustrated in Fig. 5. Our Github repository contains Gazebo world files for all 3 scenarios.

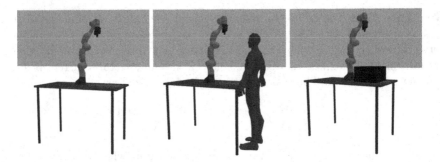

Fig. 5. The simulation environment in gazebo. From left to right: table world, human world, and case world.

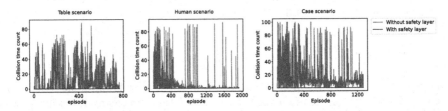

Fig. 6. Number of collisions occurring per episode, with and without collision avoidance with MoveIt. The blue line indicates that our safety layer, based on MoveIt, successfully prevents collisions throughout the learning process.

5.2   Learning Algorithm

We use a Reinforcement Learning agent from the Stable-Baselines 3 [21], that contains a set of reliable RL algorithms including A2C, DDPG, PPO, SAC and TD3. We choose PPO, as it is highly popular, compatible with continuous actions, and has many implementations. In this paper, we focus on showing that RL with ROS is possible, we do not aim at evaluating which RL algorithm performs the best. The hyper-parameters that we use for PPO in our experiments are the default values used Stable-Baselines 3, as of August 23rd, 2021, with the following changes: the policy network is MlpPolicy, the learning rate is 0.0005, the batch size is 200, and the number of steps between policy updates is 100.

5.3   Results

To evaluate our safety layer, we compare how a PPO agent learns with and without our collision avoidance method. We observe that our safety layer successfully prevents collisions, and has no negative impact on sample-efficiency:

Figure 6 shows that enabling our safety layer successfully prevents collisions, and that disabling our safety layer leads to a large amount of collisions.

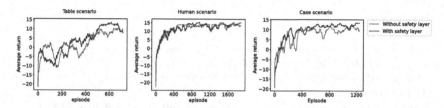

Fig. 7. Learning curves in each learning scenario. We confirm that our safety layer, that successfully prevents collisions, has no negative impact on sample-efficiency (the red and blue curves have the same shape). This shows that safety does not come at the expense of sample-efficiency with our MoveRL framework. (Color figure online)

Figure 7 presents the learning curves in our three scenarios, with and without our collision avoidance method. Avoiding collisions does not appear to have any negative impact on the agent, as the learning curves are comparable. If it has any effect, it would be a slight increase in sample-efficiency, as seen in the Case scenario. We are happy with this result, as it shows that safety in Reinforcement Learning does not come (in our case) at the cost of sample-efficiency and final policy quality.

6   Conclusion

In this paper, we presented MoveRL, a Reinforcement Learning Gym environment for robotic manipulators, that builds the widely-used ROS platform for simulated and physical robots. Thanks to the dynamism of the ROS community, advanced algorithms for planning, obstacle detection and collision avoidance are available. We leverage them in our environment to produce a method for safe Reinforcement Learning on robots. Our experiments show that our safety mechanism indeed prevents collisions while an un-modified PPO agent learns a simulated robotic task, and that our method has no negative impact on sample-efficiency.

While the deployment of our method on a physical robot remains as future work, we hope that our new software and method will allow Reinforcement Learning researchers to more easily evaluate their methods on simulated real-world robots (as opposed to unrealistic robots as available in the Gym Mujoco tasks, for instance), and will allow robotic engineers to evaluate Reinforcement Learning for the tasks in which classical planning methods show limitations.

Acknowledgments. The first author is supported by the China Scholarship Council (CSC). The second author is supported by the Flemish Government under the Flemish AI Program (*Onderzoeksprogramma Artificiële Intelligentie (AI) Vlaanderen*).

References

1. Ahn, M., et al.: Robotics benchmarks for learning with low-cost robots. In: Conference on Robot Learning, pp. 1300–1313. PMLR (2020)
2. Alshiekh, M., et al.: Safe reinforcement learning via shielding. In: Thirty-Second AAAI Conference on Artificial Intelligence (2018)
3. Brockman, G., et al.: OpenAI Gym. arXiv preprint arXiv:1606.01540 (2016)
4. Chitta, S., Sucan, I., Cousins, S.: Moveit![ros topics]. IEEE Robot. Autom. Mag. **19**(1), 18–19 (2012)
5. Dalal, G., Dvijotham, K., Vecerik, M., Hester, T., Paduraru, C., Tassa, Y.: Safe exploration in continuous action spaces. arXiv preprint arXiv:1801.08757 (2018)
6. Delhaisse, B., Rozo, L., Caldwell, D.G.: Pyrobolearn: a python framework for robot learning practitioners. In :Conference on Robot Learning, pp. 1348–1358. PMLR (2020)
7. Elbanhawi, M., Simic, M.: Sampling-based robot motion planning: a review. IEEE Access **2**, 56–77 (2014)
8. Fan, L., et al.: Surreal: open-source reinforcement learning framework and robot manipulation benchmark. In : Conference on Robot Learning, pp. 767–782. PMLR (2018)
9. Ferigo, D., Traversaro, S., Metta, G., Pucci, D.: Gym-ignition: reproducible robotic simulations for reinforcement learning. In: 2020 IEEE/SICE International Symposium on System Integration (SII), pp. 885–890. IEEE (2020)
10. Garcıa, J., Fernández, F.: A comprehensive survey on safe reinforcement learning. J. Mach. Learn. Res. **16**(1), 1437–1480 (2015)
11. Grushko, S., et al.: Tuning perception and motion planning parameters for move it! Framework (2020)
12. Hornung, A., Wurm, K.M., Bennewitz, M., Stachniss, C., Burgard, W.: Octomap: an efficient probabilistic 3d mapping framework based on octrees. Auton. Robot. **34**(3), 189–206 (2013)
13. James, S., Ma, Z., Arrojo, D.R., Davison, A.J.: Rlbench: the robot learning benchmark & learning environment. IEEE Robot. Autom. Lett. **5**(2), 3019–3026 (2020)
14. Kober, J., Bagnell, J.A., Peters. J.: Reinforcement learning in robotics: a survey. Int. J. Robot. Res. **32**(11), 1238–1274 (2013)
15. Lopez, N.G., et al.: Gym-gazebo2, a toolkit for reinforcement learning using Ros 2 and gazebo. arXiv preprint arXiv:1903.06278 (2019)
16. Moll, M., Sucan, I.A., Kavraki, L.E.: Benchmarking motion planning algorithms: an extensible infrastructure for analysis and visualization. IEEE Robot. Autom. Mag. **22**(3), 96–102 (2015)
17. Pan, J., Chitta, S., Manocha, D.: FCL: a general purpose library for collision and proximity queries. In: 2012 IEEE International Conference on Robotics and Automation, pp. 3859–3866. IEEE (2012)
18. Panerati, J., Zheng, H., Zhou, S., Xu, J., Prorok, A., Schoellig, A.P.: Learning to fly-a gym environment with pybullet physics for reinforcement learning of multi-agent quadcopter control. arXiv preprint arXiv:2103.02142 (2021)
19. Pecka, M., Svoboda, T.: Safe exploration techniques for reinforcement learning – an overview. In: Hodicky, J. (eds.) Modelling and Simulation for Autonomous Systems. MESAS 2014. LNCS, vol 8906, pp. 357–375. Springer, Cham (2014). https://doi.org/10.1007/978-3-319-13823-7_31s
20. Plappert, M., et al.: Multi-goal reinforcement learning: challenging robotics environments and request for research. arXiv preprint arXiv:1802.09464 (2018)

21. Raffin, A., Hill, A., Ernestus, M., Gleave, A., Kanervisto, A., Dormann, A.: Stable baselines3. https://github.com/DLR-RM/stable-baselines3 (2019)
22. Ray, A., Achiam, J., Amodei, D.: Benchmarking safe exploration in deep reinforcement learning. arXiv preprint arXiv:1910.01708 (2019)
23. Schulman, J., Wolski, F., Dhariwal, P., Radford, A., Klimov, O.: Proximal policy optimization algorithms. arXiv preprint arXiv:1707.06347 (2017)
24. Sucan, J.A., Moll, M., Kavraki, L.E.: The open motion planning library. IEEE Roboti. Autom. Mag. **19**(4), 72–82 (2012)
25. Tassa, Y., et al.: Deepmind control suite. arXiv preprint arXiv:1801.00690 (2018)
26. Todorov, E., Erez, T., Tassa, Y.: Mujoco: a physics engine for model-based control. In: 2012 IEEE/RSJ International Conference on Intelligent Robots and Systems, pp. 5026–5033. IEEE (2012)
27. Wachi, A., Sui, Y.: Safe reinforcement learning in constrained Markov decision processes. In: International Conference on Machine Learning, pp. 9797–9806. PMLR (2020)
28. Yang, X., Ji, Z., Wu, J., Lai, Y.-K.: An open-source multi-goal reinforcement learning environment for robotic manipulation with pybullet. arXiv preprint arXiv:2105.05985 (2021)
29. Zhu, Y., Wong, J., Mandlekar, A., Martín-Martín, R.: Robosuite: a modular simulation framework and benchmark for robot learning. arXiv preprint arXiv:2009.12293 (2020)

Author Index

Printed in the United States
by Baker & Taylor Publisher Services